SUB-SETS

Phylum Annelida

Phylum Mollusca

Phylum Echinodermata

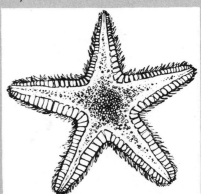

Phylum Chordata

Class Pisces

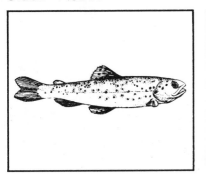

Class Amphibia

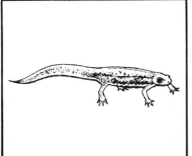

Class Reptilia

Class Aves

Class Mammalia

Sub class Monotremata

Sub class Marsupialia

Sub class Placentalia

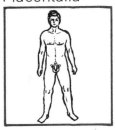

BIOLOGY BY INQUIRY

Book 2

Editorial Chairman
    John E. Dale, *Reader, Botany Department, University of Edinburgh*
Advisory Panel
    James Park, *Principal Teacher of Biology, George Heriot's School, Edinburgh*
    Alexander Pratt, *Principal Lecturer in Biology, College of Education, Aberdee*
    Avril Simpson, *Principal Teacher of Biology, Paisley Grammar School*

BIOLOGY

A course in experimental Biology for

With a Foreword by
Michael Swann, F.R.S.
Principal and Vice-Chancellor of the University of Edinburgh

HEINEMANN EDUCATIONAL BOOKS

BOOK 2

BY INQUIRY

secondary schools

Robert A. Clarke
Principal Lecturer in Biology, College of Education, Dundee

P. Rupert Booth
Formerly Head of Biology Department, The Edinburgh Academy

Peter E. Grigsby
Head of Biology Department, Strathallan School, Forgandenny, Perthshire

Jack F. Haddow
Lecturer in Science, College of Education, Dundee

John S. Irvine
Principal Teacher of Biology, Forrester Secondary School, Edinburgh

LONDON AND EDINBURGH

Heinemann Educational Books Ltd
London Edinburgh Melbourne Auckland Toronto
Singapore Hong Kong Kuala Lumpur
Ibadan Nairobi Johannesburg
Lusaka New Delhi

ISBN 0 435 59171 1
© Robert A. Clarke, P. Rupert Booth, Peter E. Grigsby,
Jack F. Haddow and John S. Irvine 1970

First published 1970
Reprinted 1971, 1973, 1974

Published by Heinemann Educational Books Ltd
48 Charles Street, London W1X 8AH

Printed in Great Britain by Morrison & Gibb Ltd
London and Edinburgh

FOREWORD

by **Michael Swann**, F.R.S.
Principal and Vice-Chancellor of the University of Edinburgh

For too long, Biology has been regarded as something of a soft option; and if we are honest, not without some justification. School Biology has tended to concentrate on factual description, and while it may have required an effort of memory, it has by no means always required a great effort of thought. Yet modern Biology is as intellectually demanding a science as any; indeed, because it lacks the clear-cut simplicity of the physical sciences, it is not easier, but often more difficult than they are.

It is only recently that there have been serious and concerted attempts to teach Biology at school in a way that reflects the real nature of the science. The most notable of these has been the now well-known Nuffield project, but this was intended specifically for English schools. Now a group of Scottish teachers and lecturers have produced, in *Biology by Inquiry*, a series in the Nuffield idiom, designed for the new 'O' and 'H' Grade Biology syllabus.

Biology by Inquiry does exactly what its title implies. By methods that mirror the research that has made Biology the most important of the sciences for the future, it enables the pupil to disentangle for himself some of the vast complexity of living things. And equally important, it cannot fail to arouse young people's interest in the one school subject that can really bridge the gap between the humanities and the physical sciences. I suspect that the popularity of Biology, which has been growing steadily in Scotland, will now grow yet faster.

The Scottish contribution to education has been a unique and important one, and it is good that the inspiration is not drying up. There have been very significant developments north of the border in recent years, both in school Physics and in school Chemistry. I believe that *Biology by Inquiry* will prove to be an equally important landmark.

ACKNOWLEDGEMENTS

The authors wish to take this further opportunity to acknowledge the stimulation given to the teaching of biology by the work of the Nuffield Biology Teaching Project. As in Book 1 of this series, several of the ideas and experiments in this volume are based on the Texts and Guides of that Project.

Also acknowledgement for permission to publish certain figures is due, as follows:

1.1, South West Optical Instruments Ltd; 1.6, 5.16, C. A. W. Guggisberg, Bruce Coleman Ltd; 1.10, Ilford Ltd; 1.13, C. Wyles; 1.14, Richard Haveley; 1.15, R. F. Lyndon; 2.8, 7.9, 7.10, 7.11, 7.13, 7.14, 10.2, and cover photographs, B. Bracegirdle; 5.1, Leonard Lee Rue, Bruce Coleman Ltd; Table 5.1, J. Murray and *British Dental Journal*; 5.5, British Dental Council; 5.9, H. Schultz, Bruce Coleman Ltd; 5.15, Ernest G. Neal; 5.17, D. Irvine; 6.2, Peter Keen, Oxfam; 6.11, National Film Board of Canada; 6.12, Contra la Faim, Oxfam; 6.13, F.A.O., Oxfam; 6.15, Kenya Information Office, Oxfam; 8.9, 8.13, Pace; 8.14, East of Scotland Blood Transfusion Service; 8.15, P. A. M. Paice; 8.18, Gene Cox; 8.19, Harris Biological Supplies Ltd; 9.2(*a*) and (*b*), Professor and Mrs Brian Hopkins; 9.14, 17.14, United Press International (UK) Ltd; 14.4(*a*) and (*b*), Oxoid Division, Oxo Ltd; 15.1, Ivor Fields Photography Ltd, Abingdon; 15.15, reproduced from *Plant Propagation* by R. C. M. Wright (Ward Lock Educational Company Ltd); 17.1, Airviews (Manchester) Ltd; 17.3, 17.4, 17.5, The National Institute of Oceanography; 17.6, Camera Press Ltd (photo by Ben Darby); 17.7, W. R. Lobb, Winchmore Irrigation Research Station, New Zealand; 17.10, Rothamstead Experimental Station; 17.11, C. D. Bingham; 17.12, Bruce Coleman Ltd; 17.13, Aerofilms Ltd; 17.17, M. J. Cotton. The cover photographs were taken by Mr Brian Bracegirdle.

Thanks are due to Dr A. F. Dyer for the unique production of Figure 2.4, to Dr J. D. Lockie and Dr D. A. Ratcliffe and the journal *British Birds* for information on golden eagles, and to Mr J. J. D. Greenwood for information about oil pollution in the Tay Estuary. Information on organo-chlorine pesticides is derived from the *Review of the Persistent Organo-chlorine Pesticides* (1964), by kind permission of the Controller, H.M.S.O.

The members of the Panel of Advisers have given invaluable help at various stages in the planning and writing of the book. The work of the artists, Design Practitioners Ltd, and of Mr H. MacGibbon and the Science Department of Heinemann Educational Books Ltd, must also be acknowledged with sincere thanks.

CONTENTS

BIOLOGY BY INQUIRY

In the earlier part of this course in Biology you will have discovered for yourself that Biology is a branch of Science which can be investigated by asking questions and by carrying out experiments to try to find the answers. In several cases, due to the variation in living organisms, you found that a particular experiment did not always give exactly the same result. In this part of the course you will spend some time investigating why organisms vary, and you will find out the use which man can make of this variation.

You have also inquired briefly into the ways in which organisms function, both as individuals and as part of ecosystems. Just as it is possible to relate the parts of a motor car such as the engine, the brakes or the steering assembly to the jobs they do, so it is possible very often, but not always, to relate the structures of organisms to their functions. You will also investigate this fascinating part of Biology in more detail. However, man is an organism, and the principles and rules found from the study of Biology affect him just as they do any other organism. In this part of the course you will find many examples of the importance of Biology to almost every aspect of man's life and behaviour.

1 SIZE AND SHAPE

1.1 Mini and maxi

When we are asked to describe an organism we often say that it is big or small, huge or tiny, but what do we really mean by these terms? Compared to a mouse, a man is big; compared to elephants, we are small. There are different ways of measuring size. Is a snake 'big' because it is 2 m long or 'small' because it is only 10 cm thick? Obviously, an organism may be big in one dimension but small in another. In investigating size, we must first decide how we are going to measure an organism, and then decide upon a suitable unit of measurement. We might measure the length of the organism in centimetres, or its surface area in cm², or the space it takes up—referred to as its volume or bulk—in cm³. If the organism is much bigger we then use the larger units, metres, m² and m³ for measuring length, area and volume.

In this chapter we shall consider the range of size of organisms. It is more difficult to measure the volumes and surface areas of living things, so to begin with we shall compare lengths. *Euglena*, seen in Figure 1.1, is a microscopic freshwater organism sometimes found in such large numbers that the water appears green. With the low power of the microscope you can make out very little detail, and, as it moves quickly with a rotating motion across the field of the microscope, it is difficult to find out much about it, even with the high-power lens. *Euglena* is not the smallest organism, nor is it of particular interest to man except for showing certain characteristics of both plants and animals, but it is convenient to use it as a unit of measurement in comparison of the lengths of other organisms. One species measures 0·25 mm in length, so 4 000 of these organisms placed end to end could lie along a metre stick. A blue whale is about 30 m long, and it is possibly the largest animal which has ever lived on our planet. This means that a blue whale is 4 000 × 30, or 120 000 times as long as *Euglena*. How many times longer than

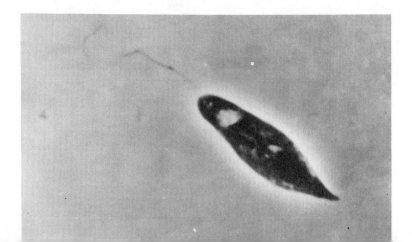

Figure 1.1 *Euglena*, as seen under the high power of a microscope

Euglena would be the largest-ever plant, the giant redwood tree of California, if it measures about 100 m in height?

Let us begin our investigations of size by calculating the lengths of a mixed collection of organisms in terms of *Euglena*.

Make out a table similar to Table 1.1. Measure the lengths or the heights of various organisms, and calculate how much longer they are than *Euglena*. The organisms you measure are likely to be different from those given in the table.

Table 1.1

Organism	Average length	No. of times longer than *Euglena*
Euglena	0·25 mm	1
Duckweed	3·0 mm	
Earwig	2·0 cm	
Adult locust		
Hamster		
Man		
Giraffe		
Ash tree		
Blue whale	30 m	120 000
Redwood tree	100 m	

How much longer than *Euglena* are the largest plant and the largest animal that you measured?

These results should emphasise the tremendous range of size which exists amongst living organisms.

1.2 Surface area and volume

You know already that organisms feed, store and use energy, grow and reproduce, and, in later chapters, we shall investigate some other vital activities. Earlier in the course you looked at stages of growth of a chick embryo, which was growing not only in length but also in every direction. We are now going to investigate some of the problems of growing bigger.

It is difficult to measure accurately the volume of a living organism, and even more difficult to measure its surface area because its shape is usually irregular. If we use a model organism with a very regular shape, for example, a cube, we can build up a table to compare the linear, surface area and volume measurements, as the model organism grows.

Figure 1.2 The cubic model organism

1. Model 1 is a cube shape, each side measuring 1 cm. This is the linear measurement of the model and it is entered in column A of Table 1.2.
2. In column B we calculate the area of one side which would be 1 cm^2, in this case.
3. As there are six sides to the cube the total surface area will be 6 cm^2. This result is recorded in column C.
4. Calculate the volume of the cube, 1 cm $\times$ 1 cm $\times$ 1 cm, which is 1 cm^3. Enter this in column D.
5. In column E calculate the ratio of surface area to volume.
6. In column F record the surface area the model has for each cm^3 of volume.
7. Complete the calculation for models 2, 3 and 10.

Table 1.2

Model organism	A Linear	B Area of side	C Total surface area	D Volume	E Ratio $\frac{C}{D}$	F No. of cm^2 of surface area for each cm^3
One	1 cm	1 cm^2	6 cm^2	1 cm^3	$\frac{6}{1}$	6
Two	2 cm					
Three	3 cm					
Ten	10 cm					

Which has the greater surface area for each cubic centimetre of volume, the large cube or the small cube? What results would you expect if you compared the ratios of surface area to volume in animals such as mouse and guinea pig?

1.3 Surfaces of animals

From our calculations we can now put forward the hypothesis that the bigger an organism becomes the less surface area it has in relation to its volume or bulk. This certainly was the case with the cubic model organisms. Let us test the hypothesis with living animals.

Three mammals of different size are required for this experiment. A mouse, a guinea pig and a girl or boy are suitable, but you may use other animals. We shall use methods of estimating the surface areas which will only give approximate results because of the difficulties in making more accurate measurements. Also, we shall substitute weight for volume, as it is easier to weigh animals than to find their volumes. We can make this substitution because the weight of an animal is generally in proportion to its volume.

1. Make a rectangle of paper which will just cover the mouse if it is wrapped up with the edges of the paper just meeting as in Figure 1.3. Pet mice which are handled frequently are suitable for this treatment. Unroll the paper, and then calculate the area by multiplying the length by the breadth. This will give the approximate surface area of the mouse.
2. Use the same method to find the surface area of the guinea pig.
3. Make six cylinders of paper to cover the head, trunk, two arms and two legs of the boy, as in Figure 1.4. Calculate the areas of the rectangles when unrolled, and add these together to give his approximate surface area.
4. Weigh all three mammals in grammes.
5. Enter your results in a table similar to Table 1.3, and enter in the last column the ratios of the surface area to the weight.

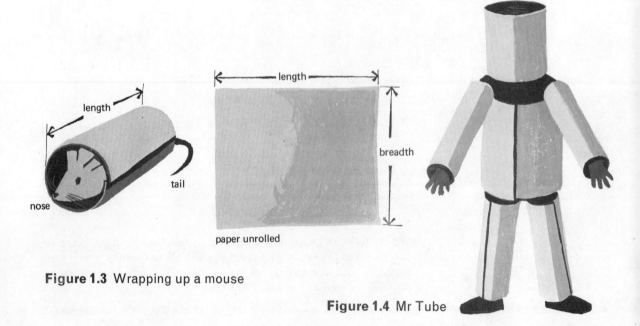

Figure 1.3 Wrapping up a mouse

paper unrolled

Figure 1.4 Mr Tube

Table 1.3

	A	B	Ratio $\dfrac{A}{B}$
	Surface area	Weight	
Mouse	cm²	g	
Guinea pig			
Boy			

Do the results support the hypothesis about the relationship between the surface area and the size of an organism?

1.4 Keeping warm and cooling off

We discovered earlier that animals produce energy, in the form of heat, from some of their food. This heat can be lost from their bodies in many ways, such as by breathing out warm air, by passing warm urine, and in sweating, when the heat of the body is used to evaporate the water. Warmth is required by the muscles before they will work properly; if too much heat escapes from the body of an animal, the working of the muscles slows down and eventually stops, and the animal dies. We shall perform an experiment to find out how the ratio of surface area to volume affects the loss of heat from animals of different sizes.

1. Take two round-bottomed flasks, one of 50 cm³ capacity and one of 500 cm³ capacity, to represent two animals of the same kind but different in body volumes.
2. Fit the flasks with stoppers and thermometers, as shown in Figure 1.5.
3. Fill both flasks with water at 90°C.
4. Record the temperatures in both flasks at intervals of 5 minutes, and tabulate the results as in Table 1.4.
5. For both flasks, draw a curve to show the temperature readings in relation to the passage of time. Draw both curves on the same sheet of graph paper.

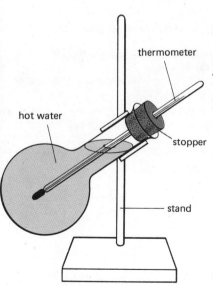

thermometer

hot water

stopper

stand

Figure 1.5 Setting up the flasks

Table 1.4

Time	Temp °C	
	50 cm^3	500 cm^3
0 min	90°C	90°C
5 ,,		
10 ,,		
15 ,,		
20 ,,		
25 ,,		

If two animals, similar in size to the flasks, were exposed to very severe cold, which one would be most likely to suffer first, other things being equal? Consider the result of this experiment and the conclusions reached in Section 1.3, and try to explain your answer.

1.5 Water loss

We shall see later that most living organisms consist largely of water. If you leave an apple in a warm room for a few weeks, some of the water escapes and the apple gradually becomes wizened and dried up. What effect will the ratio of surface area to volume have on the proportion of water lost by an organism?

1. Select two large potato tubers about the same size and two small ones about the same size as each other.
2. Carefully peel one large one and one small one, removing as thin a layer of peel as possible.
3. Weigh each potato and note the date.
4. Leave all four potatoes exposed to the air for a week and then reweigh.
5. Enter your results as shown in Table 1.5, and work out the percentage loss of weight for each potato.

Table 1.5

	A	B	C	Percentage Loss $\dfrac{C}{A} \times \dfrac{100}{1}$
	[First wt]	[Second wt]	[Loss (A−B)]	
Small whole potato	g	g	g	per cent
Small peeled potato				
Large whole potato				
Large peeled potato				

What effect has the ratio of surface area to volume on the percentage of water lost by the potatoes? What effect does the presence of the peel of the potato have on water loss?

1.6 Putting on weight

Look at Figure 1.6 which shows a mother giraffe with her young. The adult is much bigger and heavier but her legs are not much longer, although they do seem to have become thicker. You might even think the legs of the young are out of proportion to the rest of its body. Why do you think the legs do not continue to grow at the same rate as the rest of the body? You may suggest that the giraffe does not need to grow much taller in order to reach its food. However, other mammals which do not feed on the leaves of tall trees can also have young with long spindly legs which do not increase much in length as the animal grows.

The main supporting structures in the legs are the bones, and, if the legs were to grow longer, these bones would have to become longer as well. How does the length of a bone affect its strength? The following experiment will help you to find the answer. It should be performed behind a Perspex screen to prevent the possibility of splinters of glass flying off and damaging your eyes.

Figure 1.6 Giraffe and young

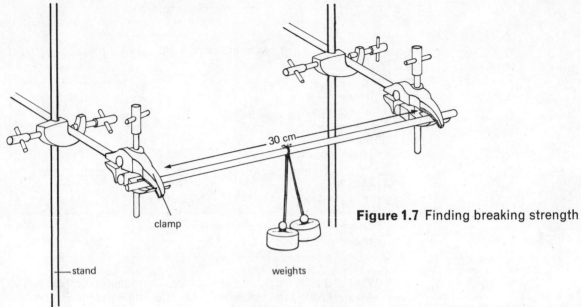

Figure 1.7 Finding breaking strength

1. Clamp a solid glass rod between two stands, as in Figure 1.7 so that exactly 30 cm of rod are exposed.
2. At the middle of the rod fasten a piece of string on to which weights can be tied.
3. Starting with 100 g, carefully add 100 g weights until the rod snaps.
4. Repeat the experiment with the same thickness of rod, but this time expose exactly 15 cm.
5. Tabulate the results as in Table 1.6.

Table 1.6

Length of glass rod	Breaking strength (weight which causes breaking)
30 cm	g
15 cm	g

You have probably found that it takes a much greater force to break the short piece of glass than it does to break the long piece. In the same way, long bones will be broken more easily than short ones, and they are less able to support greater weights. This is one of the main reasons why the length to which the legs of the adults grow is limited. Note that, in the experiment, the force was applied at right angles to the length of the rod but that this is not so in the legs of animals.

1.7 Looking at bones

Look at the drawing of the longitudinal section of the humerus of a cow, or, better still, get a humerus or a femur from the butcher and saw it in half, lengthwise, as in Figure 1.8. The humerus is the upper bone in the foreleg of a cow, while the femur is the upper bone, sometimes called the thigh bone, in the hind leg. You will notice that these bones are hollow. If the bones were to be the same length, but solid, like the glass rods used in the experiment, would they be heavier or lighter? If they were solid, of the same length, and still weighed the same, would they be thicker or thinner? Let us try another experiment to see if hollow bones offer any advantage over solid bones of the same weight. We can use glass rods and tubes to represent the bones.

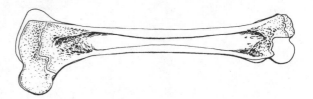

Figure 1.8 Section of humerus

1. Select glass tubing of a bore such that a length of it will weigh exactly the same as an equal length of the solid rod used in the previous experiment.
2. Clamp it as in Figure 1.7 to expose exactly 30 cm.
3. Add weights carefully as before, until the tube snaps.
4. Compare the result with that obtained for the 30 cm solid rod in the previous experiment.

What is the significance of having hollow bones rather than solid ones?

The investigation shows that a hollow tube of glass is much stronger than a solid rod of the same length and weight. The same principle applies to leg bones. The advantage is in having a strong support for the body without having to carry the additional weight which a solid bone of the same strength would entail. Look again at the section of the humerus. The wall of the tube of bone is thicker in the middle than at the ends. What benefit is there from this form of construction?

1.8 Spreading the load

Most vertebrate animals have limbs not only for support but also for moving from place to place. It could be said that their modes of life are governed to a great extent by the shapes and sizes of their limbs, and by the way the limbs are attached to their bodies, or you might argue that their limbs have developed to suit the environment in which they live. How could you decide between these two alternatives? You are now going to investigate the way in which the supporting structures affect the stability of the organism.

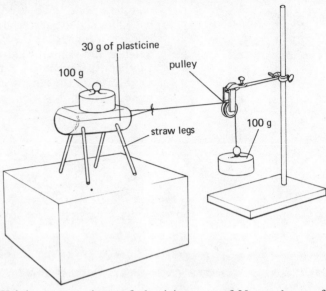

Figure 1.9 A plasticine animal

1. Weigh out two pieces of plasticine, one of 30 g and one of 20 g weight.
2. Mould 30 g of plasticine into the shape of the body of an animal, with a flat back on which weights can be placed.
3. Push four milk straws into the body to represent legs.
4. Fasten a string round the body and over a pulley as in Figure 1.9, and attach a 100 g weight to the string. If the weight pulls the animal over, you will have to adjust the position of the legs.
5. Now add weights to the animal's back until the legs give way.
6. Repeat the experiment, using the extra 20 g of plasticine in any way you choose to strengthen the legs or to keep the animal upright.
7. Replace the straw legs with other legs, each made of two half straws taped together. Test the strength of the supports, with and without the additional 20 g of plasticine.
8. Tabulate your results as shown in Table 1.7.

Table 1.7

	Wt supported
1 Straw legs	g
2 Straw legs plus plasticine	
3 Double half straws	
4 Double half straws plus plasticine	

An object is said to be **stable** when it does not fall over. The more stable it is, the more pushing and pulling it can withstand without changing its position or falling. The 100 g weight hanging from the pulley is there to test the stability of the model animal. Study the results of your experiments. Is any relationship apparent between the weight of an animal and the length and thickness of its limbs? If so, what is the relationship?

You have found that the model animal becomes more stable if the legs diverge as they leave the body. When you add weight to its back, it will either 'do the splits', or else its legs will buckle. If you use the extra plasticine to strengthen the legs in the middle and to make broader feet, it will carry more weight. From the results of the experiment in Section 1.7, we would expect the shorter legs to carry a greater weight, and short ones twice as thick will be even more efficient as weight carriers. The results from the experiment in this section confirm this.

Let us try to relate these findings to real life. The baby giraffe might be compared to our first model in the table. As the body weight increases with growth, the legs become thicker to support the extra weight, but they cannot become much longer without weakening the structure. Thus, the mother giraffe might be compared to model two. Animals like a hippopotamus and a rhinoceros have shorter and thicker legs and therefore they can support more weight. You might wonder why many young animals, such as foals, or calves, have legs which appear to be out of proportion to the rest of their bodies. Remember that in the wild they have many enemies. Shortly after birth they are able to walk and run, and their long legs enable them to keep up with their parents when fleeing from predators.

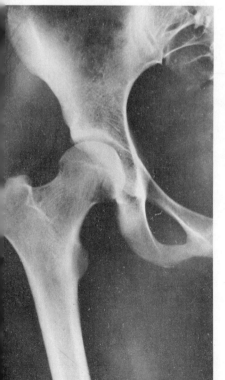

Figure 1.10 X-ray photograph of a leg bone

1.9 Stress and strain

If the legs are vertical under the animal, a force will act straight down through the legs. If the legs are splayed out for stability, and muscles are attached to the bones to pull in other directions, other forces are going to be exerted on the bones. To counteract these stresses and strains, bone tissue is not formed in a solid mass as in a plaster mould, but is laid down in layers running in different directions. The principle used in making plywood is somewhat similar. The X-ray photograph in Figure 1.10 shows the lines of stress in a leg bone. If you made a good job of cutting the humerus in the experiment in Section 1.7, you may be able to see the lines of stress in the section of bone.

1.10 More strength to the structure

When you added more weights to the back of the plasticine animal in the experiment in Section 1.8, you may have found that the legs were strong enough, but that the body gave way. The longer the back of the animal, the more readily this is likely to happen. Look at the skeleton of a rabbit or Figure 13.13 and notice how its back is arched. Much of the weight of the animal is slung from the arch. The following simple experiment can be performed to illustrate the principle of arch support.

1. Cut two strips of card 3 cm wide by 14 cm long.
2. Place two blocks of wood, 3 cm thick (books would also do) so that they lie 10 cm apart.
3. Bridge the gap with one of the strips of card so that a length of 2 cm lies on each support.
4. Add similar coins to the middle of the bridge until it collapses.
5. Bend the second card to form an arch and place in position as in Figure 1.11.

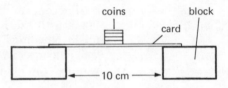

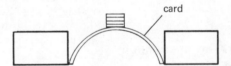

Figure 1.11 The two bridges

6. Find the number of coins required to make this structure collapse.

In which places in your own skeleton are arches present to provide strong supports? (Look at a human skeleton, if you have one in your laboratory, or at a plastic model of a skeleton in order to try to answer this question.)

Many structures used by engineers are similar to structures found in plants and animals. Figure 1.12(*a*) shows a T-girder. This is a method of strengthening a girder without adding too much to its weight. Try to find out the name and position of any bone in the skeleton in which this principle is found.

Figure 1.12(*b*) shows man's use of the arch, using a principle which you investigated earlier in this section.

Figure 1.12 Engineering
structures

(*a*) T-girder

(*b*) Sydney Harbour Bridge

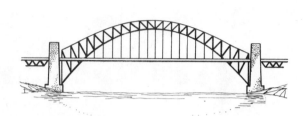

1.11 Support in plants

Animals must move around to look for food and water, for a mate and for shelter from weather and from enemies. Any weight which they put on in growing bigger and stronger has to be carried round with them. We have seen how many of the principles used by engineers to make strong, lightweight structures are also found in animal support. Plants do not move, and so they do not have to carry their weight from place to place. Some of the giant redwood trees are known to be well over 2 000 years old, and they are still growing taller and heavier. The whole weight of such a tree has to be supported on its base. The taller the tree grows, the more surface will be exposed to catch the wind, and the more leverage there will be on this base. Let us look at a growing tree and then at a dead one to see if we can find how they are strengthened.

1. Hammer 4 cm long nails into the trunk of a small tree at 50 cm intervals, starting 50 cm above ground level. At three-monthly intervals measure the height of each nail above the ground and also the circumference of the tree at that height.
2. Cut, or section, an old Christmas tree half-way between each ring of branches, and compare these cross sections.

Where does the increase in size of the trunk take place, and how does this affect support?

As the tree grows older and taller, the height of the nails above the ground level does not alter to any extent. Increase in height is caused by growth at the top of the tree. This might not be un-expected, since we found out earlier in the course that increase in length of roots also takes place at the tips.

The girth measurement at each nail increases with time, showing that there is a growth in thickness all the way up the tree. The glass

Figure 1.13 Sections of the stem of a spruce tree

rod experiment in Section 1.6 shows the need for extra strengthening as the length of a structure increases. Look at the section through the stem of a young spruce tree in Figure 1.13. As the tree becomes taller, so the base becomes broader and thus carries the increasing weight.

The age of the tree can be calculated by counting the annual rings in the bottom section. In perennial plants, like the spruce tree, where the stem does not die at the end of the season, many of the cell walls are thickened with a substance which is called **lignin.** The **wood** of a tree is largely composed of lignin, adding considerably to the strength of the trunk. As annual plants complete their life cycle in one year, they do not have as much weight to support; they do not develop woody stems and contain much less lignin. How are such stems strengthened?

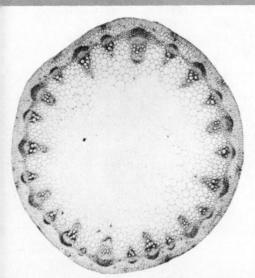

1. Take a piece of bean stem between your finger and thumb and press gently to check its strength.
2. Leave a similar piece out of water in a warm place for an hour and compare its strength with that of the first piece of stem.
3. Examine a section of a young bean stem, or other prepared slide of a dicotyledon stem showing primary growth, under the low power of the microscope. Compare it with the section of *Dahlia* shown in Figure 1.14.

In what ways are stems like those of bean and *Dahlia* strengthened?

Figure 1.14 Section of young *Dahlia* stem as seen under the low power of a microscope

The stem of the bean or *Dahlia* is composed of thousands of cells. When sufficient water is present, the cells are firm and press against one another and keep the stem rigid. When the water dries out, the stem becomes flabby. You may have observed this happening with pot plants which have not been watered. If they are given water soon enough they eventually recover their rigidity. In the prepared section of the stem you may have noticed cells with thicker walls, arranged in groups in a circle within the stem. These groups of cells act like reinforcing rods of iron which are often set in concrete walls to withstand stresses.

So far we have only considered land plants. We must also investigate those which grow in water.

1. Look at a specimen of *Elodea*, or some other aquatic plant, growing in an aquarium. What do you notice about the thickness of the stem in relation to its length?
2. Look at the section of a stem of an aquatic plant shown in Figure 1.15. The tightly packed supporting cells seem to occupy only a small part in the middle of the stem. How do you think the stem is supported, and what is the significance of the strengthening material being confined to the centre?

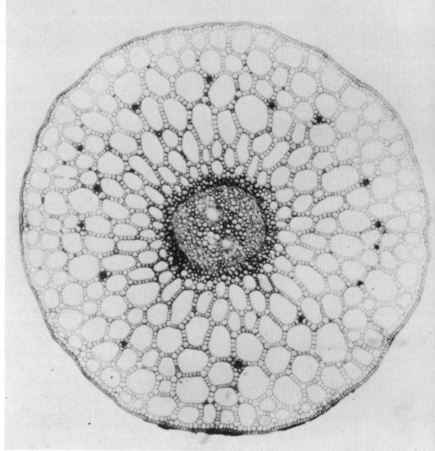

Figure 1.15 Section of the stem of a water plant (*Potamogeton* sp.), as seen under the low power of a microscope

The long thin stems of water plants are supported by the water. Notice the large air spaces in the stem (Figure 1.15), which help to keep the plant floating. If the water recedes the plant collapses and falls over. You have probably seen this happen to seaweeds at low tide. In fast-moving water, plants must bend and wave with the current. If their stems were tubular or solid, as well as being long, they might crack, but if the strengthening tissue is in the middle they are more pliable and they bend without breaking.

1.12 Size limitation

Earlier in the course you saw the graph reproduced in Figure 1.16. It shows the growth in height of a boy from birth, to the age of 18.

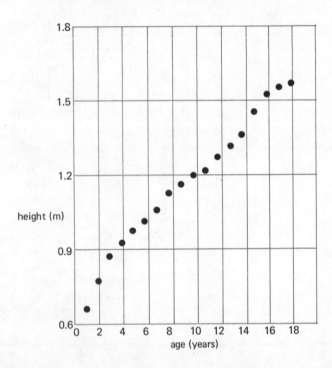

Figure 1.16 Growth curve for Montbeillard's son

The growth was fairly regular from 0·6 m at birth, to 1·6 m at 18. If this rate of increase in height had continued, a man about 2·6 m tall at the age of 36 would have been produced, and by the time he was 54 years of age, he would have been 3·6 m tall. What is the height of the tallest man you know? In land vertebrates, whether men or elephants, there is a fairly steady rate of growth to begin with, but growth gradually ceases as the animal becomes mature.

From your experiments and observations, it should now be clear that the ability to support its own weight will be one of the major factors which limit the indefinite growth of an animal. If an animal grew much bigger than an elephant, what would the legs be like? If the legs became much thicker, or much shorter, movement on them would be very difficult. At the beginning of this chapter it was stated that blue whales are possibly the biggest animals ever to have lived on this planet. Why can whales grow to this massive size in spite of the problem of their great weights? Plants, such as the giant redwood tree, which do not move, continue to grow throughout their lives.

1.13 Shape

So far, we have dealt mainly with size, and with the problem of supporting weight. We have considered different shapes of parts of the skeleton, but have not thought much about the shape of the animal. Let us now investigate how an animal's shape may be adapted to its way of life.

If you visit the swimming baths and wish to jump off the springboard, why is it better to jump in feet first or dive in head first, rather than to flop in on your stomach? The following simple experiment should help to provide an answer.

1. Cut a square of thin card with its sides about 6 cm long.
2. Hold the card in one hand and try to push the blunt end of a pencil through it.
3. Try to push the pointed end of the pencil through a similar piece of card.

In which case is it easier to push the pencil through the card? What reason can you give for this result?

In the first case, the force applied when you push is spread out over the area of the blunt end of the pencil. Thus, a considerable force is needed to push the pencil through the card. In the second case, the force is concentrated in the very small area of the point, which goes through quite easily. Similarly, water will offer less resistance to the entry of your body if you concentrate the force of your dive on a small area when you jump in. Once you are in the water, if you walk forward, you press against it with a large surface area, but, if you swim, you reduce this area and move more easily. What other medium offers a resistance to the movement of animals? Which shape offers the least resistance to movement?

Compare the speeds with which different plasticine shapes will sink through water. If you embed a small screw-top aluminium canister (such as those used by chemists to hold tablets) in the plasticine, you can increase the buoyancy of the model and have more time to watch the effect of its shape on the speed at which it sinks. A canister of about 40 cm^3 capacity and 100 g of plasticine make a suitable combination, but you should experiment with different proportions. Figure 1.17 shows three suggested shapes.

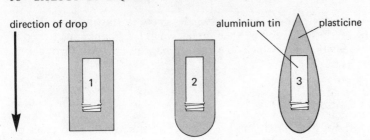

direction of drop

aluminium tin   plasticine

Figure 1.17 Suggested shapes made from plasticine

A class competition could be organised to design the shape which sinks fastest. Each group of pupils would observe a code of rules, such as:

1. The same amount of plasticine must be used in each case.
2. Each buoyancy tank must have the same capacity and be full of air.
3. Competing models should be dropped simultaneously into similar cylinders of water, and a note taken as to which reaches the bottom first.
4. The designers should be allowed a trial drop.

What is the ideal shape for a fast-moving water animal? Are animals which live in water the only ones which have a shape modified in this way for fast movement?

1.14 Flow and drag

In the previous experiment you probably found that if the plasticine is moulded into a torpedo-shape round the canister, slightly blunter at the front and more tapered to the rear, it will sink more quickly. Some animals, such as trout, stay motionless for long periods and let the water flow past them, while at other times they move rapidly through the water. Whether the fluid moves round the motionless animal or whether the animal moves through the fluid, the stream-lined shape will offer the least resistance to the flow of the fluid. You can investigate the effect of shape on the flow of fluids in the following experiment.

1. Make flat plasticine or wooden shapes similar in outline to those used in the last experiment.
2. Lay the shapes on a sloping tray. See Figure 1.18.
3. Put some potassium permanganate crystals in a strip of muslin at the top of the tray and allow water to flow through it and past the shapes.
4. Make drawings to show how the different shapes disturb the parallel lines of the flowing liquid. This disturbance is known as turbulence. What relationship is there between the shape of the model and the amount of turbulence produced?

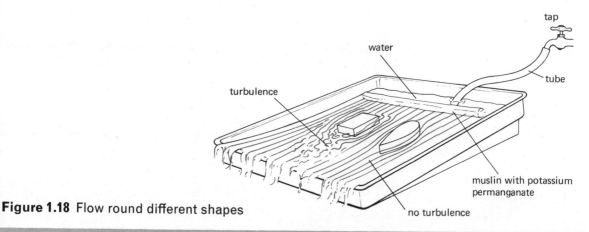

Figure 1.18 Flow round different shapes

The pressure in front of the shape decreases as the 'nose' becomes more streamlined. If the 'tail' is square, the water is likely to flow straight past, causing a low pressure area which will tend to pull the model backwards. This is known as drag. If the tail comes to a point, the water flows gently together again, and drag is eliminated. The shape at both ends of the model is therefore important.

Air behaves just like water, although it does not offer so much resistance. When a hawk dives through the air, it tucks in its legs and folds back its wings and thus the least possible resistance is offered. Try to observe how a duck lands on the water, or how a bird alights on a perch, such as the branch of a tree or on a ledge on a building. The bird splays out its wings and tail and feet and produces the maximum drag at the moment of touch-down.

Looking Back at Chapter 1

1. Small organisms have a greater surface area to volume ratio than large organisms.
2. The rate of loss of water and of exchange of heat at the surface is greater in an organism with a high surface area to volume ratio.
3. The larger an organism becomes, the more weight there is to be supported. Problems of support are greater in animals, which move, than in plants, which are stationary.
4. The shape and form of supporting tissues is modified to support the increasing weight of the organism as it grows.
5. Many engineering principles used by man are to be found in supporting structures of animals: for example, arches and tubes. These structures may also help to overcome other stresses.
6. The most useful structures may have to be a compromise between those which give greatest stability and those which give greatest strength.
7. Growth in height of plants takes place at the stem tip, the apex. The extra weight of land plants, due to growth, is supported by an increase in the girth of the stem. In some cases support is also

given by the lignification of certain tissues in the formation of wood.

8. The structures of aquatic plants and animals are further modified, as they are supported by the water; weight is no longer a major factor which limits their size.

9. The shapes of moving organisms may be adapted to their way of life.

CELLS GROWING AND DIVIDING

2.1 Organisms and cells

You have already found that plants and animals are made up of small structural units called cells, rather as a house is built of bricks. Figure 2.1 shows cells from the thin skin found inside an onion bulb, and also cells scraped from the lining of the human cheek. Earlier in the course you carried out experiments to observe cells like these for yourself, so you should remember the names of the parts labelled. What are they?

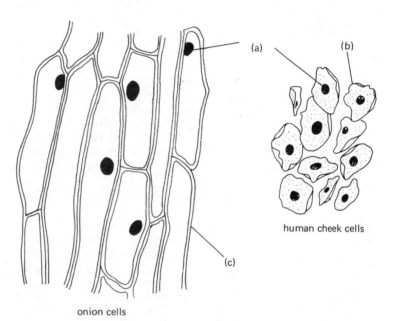

human cheek cells

onion cells

Figure 2.1 Onion cells and human cheek cells

Nearly all cells have a nucleus (labelled 'a' in Figure 2.1), which can be thought of as the control centre of the cell, governing its growth and the activities which go on inside it. The outermost layer of living material forms the very thin cell membrane ('b'). This is not always easy to distinguish in plant cells, as here there is an additional thicker structure, the cell wall ('c'), which encloses the cell and has the cell membrane pressed against its inner surface.

In fact, the cell membrane is only about 0·01 micron thick (one micron, 1μm, is one micrometre i.e. 10^{-6}m), and so it is far too thin to be distinguished using an ordinary light microscope. The sharp border which you see round an animal cell, when viewed under the microscope, is due to the interface, or boundary, between the cell and the substance in which it is mounted. It is therefore more accurate to think of 'b' as showing the *position* of the cell membrane.

The cellulose wall is thick enough to be seen under the microscope, and it has the effect of enclosing the plant cell in a fairly rigid box which gives support and protection. This is a very different arrangement from that found in animals, many of whose cells are soft and pliable.

2.2 Numbers and sizes of cells

When you looked at cheek cells, you probably found that you had scraped several dozen cells on to the slide. If you scraped too hard, you might have obtained a solid mass consisting of several hundred or even several thousand cells. What does this suggest about the total number of cells in your body? Someone has calculated that an adult human has something like sixty million million cells in his body. What is the origin of all these cells?

The majority of living organisms, like ourselves, begin as a single fertilised egg cell. So, in the course of growth and development there is a great increase in the number of cells in each individual. How is this increase brought about? You may have seen some of the early stages in the process by observing the developing eggs of *Pomatoceros*, or some other organism. You now know that growth is accompanied by a repeated division of cells, hence the increase in numbers.

Cells are not, of course, all the same size. You will have noticed that onion cells are rather bigger than your cheek cells. If you have an eyepiece micrometer, you can compare the size of these and any other cells you look at. How could you use the eyepiece micrometer to measure the actual sizes of cells?

Another way to make a comparison of cell sizes is as follows.
1. Set up the microscope on a well-illuminated sheet of white paper, and focus the cells clearly.
2. Look down the microscope with one eye and keep the other eye open. You may find this difficult at first, but after a little practice what you see down the microscope appears against the background of the white paper.
3. Lay a rule on the paper across the image of the cells, and measure the apparent size of the cells.
4. Make a table of the cell sizes you measure, noting particularly the smallest and the largest cells.

What assumptions would you have to make if you wished to estimate cell volumes from your measurements?

The smallest cells are found amongst the bacteria, some of which are less than 1 micron in diameter. By contrast, the yolk of the ostrich's egg ranks as the largest cell, having a volume of half a litre. Egg yolks however are exceptional cases, since they consist mainly of a store of food for the developing embryo.

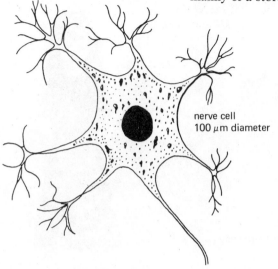

Figure 2.2 Comparative sizes of cells

nerve cell
100 μm diameter

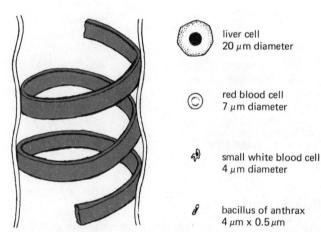

liver cell
20 μm diameter

red blood cell
7 μm diameter

small white blood cell
4 μm diameter

bacillus of anthrax
4 μm x 0.5 μm

portion of xylem vessel —100 μm diameter
N.B. This is a small example of this type
of cell. It would have a length, on this
scale, of 1m.

If egg cells are discounted, the largest animal cells have a diameter of about 100 microns. Some unicellular organisms, such as *Amoeba*, are about this size, as are some of the nerve cells of our own bodies (though these may have fine nerve fibres growing out of them reaching a length of up to a metre). The smallest cells of our bodies are certain white cells in the blood, which are 3–4 microns in diameter. Some of the cells from the wood of plants may be 1 mm long. Fibres from the ramie plant, which at one time were used to make the paper for £5 notes, may reach a length of 55 cm. Comparison of cell sizes is shown in Figure 2.2.

Thus the size range among cells, though considerable, is less than that which you found for living organisms in Chapter 1. From this it follows that large organisms will generally have more cells than smaller ones. This will apply not only to large and small members of a species but also to the young and adult stages of the same individual, as shown in Figure 2.3.

Human adult

Figure 2.3 Body size and cell number

Human baby

Single fertilised
egg cell

•

Weight
0.00003 g

Weight 3 kg
Number of cells:
2 000 000 000 000

Weight 73 kg
Number of cells:
60 000 000 000 000

2.3 Why do cells divide?

This raises the problem of what determines the size to which a cell will grow before it divides and becomes two cells. In Chapter 1, your measurements of cubic model organisms showed that, if some object of fixed shape increases in size, its surface area to volume ratio decreases. How does this affect a growing cell? Respiration in a unicellular organism illustrates one of the factors which may sometimes be involved. The cell must obtain a supply of oxygen and food, and it must be able to get rid of waste material produced. These exchanges between the cell and its surroundings must occur through the cell membrane. Thus, as the cell enlarges, each unit area of its surface will have to meet the demands of an increasing volume of living material within the cell. One could argue that, perhaps, when the cell reaches a certain size, exchange of materials cannot go on quickly enough. If division now occurs, producing two smaller cells, the surface area to volume ratios of the new cells will be greater. How may this affect the exchange of materials?

For a cell in a tissue surrounded by other cells, the problems are not quite the same. Why is this? Size is still an important factor, as also are the position of the cell and the level of activity within it, but it has not been found possible to say exactly what governs the onset of cell division in multicellular organisms.

2.4 Binary fission in micro-organisms

Some very small organisms consist of one cell only and so are known as unicellular, or single-celled. All bacteria come into this category; so do many microscopic organisms, some of which you have already seen. The various kinds of yeast are unicellular fungi, and *Pleurococcus*, which forms the green powdery material often found on fence posts, walls and tree trunks, is a unicellular green plant.

Earlier in the course you found that unicellular organisms often abound in water.

Examine under the microscope drops of water from various sources, and look for unicells. Rock pools, stagnant puddles, the bottoms of ponds, and any tanks or aquaria that there may be in the laboratory are all worth investigation. The following key will enable you to decide the group of organisms to which any unicell belongs.

Some unicells found in water

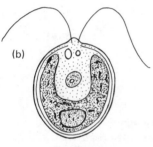

(b)

Chlamydomonas

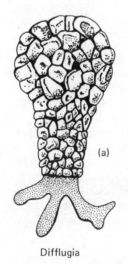

(a)

Difflugia

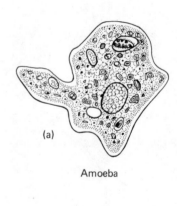

(a)

Amoeba

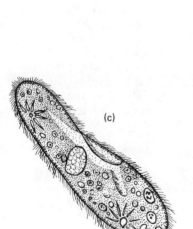

(c)

Paramecium

Key to some unicells found in water

Unicells of no fixed shape, moving by blunt, flowing extensions of cytoplasm	Amoebae (*a*)
Not as above	1

1. Moving by one or two whiplike processes (flagella), often green;

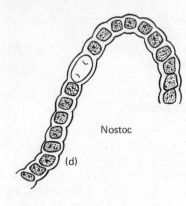

Nostoc

(d)

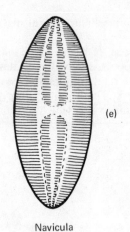

(e)

Navicula

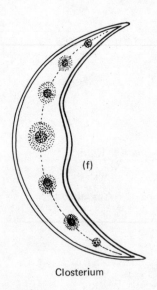

(f)

Closterium

sometimes several cells adhering together to form a colony	Flagellates (*b*)
Not as above	2
2. Cells showing movement or filter-feeding by very numerous, tiny hair-like processes (cilia)	Ciliates (*c*)
Not as above	3
3. Cells with green or golden brown colouring in one or more distinct structures (chloroplasts) clearly distinguishable within the cell	4
Cells with a blue-green colour distributed evenly through the cell. Cells often in rows or clusters	Blue-green algae (*d*)
4. Cells enclosed in a box-like shell, often finely patterned, usually golden-brown in colour and with no obvious means of movement	Diatoms (*e*)
Single cells divided into two identical halves	Desmids (*f*)

Most of these organisms reproduce simply by dividing into two similar units which are, of course, smaller than the original cell. The process is known as **binary fission.** Thus, by dividing, one such unicell is converted into two, all its material being passed on to its offspring. How does this differ from reproduction in larger organisms, such as flowering plants, locusts, fish, frogs, and ourselves? Binary fission is one example of asexual reproduction, that is, reproduction in which no sex cells are produced, and only one parent is required to give rise to the next generation.

It is not usually easy to watch binary fission taking place, though prepared microscope slides and films can be used to demonstrate the process. However it is easier to make observations on various organisms to show that increase in cell number is, or has been, taking place.

1. You are provided with a number of petri dishes containing sterile nutrient agar, which is used to culture micro-organisms.
2. Expose the agar plates, to collect micro-organisms in a variety of ways, such as
    (i) exposing a plate directly to the air
    (ii) allowing a fly or other insect to walk about on the plate
    (iii) placing two drops of milk on the plate
    (iv) placing on the plate two drops of water in which some fresh soil has been shaken up.

3. Replace the lids and keep the plates at a temperature of about 35°C for two or three days.
4. Examine the plates for colonies of bacteria. These show up as circular, slimy, semi-transparent patches of various colours. Some moulds may also grow, but these form thicker-looking patches which are opaque and usually white or greenish in colour.
5. The next step is to sub-culture the bacteria, setting up pure colonies from small pieces of those which have grown. Have ready a number of sterile plates of nutrient agar and a loop of nichrome wire. Hold the loop in the Bunsen burner flame for a few seconds until it glows red hot, then remove it and allow it to cool. Why is this heating followed by cooling necessary? Remove the lid from an infected agar plate and scrape lightly at a bacterial colony with the loop. Remove the lid quickly from a sterile plate and touch the loop lightly on the surface of the agar in one spot. Replace the lid immediately.
6. Incubate these cultures as before. Inspect daily for bacterial colonies. When any occur, measure their diameter each day with a pair of dividers. Why does the diameter of the colony give a good measure of its size? What have you found about the rate of increase of a bacterial colony? Why do you think the growth of the colonies may slow down after a while?

How, do you think, the increase in size of the colonies has come about?

Bacteria can be seen under the microscope, though they are very small, but you are not likely to see any direct evidence of binary fission.

1. Transfer a small piece of bacterial colony to a drop of water on a microscope slide, using a wire loop as in the previous experiment.
2. Mix the bacteria and water, spreading the mixture to a thin layer, and dry quickly by waving the slide to and fro a few centimetres above the top of a Bunsen burner flame. Do not let the water steam.
3. Immerse the slide in a staining jar or small beaker containing a one per cent solution of gentian violet, for two or three minutes.
4. Remove the slide and wash it well in a stream of running water from a tap. Dry the slide. Make sure you know on which side of the slide the bacteria are situated, otherwise it is easy to wipe them off, or to set the slide upside-down on the microscope stage.
5. Examine the slide under the high power of the microscope.
6. Repeat this examination on two more occasions during the growth of the bacterial colony. Are the bacteria the same size and shape when the colony is large as when it is small? What can you conclude about the number of bacteria composing the colony at different stages in its growth? Would you agree that increase of size of the colonies has been due to cell division?

2.5 Cell division in larger organisms

As we noted in Section 2.2, growth in multicellular organisms involves an increase in number of cells by cell division. The growing tip of a young onion root is suitable material in which to see this process taking place. You may have looked at cells in a root tip before, but this time we are going to concentrate on cells which are dividing, and we will use a stain which will show up important structures inside them.

1. Cut off 0·5 cm from the end of the root tip and place it in a little M hydrochloric acid in a test tube which has been heated to 60°C. Leave for 10 minutes.
2. Wash the root tip in water and place it on a microscope slide. Remove excess water.
3. On to this tip place a small drop (0·5 cm diameter) of orcein stain. There should be sufficient stain to prevent the preparation drying out, but not enough for material to be lost when the cover slip is lowered.
4. Tap the root tip with the end of a brass rod until no particles can be seen. Ideally, there is now a suspension of separated cells. Remove any particles big enough to be seen.
5. Lower a cover slip, and leave for 10 minutes.
6. Place the slide between sheets of blotting paper, and avoiding lateral movement, press the cover slip firmly with your thumb.
7. Examine the preparation carefully under the high power of the microscope, paying particular attention to the cells that were a little way back from the tip of the root.

Look for any cells in which the nuclear material has an unusual form. Compare these cells with the photographs shown in Figure 2.4 and see how many of the stages shown there you can distinguish.

The nuclei in the cells you have observed are undergoing a type of division called **mitosis.** This occurs both in binary fission in unicells and during growth in multicellular organisms. Mitosis is a process involving gradual but regular changes in the thread-like structures called **chromosomes.**

Look at the upper centre photograph in Figure 2.4. What is the appearance of the chromosomes? Are they all the same size? Are they single structures? Have they taken up the stain all over? Try to count the number of chromosomes in a cell in your preparation. If you find this difficult, count the number using the photographs in Figure 2.4. The number of chromosomes in a cell is the same for all members of a species although the chromosome number, as it is called, varies from one species to another. In man, this number is 46. What is the number in onion?

The chromosomes are not separately visible in the nucleus of a cell which is not dividing. When a cell is about to divide, the chromosomes first appear as a tangled mass of fine threads in the nucleus,

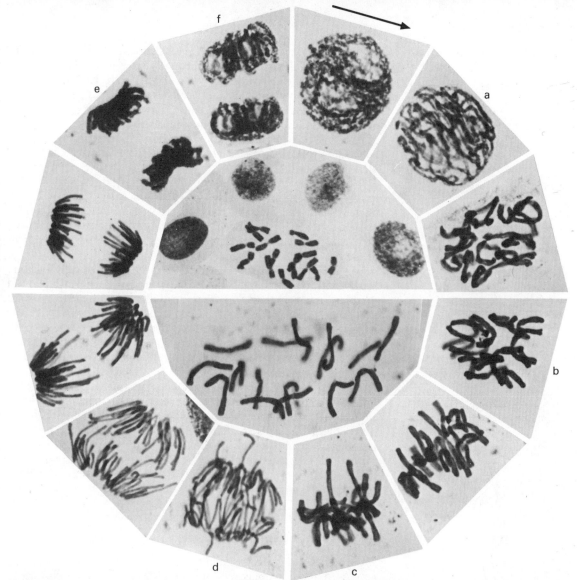

Figure 2.4 Stages in the division of nuclei of cells of onion root. Low power magnification for upper centre diagram: remainder high power magnification. Note that the time intervals between successive stages shown in the 'clock' are not equal

as shown in Figure 2.4(*a*). Look at Figure 2.4(*b*). What change of shape has taken place in the chromosomes by the time this stage is reached? Note that, by this stage, the nucleus is no longer a single discrete unit within the cell, as it is in Figure 2.4(*a*).

Each chromosome is in fact split lengthways into two identical halves called **chromatids,** although these are not always distinguishable up to the stage shown in Figure 2.4(*b*). How do these chromatids behave? Firstly, the chromosomes become arranged in a more or less regular fashion, as shown in Figure 2.4(*c*). Next, the chromatids, which can now be considered to be daughter chromosomes, separate from their partners and move in opposite directions, as shown in Figure 2.4(*d*) onwards.

What has happened by the time stages (*e*) and (*f*) are reached? Eventually, a new membrane forms around each of the two newly formed nuclei and nuclear division is complete. What further changes have to occur for cell division to be completed?

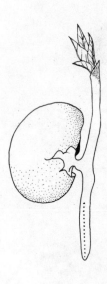

(1)   root tip marked
      at 2 mm intervals

In this way two cells have formed from the original one. The nuclear material has been divided equally between them, since each of the daughter cells, as they are usually called, receives one half of each chromosome from the parent cell. The number of chromosomes in each of the cells is thus the same. Now, if either of these cells divides again, each of its chromosomes will be seen to consist not of one, but of two chromatids. This shows that during the period between mitotic divisions, each chromatid forms another chromatid identical to itself.

Why is it so important to ensure this precise similarity in the nuclei of cells as an organism grows? What is the function of the nucleus? All the activities of the cell, such as respiration and protein synthesis, are under the control of the nucleus. At mitosis, then, each daughter cell gets an exact copy of the control mechanism of the cell.

When would mitosis not be an appropriate type of cell division? If all divisions in the life cycle were by mitosis, fertilisation would double the chromosome number of each generation. How would this come about? The fertilised egg cell would contain twice the usual number of chromosomes and the same would apply to all cells derived from it by mitosis in the course of the organism's growth. In this way, in a few generations, the nucleus would become too large to function normally.

This problem is avoided, since gamete formation involves a different kind of cell division called **meiosis,** or **reduction division.** In this, the chromosomes do not behave as in mitosis but are shared out between the cells so that each gamete receives half the usual number of chromosomes for the species. This number is given the symbol n. The usual number of chromosomes is restored in the fertilised egg ($2n$), and in all cells which are derived from it by mitosis in the course of growth and development.

2.6 Cell enlargement

Figure 2.5 shows an experiment you have seen in which a growing root is marked with a row of equidistant dots and allowed to continue growing for a few days.

In which region of the root does elongation occur?

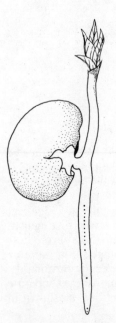

(2)   marked root tip after
      two days further growth

Figure 2.5 Experiment to show region of elongation in a growing root tip

What do you suppose has happened to the cells in the elongating region? You may have noticed these cells while you were observing mitosis, but, if not, another preparation can be made quickly.

1. Place about 1 cm length of root tip on a microscope slide and add a drop of iodine solution.
2. Cover carefully with a cover slip. Wrap the slide and cover slip in two or three layers of paper towel and squeeze between the thumb and finger to spread out the cells.
3. Examine under the microscope, and compare the size and shape of the cells in the elongating region with those where cell division is occurring in the tip of the root.

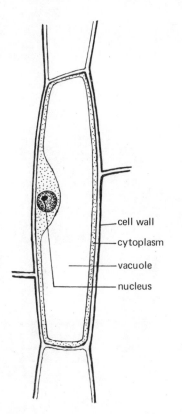

cell wall

cytoplasm

vacuole

nucleus

How has the increase in size of these cells occurred? One obvious part of the answer is that they have absorbed food materials and used them to increase the amount of living material in the cell. Examine the cells and Figure 2.6 carefully, and try to find another feature, not seen in the dividing cells, which may have contributed towards the size increase.

Though it is not always easy to see in a simple preparation, most of the size increase of the elongated cells is due to the absorption of a considerable amount of water, which forms a reservoir-like structure called the **vacuole** in the centre of the cell. The vacuole is bounded by a thin membrane similar to that enclosing the whole cell. The living material, or cytoplasm, forms a thin layer lining the cellulose wall.

The water is absorbed by a process which is discussed in Chapter 4. The cell wall will enlarge to allow elongation to take place, and most of the size increase will be along the axis of the root because of the inward pressure of the surrounding cells. Since the region of the root above the elongating region is held firmly in the soil, what will be the effect of the elongation of these cells?

Vacuolation does not occur in animal cells.

Apart from growing larger, in what other ways do cells change after they have been formed by mitosis? We can answer this question by examining an older region of a plant to see the kinds of cells which it contains.

Figure 2.6 Elongated cell from growing root

1. Place the portion of stem provided in a drop of 0·5 per cent ammonium oxalate solution on a microscope slide.
2. Lower a cover glass on to the preparation.
3. Tap gently with the handle of a mounted needle to separate the cells.

4. Make drawings of the different types of cells you can see. Compare them with those shown in Figure 2.7.
5. Draw up a table of the relative sizes of different types of cells. Details of their functions will be considered in Chapter 8.

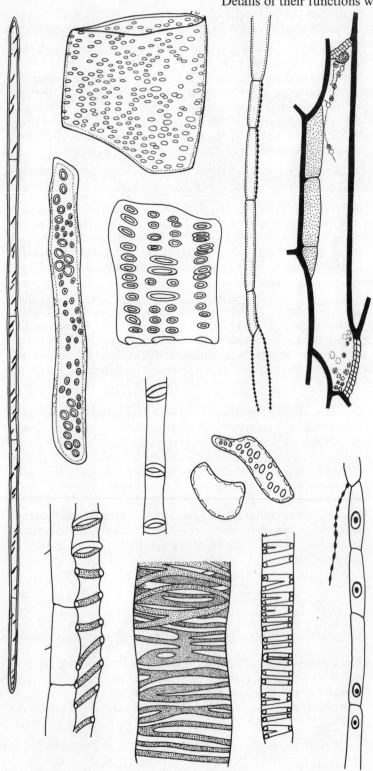

Figure 2.7 Types of cells from mature plant tissues

Your observations have shown that not only do cells grow after their formation by mitosis, but also they develop distinctive structural features, and more mature regions of an organism will contain a variety of different types of cells. These will have different parts to play in the life of the organism, but cells of the same sort are grouped together to form regions known as tissues. The development of the special structures and functions of cells and tissues is known as **differentiation.**

Differentiation also occurs in animal cells. You have already seen cheek cells. The structure of muscle tissue provides a striking contrast.

1. Place a small piece of muscle in a drop of water on a microscope slide.
2. Using mounted needles, separate the muscle fibres. Start with the needle points together in the middle of the muscle and pull them lengthways along it in opposite directions, separating the muscle into a mass of fine fibres.
3. Lower a cover slip on to the preparation and examine, first under the low power and then using the high power of the microscope, and compare with Figure 2.8. Notice the light and dark bands, or striations across the fibres. These are due to the particular arrangement of proteins within the fibres, which gives them the special property of being able to contract.

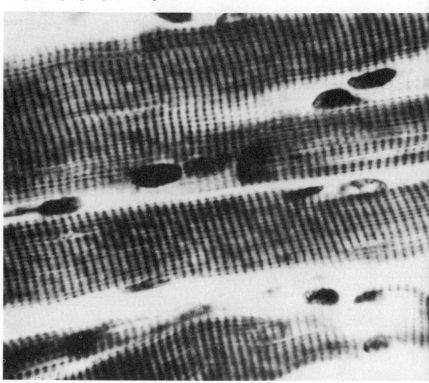

Figure 2.8 Skeletal muscle fibres as seen under the microscope

From these studies, and from observations you may have made on other cells, you will now appreciate that, while most cells have certain features in common, many types of cells are present in a mature organism, and each has its own particular structure. Further studies will show how these special structural features are related to the functions which are performed by different types of cells in an organism.

Looking Back at Chapter 2

1. All organisms are composed of cells, which are small masses of cytoplasm, each bounded by a membrane and containing a nucleus. Plant cells, in addition, are enclosed in a more rigid outer wall of cellulose, and in many cases contain a fluid-filled vacuole.
2. Cells vary in size, and, as an organism grows, its cells divide, by the process of mitosis.
3. Cell division by binary fission is a common method of reproduction in unicellular organisms.
4. During mitosis, thread-like structures called chromosomes may be seen in the cell. At mitosis, each chromosome consists of two chromatids. During division one of these goes to each daughter cell.
5. Following division, cells enlarge. In plant cells, enlargement is often accompanied by vacuolation.
6. Cell growth also involves differentiation, in which the cells develop special structural features which are related to their function.

CELLS AT WORK

3.1 The chemical nature of cells

What structural features are common to cells? You have seen in Chapter 2 that many different types of cells exist, but that most cells have an enclosing membrane and a nucleus controlling the cell's activities, while the cytoplasm accounts for the rest of the living material. Is it reasonable to suppose therefore that most cells are rather similar in chemical composition?

Table 3.1

Various elements in mature maize plants, expressed as percentages of total dry weight

Element	Per cent of total dry weight
oxygen	44·43
carbon	43·57
hydrogen	6·24
nitrogen	1·46
phosphorus	0·20
potassium	0·92
calcium	0·23
magnesium	0·18
sulphur	0·17
iron	0·08
silicon	1·17
aluminium	1·11
chlorine	0·14
manganese	0·04
undetermined elements	0·93

All living cells contain water; most of the other chemicals present are **organic** substances. Organic compounds have large, sometimes very large, molecules. These always contain carbon atoms, often in very large numbers. Hydrogen, oxygen and nitrogen are other elements commonly found in organic compounds. From your knowledge of food tests, what are the three most important groups of organic compounds in the diet of man and other animals? Animals obtain these substances from the animal or plant material which they eat. By what process does the green plant build complex organic material?

These organic substances, which are manufactured or taken in as food by all living organisms, are found in every cell. The exact nature and proportions of the proteins, carbohydrates and fats will vary from one type of cell to another, but they are essential components for the life of each cell.

In addition, living cells contain small amounts of a variety of inorganic substances. Table 3.1, page 35, shows results from an analysis carried out on material from dried mature maize plants. The material is prepared from plants which have been carefully washed and heated to a temperature just below 100°C until there is no further loss in weight. Why is the washing necessary? What substance is removed from the plant material before the analysis begins?

What compounds will mainly account for the first four items in the table? What proportion, approximately, of the dry weight of the plants is accounted for by inorganic materials?

3.2 What goes on in cells?

Living things, as you know, are distinguished from non-living not only by their structure and composition, but by their activities, that is, by the various things they do. What examples of these can you think of? All these activities of living things depend ultimately on chemical activity in the cell. By what process do living cells release energy? For what purposes is the energy used?

There is ceaseless chemical activity going on within living cells. The sum total of chemical reactions occurring in a living organism we call **metabolism**. Some of the reactions involve building up complex substances, starting from simpler ones, while in other reactions complex molecules are broken down into smaller, simpler molecules. You should be able to think of at least one example of each of these types of reaction in a living cell.

3.3 Large molecules from small

You have learned that, in a green plant, the sugars produced in photosynthesis are often converted into starch. Sugars and starch are both carbohydrates, but the molecule of starch is very much larger than the molecule of a sugar such as glucose, because it consists of several dozen glucose molecules joined together. The conversion of sugar to starch is thus a building up or synthetic reaction.

It is quite easy to synthesise starch in the laboratory.

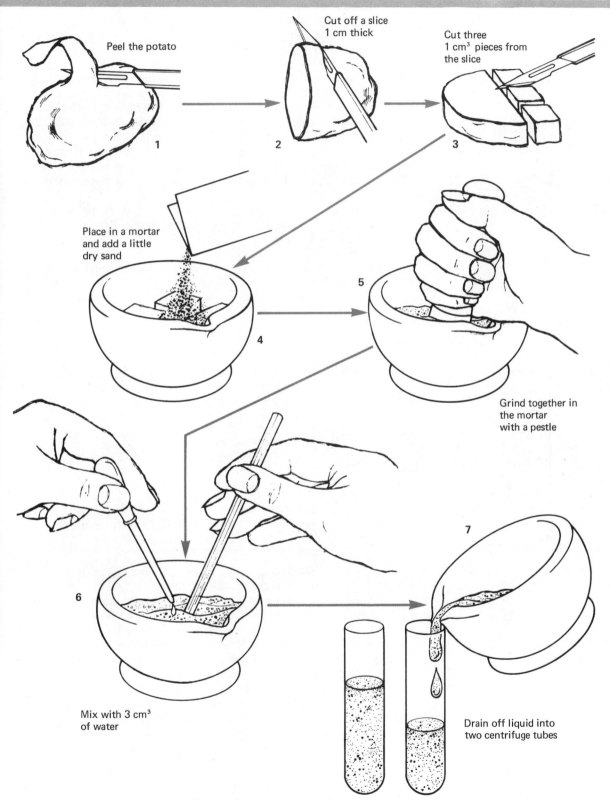

Figure 3.1 Preparation of potato extract

1. Cut three 1 cm cubes of tissue, without skin, from a raw potato and grind with a little clean sharp sand using a pestle and mortar. Do not grind for too long, but just enough to break up the potato tissue.
2. Add 3 cm³ distilled water and stir gently with a clean glass rod.
3. Drain the liquid off into two centrifuge tubes, putting equal amounts in each, and centrifuge the tubes for 5 minutes. What has happened to the particles of solid matter in the tube?
4. Using a syringe or fine pipette, remove a small drop of the clear liquid on to a tile and test it with iodine solution. If a blue colour results, centrifuge and test again, and keep repeating this procedure till the liquid in the tube is shown to be free from starch. Why is it important to ensure that the potato extract is starch-free?
5. Now set up a spotting tile with three rows of drops as follows:
   Row A—4 drops of a one per cent solution of glucose-1-phosphate which is a form of a sugar.
   Row B—4 drops of distilled water.
   Row C—4 drops of equal volumes of distilled water and glucose-1-phosphate.
   The arrangement of drops on the tile is shown in Figure 3.2.

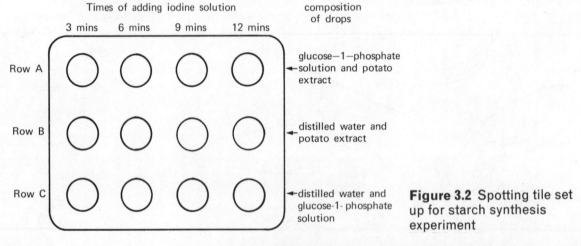

Figure 3.2 Spotting tile set up for starch synthesis experiment

If you are working in pairs, one person can set up the tile while the other prepares the starch-free potato extract.
6. Now note the time, and put one drop of the starch-free potato extract into each of the drops in rows A and B on the tile. Do not add any potato extract to the drops in row C.
7. After three minutes add a drop of iodine solution to the first drop in each row. After a further three minutes add a drop of iodine solution to the second drop in each row. Repeat after a further three minutes for column three, and then three minutes after that repeat for column four. After each addition of iodine, note and record any colour changes which occur.

Has starch been formed in any part of the experiment? What does the experiment show to be necessary for starch formation?

3.4 Enzymes

What part was played by the potato extract in bringing about the synthesis of starch from glucose-1-phosphate? The experiment shows that the glucose-1-phosphate by itself will not change into starch, although glucose contains all the elements necessary to produce starch since both are carbohydrates. You may have carried out experiments in your Chemistry course in which a substance played a similar part to that of the potato extract in our experiment. What term is applied to such a substance?

The potato extract acts as a kind of catalyst, that is to say, it brings about a reaction which would otherwise not occur under the conditions of the experiment. What other characteristics do catalysts show? The substance in the potato extract which acted as a catalyst is called phosphorylase, and it belongs to a class of substances known as enzymes. Enzymes are organic catalysts, produced in the living cells of animals and plants. They are responsible for controlling the enormous variety of chemical reactions which go to make up the metabolism of an organism, which we referred to in Section 3.2. Most enzymes act within the cells in which they are made but grinding up the potato, in the experiment, released the phosphorylase from the cells. Most cells contain large numbers of different enzymes. In the remainder of this chapter we shall investigate some reactions catalysed by enzymes and the ways in which they are affected by changes in conditions.

What part may be played in the life of the potato plant by the reaction you investigated in the experiment?

3.5 Chemical breakdown by an enzyme

At what stage in the life of a potato plant is the reaction we have investigated likely to 'go the other way'? Many plants store starch as a food reserve, not only in underground storage organs like the potato tuber, but also, very commonly, in their seeds. When the seeds germinate, or when growth begins from the storage organ, carbohydrates are needed to provide energy and to contribute to the material of new cells, such as their cellulose walls, in the growing regions of the plant. For these purposes, starch food reserves are first converted into sugars by enzyme action. In the next experiment you will investigate this conversion of starch into sugar.

1. You are provided with petri dishes containing agar made up with a small quantity of starch. Confirm the presence of starch by removing a small piece of agar and adding it to a little dilute iodine solution in a watch glass.
2. Now take the cereal grains which have been soaked in water for 18 hours and remove the husks from the grains. Cut carefully across a grain, as shown in Figure 3.3, to separate the endosperm, the starch food reserve, from the embryo, which is the part from which the new plant will develop.

Figure 3.3 Removing the embryo from de-husked grain

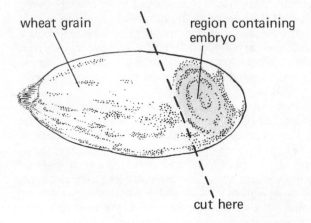

wheat grain

region containing embryo

cut here

The embryo lies at the end which is usually less tufted in appearance. If you have difficulty in distinguishing the different regions of the seed, cut it in half lengthways. The embryo may be distinguished from the whiter endosperm by its slightly greyish appearance.

3. Place the embryo in the centre of the starch agar plate in the petri dish. Set up another plate in the same way, using the endosperm in place of the embryo, as shown in Figure 3.4. Cover the plates and leave them in an incubator at 35°C for three days.

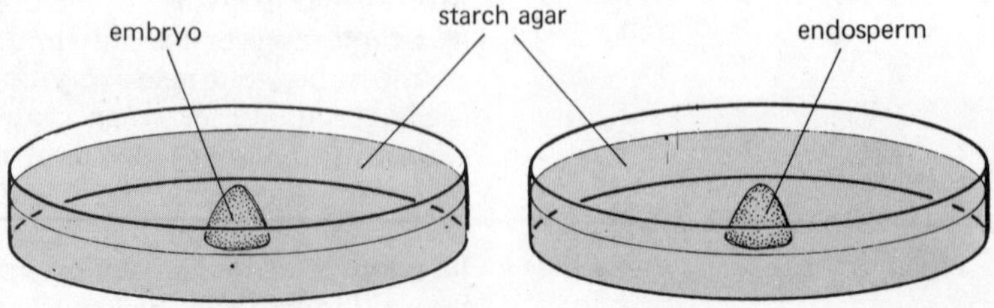

embryo   starch agar   endosperm

Figure 3.4 Endosperm and embryo on starch agar plates

4. Take out the petri dishes and carefully remove the embryo and endosperm with a pair of forceps. Using a pipette, flood the surface of the plates with dilute iodine solution. Leave this for a few minutes until a blue-black colour has developed, and then carefully wash away the iodine with a gentle stream of water from the tap.

5. Note the distribution of the blue-black colour on the two plates. Where is the blue-black colour present, and where is it absent? What is the explanation of the results obtained?

3.6 A very common enzyme

Most enzymes are specific, that is to say, they catalyse the reactions of only one substance or closely related group of chemical substances. We often speak of an enzyme and its **substrate,** the substance on which it acts, fitting together rather like a lock and key.

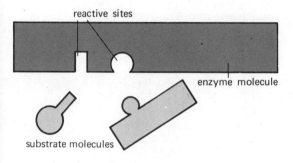

A   before reaction

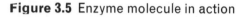

Figure 3.5 Enzyme molecule in action

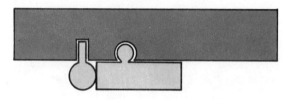

B   during reaction

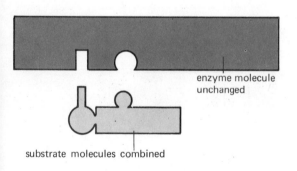

C   after reaction

Nevertheless, many enzymes are widespread in the living world, catalysing the same reaction in a great variety of plant and animal tissues. This is not really surprising for we have seen there are many structural and chemical similarities in different types of cells. These similarities extend to chemical reactions as well, many of which are common to the majority of living cells, and hence the enzymes controlling them are equally widespread. What sort of reactions might come into this category?

Catalase is an enzyme found in many different animal and plant tissues. It catalyses the breakdown of hydrogen peroxide into water and oxygen. What would you expect to notice on adding tissue containing catalase to a solution of hydrogen peroxide? How could you make a rough comparison of catalase concentration in various tissues? The following experiment is one method of doing this.

1. Set up a rack of clean test tubes, and half fill each tube with a 5 per cent solution of hydrogen peroxide.
2. Using forceps, drop pieces of plant or animal tissue into the tubes in turn, using a different kind of tissue for each tube, as shown in Figure 3.6. Potato, apple, carrot, turnip, onion, meat, liver and blood are all suitable tissues.
3. Observe and record the results in each case. Which tissue appears to have the greatest effect on the hydrogen peroxide? The results could indicate different amounts of catalase in the materials used. In what other way could the results be interpreted?

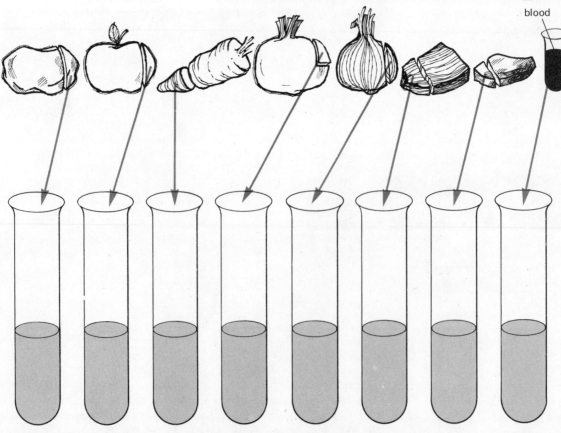

Figure 3.6 Investigating the enzyme catalase

3.7 Effect of temperature on enzyme activity

For the following experiments, select one tissue which the previous experiment showed to have a high catalase activity.

1. Set up test tubes half full of 5 per cent hydrogen peroxide solution as follows:
   Tube A: in a mixture of ice and water in a beaker,
   Tube B: in a beaker of water at 40°C,
   Tube C: at room temperature.
2. Add a small piece of the selected tissue to each tube and note the result. What can you deduce about the effect of temperature on enzyme activity?
3. Next boil a small piece of the selected tissue in water for 5 minutes. Allow it to cool and add it to some hydrogen peroxide solution. Note the effect. What effect do you think boiling has had on the catalase?

3.8 The chemical nature of enzymes

We have now learned a good deal about enzymes. We know that they are catalysts produced in living cells, that they are specific for particular reactions, that they are inactivated by heat, and that they are highly sensitive to the conditions of temperature under which they work. Notice however that enzymes themselves are not 'living'. Some, at any rate, of the tissues you used in Section 3.6 were no longer alive, and there may be, in your school laboratory, some enzymes in powder form which are just as effective as the living tissues from which they were extracted, though the powdered enzymes may have been in their bottles on the shelf for many months or even years.

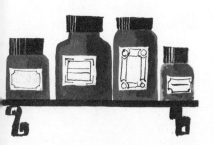

What kind of chemicals do you suppose enzymes might be? Remember that they are essential components of all living cells, and are specific catalysts. Enzymes might belong to any of the categories of organic compounds found in living cells. Simple tests will quickly demonstrate which.

1. Shake up a little powdered enzyme, such as pepsin or diastase, with 5 cm³ of water in a test tube, and add a drop of iodine solution.
2. To a little powdered enzyme in a test tube add 5 cm³ of Benedict's solution and heat gently to boiling.
3. Shake up a little of the powdered enzyme with 3 cm³ of ethanol in a test tube and allow to stand and settle for a few minutes. Pour off 2 cm³ of the ethanol into another test tube and add an equal volume of cold water.
4. To a little of the powdered enzyme in a test tube add about 3 cm³ of distilled water and two or three drops of Millon's reagent.

Warm gently in a Bunsen burner flame.

For what groups of organic compounds are these the tests? Note the results of the test in each case. To which groups of organic compounds do your results indicate that enzymes belong?

Apart from water, proteins are amongst the most abundant components of living cells. All enzymes are proteins, but it is important to note that the reverse is not true. Not all the proteins in living cells are enzymes. You will already know that proteins are essential in our diet for the building up of new material in growth and for the replacement of body tissues such as muscles. One important aspect of this growth and maintenance is the provision of the enzymes necessary to control the chemical activities which go on in living cells.

The fact that enzymes are proteins explains the effect of boiling which you noticed in Section 3.7. Enzymes, like all proteins, are chemically altered by heat in a way which cannot be reversed. One simple example of this is seen in cooking an egg. Eggs are rich in protein, and the high temperature in cooking coagulates the proteins, making a hard opaque material from what was originally a clear fluid. The egg does not become raw again if you let it cool down. Enzymes are similar. High temperatures alter them (they are said to become **denatured**) in such a way that they can no longer carry out their catalytic activities. This denaturing of proteins is part of the reason why high temperatures are lethal for living plants and animals.

Looking Back at Chapter 3

1. All living cells have certain structural features in common, and they contain water, proteins, carbohydrates, fats and a variety of inorganic substances.
2. A living cell is characterised by ceaseless chemical activity going on within it; this constitutes the cell's metabolism.
3. These chemical reactions are controlled by organic catalysts which are produced within the cell and are known as enzymes.
4. Enzymes, which are proteins, are specific in their effect, though many are widespread, catalysing the same reaction in various plant and animal tissues.
5. Enzymes are inactivated by high temperatures, and are sensitive to the conditions of temperature under which they act.

4 WATER AND LIVING THINGS

4.1 Mainly water

In Section 1.5 you investigated the loss of water from large and small potatoes. Clearly, the potato tubers must have had a quantity of water in their tissues. You will already know that all living things contain water, but you are now going to determine the actual amount of water present in various tissues.

In this experiment you can use a variety of tissues, such as fresh potato, cabbage, carrot, raw steak or minced beef. Whichever you use, the method is as follows.
1. Weigh a porcelain basin, or similar shallow vessel.
2. Reweigh the basin containing chopped-up fresh material. What can we derive from these two weighings?
3. Allow the tissue to dry by leaving the basin aside for several days, or by placing it in a drying oven at 80°–90°C for a few hours.
4. Cool and reweigh and then continue the drying process.
5. Repeat until there is no change in weight.
6. Calculate the loss in weight. What does this loss represent?
7. Finally, calculate the percentage of water which was present in the fresh tissue.

In this experiment you have obtained your result by dehydrating tissues. Now, starting off with dry, dormant seeds, such as beans, peas, or cereals, how could you determine the amount of water which they absorb in order to become active and begin to germinate? Think out and write down each step of the experiment before you start to carry it out.

You may be surprised that your results, and those of others in the class using different materials, indicate that most tissues contain a very high percentage of water.

Figure 4.1 shows the percentage of water present in a variety of living things.

In general, a living organism may have between 60 and 95 per cent of its weight made up of water. From the data given in Figure 4.1, what percentage of water, approximately, will be present in the human body? Which parts of the human body do you think will

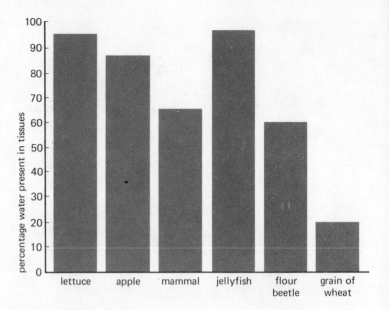

Figure 4.1 The water present in some living things

have a larger percentage than this, and which parts will have a lower percentage?

Very few active cells can survive **desiccation,** drying out, but plants such as lichens and mosses often revive and grow well even after a long period of drought. We shall now consider some reasons why water is so important within the body of an organism.

4.2 Why is water important to living things?

In order to answer the question which is the heading of this section, we shall inquire into the part played by water in (*a*) synthesis of chemical materials, (*b*) reproduction of living things, (*c*) temperature control, especially in man, (*d*) transport of materials and chemical action and (*e*) lubrication.

(*a*) *Synthesis.* You have already found that, in photosynthesis, carbohydrate is made from the combination of carbon dioxide and hydrogen. The hydrogen comes from water which is present in the green plant. Water is also involved in the chemical processes by which proteins and other compounds are formed in living things.

(*b*) *Reproduction.* Earlier in the course you have seen that water plays an important part in sexual reproduction. For example, the gametes of an animal such as *Pomatoceros*, or of many fish, are simply released into the water in which the animal lives. In land animals, reproduction also involves water, since the male gametes, after being inserted into the female's body, must move in a moist tube towards the ovum. Further, during development, the embryo of a mammal is enclosed in a bag, the amnion. What is present in the amnion, and what is its purpose?

In those land plants which have flowers, fertilisation occurs when the male gamete reaches the ovule, after passing down the pollen tube which grows within the style. However, in land plants which do not have flowers, other life cycles and methods of fertilisation occur. For example, sexual reproduction may take place only in wet weather, when it is then possible for the sperm to swim on the surface of the plant towards the ovum.

(*c*) *Temperature control.* The following experiments will help to explain how your body temperature is kept fairly constant, even when you are undergoing strenuous exercise.

1. Set up three thermometers in a stand, wrapping a little cotton wool round the bulb of each.
2. Note the temperature, which should of course be the same on each thermometer.
3. Leave the first untreated, add a few drops of water to the cotton wool of the second, and a few drops of ethyl alcohol to the cotton wool of the third. Both the water and alcohol should be at room temperature at the start of the experiment.
4. Record the temperatures at intervals of 5 minutes for at least half an hour.

Which thermometers showed a fall in temperature? For which was the fall greatest? Try to account for this fall in temperature, bearing in mind that the entire apparatus was at room temperature to begin with. To help you to arrive at an explanation, observe what happens to the temperature when the cotton wool is nearly dry again.

Loss of heat due to evaporation is a method of temperature control which occurs in many living things. For example, on a hot summer's day, bare earth and stones may be very hot indeed, but the vegetation nearby which has been exposed to the same heat from the sun is cool. Why may this be so? You should be able to think of at least two reasons.

You will learn more about water in plants in Chapter 8. Now you are going to study the sweat pores of your own body. The production of sweat is one of the mechanisms in the body preventing body-temperature rising to a dangerously high level when we are very active in very warm surroundings.

Carry out the experiment as outlined in Figure 4.2.

Dry starch and dry iodine do not react to produce a colour. What has been exuded by the skin allowing the colour change to occur? What do the dark dots represent?

Repeat this experiment after vigorous exercise. Compare the dark marks with those previously obtained. What can you deduce about the relationship between activity and output of sweat by the skin?

1. Rub the skin of the palm of the hand with
   iodine solution, (i)
   Allow to dry.

2. Press a piece of starch paper on to the iodine-
   stained skin, (ii)

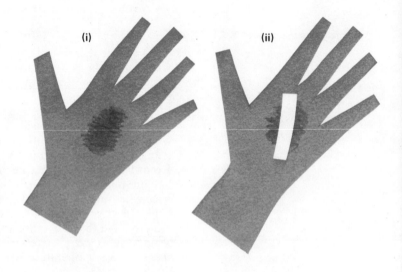

(i)   (ii)

Figure 4.2 Investigating sweat pores in the skin

3. Hold in position for 5 minutes.
   Remove the paper and examine it.

The results of these experiments indicate one way in which the temperature of the body may be kept from rising above normal. In addition, the presence of water in the tissues of an organism makes it less susceptible to any sudden change of temperature which may occur in its environment. Water is slow to cool down and slow to heat up. Could water therefore be described as a good or as a bad heat insulator?

What did you learn in Section 1.4 about the effect of size on the heat retention or heat loss by an animal?

(d) *Transport and chemical action.* Of all the liquids known, water is able to dissolve the most substances. Why would it be reasonable to think that water is important in the transport of food and waste products within the bodies of organisms? Another point to remember is that most of the chemical reactions in an organism occur in solutions in which water is the solvent.

(e) *Lubrication.* You may have seen that in a dissected animal, such as a rat, the internal organs are covered by a film of mucus, which contains a great deal of water, and which has an important function as a lubricant. What would cause friction between internal organs and how does the mucus reduce this friction?

From the five points which we have discussed, you will realise that water is an extremely important component of living things.

We shall now consider the movement of water and other substances within cells and tissues.

4.3 Movement within a liquid

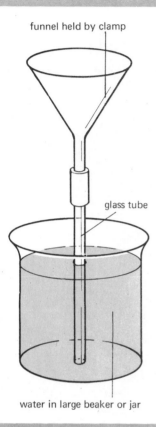

funnel held by clamp

glass tube

water in large beaker or jar

In this experiment you are going to study the movement of a coloured substance, potassium permanganate, in water.

Set up the apparatus shown in Figure 4.3 in a place in the laboratory where it can stand undisturbed for a day or two. After the water in the beaker has become still, pour a little potassium permanganate solution gently into the funnel.

Where is most of the potassium permanganate concentrated? Observe the apparatus at intervals of two or three hours, if possible, and note the spread of the potassium permanganate as indicated by the colour of the water. Finally, observe again after two or three days. Is there a concentration of colour at any point, or is there a uniform spread of colour? What must have happened eventually to the potassium permanganate which was concentrated originally in one part?

Figure 4.3 Apparatus to investigate movement in a liquid

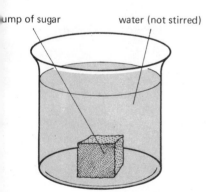

lump of sugar   water (not stirred)

Figure 4.4 Concentration and diffusion

When molecules are free to move about in a medium, they eventually become uniformly dispersed and randomly spread out, even if they start off from a high concentration. This gradual movement is known as **diffusion.** The difference in concentration from high to low is called a **concentration gradient.** Just as a ball will roll down a slope or gradient, so molecules will tend to move from a region where the concentration is high to a region where those molecules are in low concentration.

Look at Figure 4.4. Where is the sugar concentration greatest, and where is it lowest? In which direction will the sugar molecules gradually diffuse? When will this diffusion end?

Consider the water in this example. Where is the water concentration lowest, and where is it highest? In which direction will water molecules tend to diffuse? We do not usually think of water as having a concentration in this way, but it is important to realise that all molecules which are free to move will diffuse along a concentration gradient.

4.4 The entry and exit of water

The process of diffusion applies to soluble substances in a liquid and also to gases in air. As it is very important in many life processes, we shall now investigate a particular example by means of living tissues, and by a model of a cell.

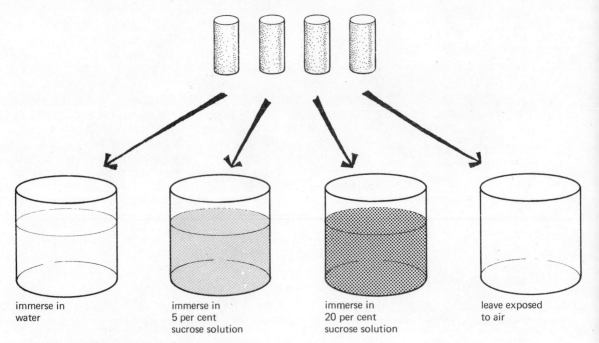

immerse in water

immerse in 5 per cent sucrose solution

immerse in 20 per cent sucrose solution

leave exposed to air

(i) Cut 4 uniform pieces of fresh potato, using a cork borer.

(ii) Trim the 4 pieces to exactly the same length.

(iii) Treat the 4 pieces as shown above.

Figure 4.5 Investigating the effect of different solutions on potato tissue

(a) *Living tissues*

Figure 4.5 indicates the stages in setting up this experiment. After 1–2 days of treatment, test the four pieces of potato in the following ways.

1. Feel each piece and decide whether it is firm, or soft and flabby. Piece number 4 has lost water, in this case by drying out. Which of the other pieces feels most like it? What does this indicate may have happened to that piece?

2. Compare the lengths of the four pieces, noting carefully any difference in size from the original length. What evidence is there that substances may enter or leave the potato tissue? We shall now inquire into the explanation of this by setting up a model of a cell.

WATER AND LIVING THINGS 51

(b) *A model of a cell*
1. Cut a 15–20 cm length of cellulose tubing.
2. Wet it, and then tie a knot firmly at one end, thus making a long bag, open at one end.
3. Pour in 20 per cent glucose solution to half fill the bag.
4. Tie a knot at the top of the bag, after carefully squeezing out the air. Rinse off any drips of glucose which may be on the outside of the bag.
5. Dry the outside of the bag, weigh it with its contents, and note to the nearest 0·5 g.
6. Immerse the bag in water.
7. Using water in a second bag instead of glucose, repeat the weighing and then immerse it in 20 per cent glucose solution.
   The apparatus at this stage is shown in Figure 4.6.

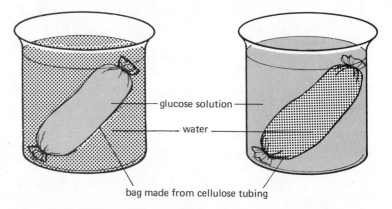

glucose solution

water

bag made from cellulose tubing

Figure 4.6 A model of a cell

After 30 minutes remove both the bags and reweigh them. What precaution must be taken before weighing?

Then replace the bags in their respective vessels and, if possible, after a further 30 minutes weigh the bags again. If necessary, this second weighing can be done 1–2 days later.

Which bag increased in weight and which decreased? What evidence is there that the cellulose, which forms a kind of membrane, did not allow completely free passage of both water and glucose molecules into and out of the bags? What general conclusion can be reached about the direction of movement of molecules in relation to the glucose solution?

This movement of a solvent such as water through a special membrane, in this case the walls of the cellulose tubing, into a solution is an illustration of one of the ways in which water moves from cell to cell within tissues. The process is known as **osmosis.**

In order to explain osmosis we shall use what you know about diffusion and concentration gradients. Look at Figure 4.7(a), which shows a diagram of a cell in water. Cellulose membranes and the membranes of living cells are capable of restricting or allowing the passage of substances. This control depends partly on the sizes of the molecules separated by the membranes.

For this reason such a membrane can be described as **selectively permeable** or semi-permeable. In this example it allows the passage of the smaller molecules of water but restricts the passage of the larger glucose molecules.

It should be noted that the cellulose cell walls found in plants do not restrict the entry or exit of substances in this way.

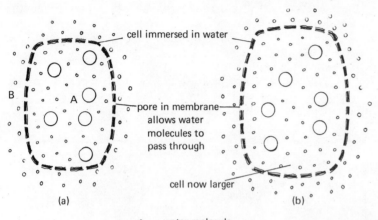

cell immersed in water

pore in membrane allows water molecules to pass through

cell now larger

(a)   (b)

o   water molecule

◯   glucose molecule

Figure 4.7 A model cell (*a*) before osmosis (*b*) after osmosis (sizes of molecules and cell not to same scale)

Of the two places, marked A and B, which has the higher concentration of glucose? There will be a tendency for the glucose to diffuse out and disperse. Why does this not happen?

Of the two places, A and B, which has the higher concentration of water? As a result of this concentration gradient, in which direction will the water molecules diffuse? What will be the result of this? Figure 4.7(*b*) shows the result of the cell membrane being permeable to water but not to glucose molecules.

4.5 Investigating the membrane

The action of the membrane in controlling the movement of substances through it is not fully understood. Indeed, the description given of osmosis in the previous section is inadequate, and we are now going to find out more about the membrane's properties.

Set up the apparatus as shown in Figure 4.8, making sure that any drips of glucose solution have been rinsed off the outside of the bag before it is immersed in the water in the boiling tube.
1. Remove a sample of the water from the boiling tube immediately the bag is immersed.
2. Test this sample to find if glucose is present.
3. Withdraw further samples and test after 5, 10 and 15 minutes.

Has any glucose appeared in the water in the boiling tube? How must the previous statements about the membrane's properties be amended? In what way is the result of this experiment in keeping with what you have found out about diffusion and gradients?

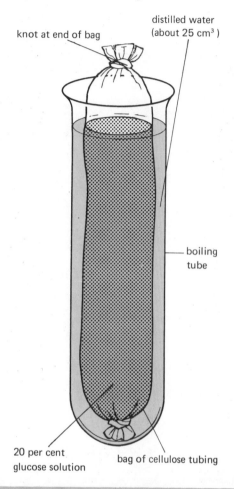

Figure 4.8 Apparatus to investigate a membrane

It will now be clear to you that the membrane is not impermeable to the glucose. It appeared to be so, however, because the rate of diffusion of the glucose molecules was much slower than the rate of diffusion of the water molecules. Many more molecules of water went through into the solution than glucose molecules into the water in the other direction. Why do you think this happens?

You are now going to find out more about the membrane of living cells of beetroot. In this plant, the deep red pigment is retained within the vacuoles of the cells by the vacuolar membrane, but it may escape under certain circumstances.

1. Set up 10 test tubes, each one-third full of water. Maintain each at a fairly constant temperature, the first at 10°C, the next at 20°C and so on at intervals of 10 degrees.
2. Set up 3 more test tubes. Add ethyl alcohol to the first, ether to the second and concentrated hydrochloric acid to the third.
3. Use an 8 mm diameter cork borer to prepare 13 similar cylinders, or 'plugs', of fresh beetroot, each small enough to go into a test tube.
4. Wash the plugs of beetroot in cold water until they stop 'bleeding'. Why does some pigment come out of these tissues?
5. Now place a plug of beetroot in each of the 13 test tubes which you have set up.
6. Observe and note the appearance of the bathing-medium after 2 minutes, 5 minutes and 15 minutes. Record your observations in Table 4.1.

Table 4.1

Bathing medium	Appearance of medium		
	after 2 min	after 5 min	after 15 min
Water at 10°C			
20°C			
30°C			
40°C			
50°C			
60°C			
70°C			
80°C			
90°C			
100°C			
Ethyl alcohol			
Ether			
Conc. acid			

What information does the experiment provide about the effect of temperature on the membrane? What has been shown about the effect of alcohol, ether and acid?

You used non-living material, cellulose, as the selectively permeable membrane in osmosis experiments. From the experiment using beetroot plugs, you have obtained evidence that the cell membrane has some of the characteristics of living things; for example, it can be destroyed at temperatures above about 50°C and it can be destroyed by certain chemicals. It is in fact composed of materials which are capable of selectively controlling the passage of substances into, or out of, the cell. In the case of plant cells, the substances move into, or out of, the vacuoles.

4.6 Some results of osmosis in models

You are now going to set up two experiments which will help you to appreciate an important consequence of water movement by osmosis.

(*a*) A simple osmometer

1. Set up the apparatus as shown in Figure 4.9.

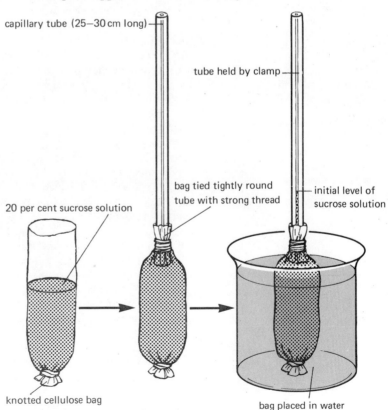

capillary tube (25–30 cm long)

tube held by clamp

bag tied tightly round tube with strong thread

initial level of sucrose solution

20 per cent sucrose solution

knotted cellulose bag

bag placed in water

Figure 4.9 A simple osmometer

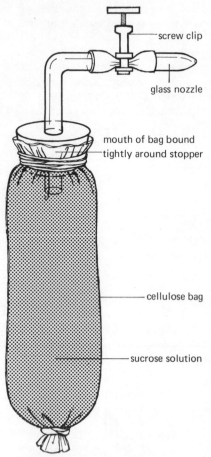

Figure 4.10 Investigating pressure due to osmosis.

2. Mark the initial level of the sucrose solution.

3. Mark the level at intervals of 10, 20 and 30 minutes.

In what direction did the level move? Is there now more or less water inside the bag than initially? What evidence is there of a pressure in operation?

(*b*) Assemble the apparatus shown in Figure 4.10 and, after screwing down the clip firmly, place the bag in a large beaker of water.

Observe after a few hours, and also after a day or two. What is the appearance of the bag? Feel it carefully. Is it firm or flabby? After what you have already learned, you should find it easy to explain the changes which have taken place in the apparatus.

Now, support the glass nozzle and point it away from yourself, but not towards anybody else. Unscrew the clip as quickly as possible. Observe what happens and explain the result.

Look again at the apparatus shown in Figure 4.9 as it is finally set up. We can say that, because of osmosis, water tends to move up the tube. Now, suppose that we move a tightly-fitting plunger down the bore of the tube, and by means of the plunger exert a pressure which tends to prevent movement of water up the tube. The pressure that must be applied to prevent water just moving up the tube is said to be equal to the **osmotic pressure** of the solution in the cellulose bag. (Osmotic pressure is sometimes called **osmotic potential.**) We can think of osmotic pressure as the pressure exerted when water moves across a selectively permeable membrane into a more concentrated solution. If we increased the concentration of the sucrose in the cellulose bag what would happen to the osmotic pressure? What difference would this make to the results observed in the experiment?

Water enters cells by osmosis, and as you have already seen in the work of Section 1.11, the presence of water can be of importance in maintaining shape by supporting the soft parts of an organism. Why should this be so? To help you to arrive at an explanation, consider how the appearance and shape of an inflated tyre serves as a model of the way in which the shape of a cell is maintained due to water taken in by osmosis.

A plant cell which is distended by the intake of water is in a state of **turgor,** and is said to be **turgid.** Why, do you think, does the cell not burst as the pressure increases? To answer that question, bear in mind that the wall of a cell will exert a pressure tending to maintain the shape of the cell. If the cells of a plant lose turgor, what will be the effect on the leaves and other non-rigid parts?

Like the non-living cellulose used in the model, Figure 4.6, the membrane of a cell is responsible for osmotic properties.

The cell may be able to take in, across its membranes, substances which are present in small concentrations in the environment and may build up a high concentration within itself. This involves the movement of substances against the concentration gradient, and is described as **active transport.** For example, in some seaweeds the vacuole contains a high concentration of iodine which is extracted from sea-water, though it exists there in a much lower concentration.

From what we have discussed, it will be clear that the cell membranes are very important parts of an organism. Cell walls, which occur only in plant tissues, are not the boundaries which regulate what enters or leaves the cell. It is the cell membrane, found in every plant or animal cell which forms the regulatory boundary.

Looking Back at Chapter 4

1. A high percentage of water is present in the bodies of plants and animals.
2. Water is very important to living things in a wide variety of ways because of its chemical and physical properties.
3. A solute moves in a liquid by diffusion, the movement being along the gradient from a high concentration of the solute to a low one.
4. Water can pass through a selectively permeable membrane into a solution, the process being called osmosis.
5. The membranes of cells are selectively permeable. They can control the entry and exit of various substances, but they are destroyed by heat and by certain chemicals.
6. As a result of taking in water by osmosis, a pressure is built up. This pressure helps to keep cells turgid and thus maintain the shape of soft parts of plants and animals.

OBTAINING FOOD

5.1 Plants, animals and their food

In Chapter 2 we recalled that organisms are composed of cells which grow in size after they increase in number by division. Chapter 3 dealt with some of the chemical activities which go on in the cells during metabolism. For life processes to take place, the cells require constant supplies of building materials, and fuel in the form of food. You know that green plants contain the pigment chlorophyll, which enables them to make food by a chemical action utilising carbon dioxide and water and light energy. What name is given to this process? This kind of feeding is called **autotrophic**; the food is manufactured by the plant from simple non-living, inorganic material.

Animals cannot make food in this way. To obtain food they either have to eat green plants, in which case they are said to be herbivores, or they eat other animals, and are then called carnivores. If they eat both plants and animals, they are known as omnivores. When an organism feeds on other living material, or on dead organic material, its nutrition is said to be **heterotrophic.** We can sum this up by saying that autotrophs are food producers while heterotrophs are food consumers. When dealing with food webs earlier in the course, you met the terms producer and consumer. In this chapter we are going to investigate some of the ways in which the consumers obtain their food.

5.2 Man and his food

Man belongs to the group of animals classed as mammals. For some time after their birth the only food of young mammals is milk, suckled from the mother. As mammals mature they require foods other than milk, and hence carnivores, herbivores and omnivores must all be able to obtain or capture food, and then cut, tear, or crush it before it is swallowed and digested. **Teeth,** the structures which do these jobs, have become specialised in different ways, depending on the kind of food which the animal eats.

5.3 Tooth types

How do you use your teeth in eating? The following experiment should help to answer this question.

1. Take two pieces of bread, one piece soft, and the other a tough crust or heel slice.
2. First eat the soft bread, and then the crust, noting down everything you do in the process of eating the separate pieces up to the moment of swallowing.
3. Which teeth are responsible for particular jobs in the process of eating?

As you have found now in eating the bread, not all teeth have the same function.

The number and different kinds of teeth possessed by an animal constitute its **dentition.** The teeth are given different names depending on how they are used. For example, when you bit into the soft bread you probably used your front teeth, bringing the sharp edges of the top set against those of the lower set. These teeth are called **incisor** teeth; there are four in both jaws. What cutting instrument does the word incisor remind you of? When you tried to cut the crust, your incisors might not have been able to bite through the tough outer layer so perhaps you moved it slightly to the side of your mouth, grasped it with the pointed teeth next to the incisors and tore a piece off. These pointed teeth, of which you have two in each jaw, are called **canines.** What sort of animals have large canines? (Figure 5.1 will suggest others.) When you cut the bread, or tore the crust, you probably moved the piece further back and ground it

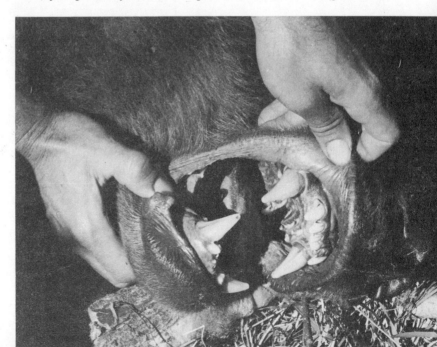

Figure 5.1 The mouth of a brown bear

between your double teeth, which are called **molars.** When you possess a full set of permanent teeth, you will have five molars on each side of your upper and lower jaws. How many teeth should an adult have in a complete set? We usually divide the molars into two groups. The back three on each side are known as the true molars, while the two in front of these next to the canines are called **premolars.** You may remember having an early set of teeth, most of which you lost while you were at the primary school stage. Such teeth are called the milk teeth and they include premolars but no molars. How many teeth should you have had in your first set?

5.4 Dental formula

Just as in Chemistry, where it is useful to summarise information by means of chemical formulae, the dentition of a mammal can be represented by a **dental formula.** Here are two ways of writing down the dental formula for an adult man.

$$i \frac{2}{2} : c \frac{1}{1} : pm \frac{2}{2} : m \frac{3}{3} \quad \text{or simply} \quad \frac{2 \; 1 \; 2 \; 3}{2 \; 1 \; 2 \; 3}$$

Look at the human skull in Figure 5.2, or refer to the previous paragraph, and try to decide what the symbols stand for and how we arrive at this formula. Then write down the formula for a set of human milk teeth, shown in Figure 5.3.

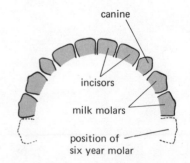

Figure 5.3 A set of milk teeth

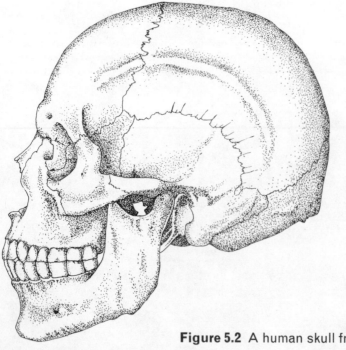

Figure 5.2 A human skull from the side

5.5 Tooth structure

Although they vary so much in shape, mammals' teeth all have the same basic structure. You are now going to investigate this structure.

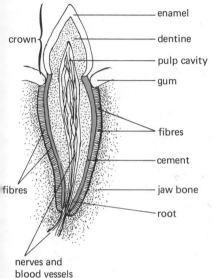

enamel

crown

dentine

pulp cavity

gum

fibres

cement

fibres

jaw bone

root

nerves and
blood vessels

1. Cut or break open the tooth of any mammal. Compare it to the plan of the human incisor tooth shown in vertical section in Figure 5.4.
2. Try to construct a drawing of the vertical section of the tooth you have cut open, and name the different parts.

Figure 5.4 Vertical section of human incisor tooth

Most of the tooth is of fairly hard material called **dentine,** with a small cavity in the middle which contains blood vessels and nerves in the living tooth. These enter the tooth through an opening at the base of the root. The root, which may be single or double, anchors the tooth in its socket in the jaw. The part of the tooth above the jaw is coated with a protective layer of hard **enamel,** while the root is coated with **cement.** Small fibres attach the cement of the tooth to the bone of the jaw. This attachment allows for a little 'give' and also acts as a shock absorber. If you look at a jaw which has had all the flesh removed, you will see that the teeth do not fit tightly into the sockets.

5.6 Good teeth or bad?

It has been estimated that only two people out of every hundred in this country have perfect teeth; the others have teeth which are damaged or decayed to some extent. Sometimes a dentist can remove the decayed part by drilling, and then he adds a new protective

coating or filling to prevent further decay. If the decay goes too far the tooth may have to be extracted. Let us now investigate the condition of the teeth of the pupils in your class.

Make a survey of your class to find out the number of teeth decayed, filled or extracted in each person's mouth. Use your results to construct a histogram.

How do your findings compare with the dentists' estimate of the condition of teeth throughout the country? Remember that the dentists' estimate will be based on a much larger size of sample than your findings.

5.7 Tooth decay; its cause and prevention

We shall now try to find what causes tooth decay, and also find ways of preventing it, or at least of slowing down the process.

---

1. Take a tooth extracted from any mammal, such as a sheep or a human, and prod it with the sharp point of a needle or with forceps. If the tooth is in good condition you will find that it is hard.
2. Leave it to soak for two or three days in dilute hydrochloric acid.
3. Wash the tooth carefully and examine it, prodding with the forceps. How has the acid affected the tooth?

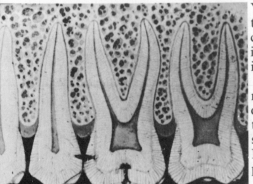

You will probably find that where the enamel has been removed the tooth begins to get eaten away. You may even see bubbles of gas coming from the tooth. Try to find out what the gas is. If the tooth is left long enough, or if the acid is strong enough, even the enamel is destroyed and the tooth crumbles away if prodded.

If food particles become lodged between the teeth and are not removed, bacteria in the mouth feed on them and multiply, breaking down the foodstuffs and liberating acids. These acids will attack the teeth, much more slowly than the hydrochloric acid but just as surely. Figure 5.5 shows the progress of decay in a molar tooth. Notice the abscess forming at the base of the root in the third picture.

Figure 5.5 Progressive decay of a molar tooth

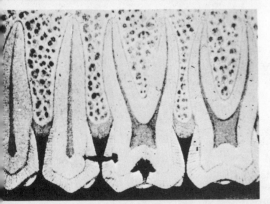
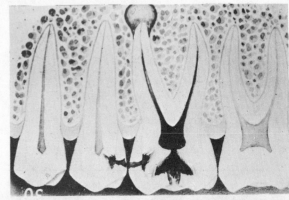

Brushing the teeth removes food and bacteria from the mouth. What effect will brushing have on the amount of acid present around the teeth? How does toothpaste help in fighting tooth decay? The following experiments may provide an answer to the last question.

1. Place a few drops of dilute hydrochloric acid in the first depression of a spotting tile.
2. Dip the end of a piece of blue litmus paper into the acid and then lay it in the next depression.
3. Place a few drops of dilute potassium hydroxide solution in the third depression and transfer the alkali by means of a glass rod, a drop at a time, on to the wet end of the litmus paper. Note any colour change.
4. Dip four more pieces of blue litmus paper into the acid and place one on each spot in the second row, as in Figure 5.6.

Figure 5.6 Testing toothpaste

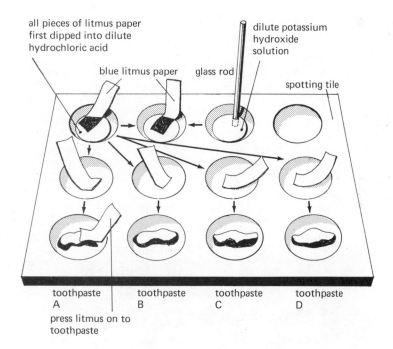

all pieces of litmus paper first dipped into dilute hydrochloric acid

dilute potassium hydroxide solution

blue litmus paper   glass rod

spotting tile

toothpaste A   toothpaste B   toothpaste C   toothpaste D

press litmus on to toothpaste

5. Squeeze a 1 cm length of toothpaste on to the first spot on the third row.
6. Transfer a litmus paper from row two to the toothpaste and press. Note the time for any colour change to take place.
7. Repeat with different brands of toothpaste.

What effect does toothpaste have on acid? How might this reaction help in preventing tooth decay?

Blue litmus paper turns red in acid, but changes back to blue as the potassium hydroxide reacts with it, that is, neutralises the acid. The potassium hydroxide is an alkali, and you may find that some of the toothpastes are also alkaline. They thus neutralise the acid, though you probably found that they took much longer to do so. Some toothpastes may not be alkaline at all. When you consider the short time that the paste is in contact with the teeth before being rinsed away, you will realise that there is not enough time for much chemical action to take place.

Let us now see if there is any other component in the toothpaste which might be more important.

1. Squeeze a 2 cm length of toothpaste into a clean test tube and half fill the tube with distilled water.
2. Shake for two minutes.
3. Place a drop of the liquid on a slide and observe under the low power of the microscope.
4. Leave the test tube standing for 5 minutes and examine the liquid.

From these observations, try to deduce another way in which toothpaste may help in the cleaning of teeth.

Under the low power of the microscope you will see masses of tiny particles which do not dissolve in water. They hang in suspension in the water and eventually sink as a sediment to the bottom of the test tube. These tiny particles help to scrape from the teeth the surface scum which contains the harmful bacteria. The powder is said to be abrasive. Similar powder with much bigger particles is used to clean sinks and bathtubs, but such large particles would damage teeth.

Certain brands of toothpaste contain ingredients which kill bacteria, but, as with neutralisation, the toothpaste is not usually in the mouth long enough to be really effective. The most important part of the operation of cleaning the teeth is the actual brushing, which deals with the bacteria and food particles physically rather than chemically. You may have heard of people who use salt, or even soot, instead of commercial toothpastes, as a fine abrasive when brushing their teeth. Why do you think that it is good to eat an apple at the end of a meal?

5.8 Fluoridation

Drinking water comes mainly from rainfall and contains dissolved gases such as carbon dioxide and also varying concentrations of mineral salts, depending on the nature of the ground over which the water flows on its way to the reservoir. Calcium fluoride is one of the salts found naturally in the drinking water of some towns.

For many years scientists have been aware of the fact that people living in towns where there were traces of fluoride in the water suffered less from dental caries than those whose water supply did not contain any. For example, West Hartlepool, a town in the north of England, has had for many years a water supply with a fluoride concentration of approximately two parts per million. The city of York, 45 miles away, is similar in many ways to West Hartlepool, but has no naturally occurring fluoride in its water. In 1967, dentists made a thorough examination of the teeth of a random sample of 5-year-old children from each community. The results are shown in Table 5.1.

Table 5.1
(results of dental examination of random sample
of schoolchildren in 1967)

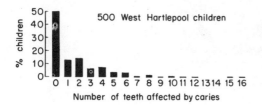 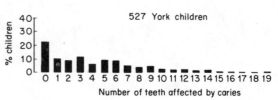

What do you conclude about the effect of fluoride in drinking water on the condition of the teeth of young children?

At most waterworks, skilled water engineers add carefully calculated amounts of chlorine to the water in order to kill dangerous bacteria which may cause disease. In the same way some towns have fluoride added to the water supply in controlled amounts.

In Kilmarnock, in Scotland, after five years of fluoridation of the water supply, dental decay in young children was reduced by half. Unfortunately, most people have shown little interest in these statistics, and very often they have fought against having fluoridation, although there is no evidence of any harmful effects on people drinking water which contains such small amounts.

Try to find out more about other towns which do have fluoridation, so that you can discuss scientifically the reasons for or against the fluoridation of all drinking water.

Well-controlled studies have also shown that regular brushing of teeth with fluoride toothpaste produces a reduction in the incidence of dental caries, and this kind of toothpaste is probably more efficient than some of the other types which you have experimented with previously.

5.9 Dentition in other mammals

(a) The dog as a carnivore
The best way of investigating how an animal uses its teeth is to watch it eating. Dogs are flesh-eaters, carnivores. If you keep a dog as a pet you may sometimes get 'lights' (lung tissue) from the butcher for dog food.

Watch a dog eating 'lights', or some other piece of meat, and consider the sequence of actions just as you did with the bread in your own case. If you cannot observe a dog in the class-room, then look at a dog's skull, Figure 5.7. Compare it to a human skull as shown in Figure 5.2.

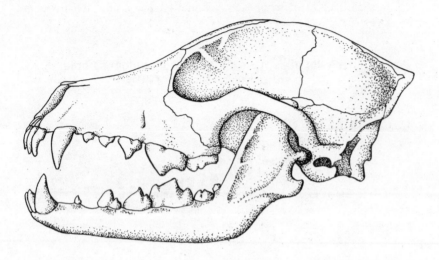

Figure 5.7 A dog's skull

Record the way in which the dog uses its teeth, just as you did previously when you noted how your own teeth were used in eating.

Which teeth stand out most? You will probably say the canines, which are used to kill prey and to tear flesh. The incisors, six in each jaw, seem small but they are sharp and are used for scraping meat off the bone. The double teeth are difficult to separate into molars and premolars. Look for the large triangular teeth on each side of each jaw. These are called **carnassial** teeth; the carnassial tooth in the upper jaw is the fourth premolar, while that in the lower jaw is the first molar. They do not meet to grind or chew, but slide past each other like the blades of a pair of scissors. When a lump of 'lights' or other tough meat is torn off, it is passed to the side of the mouth and sheared through by the carnassial teeth, then swallowed without further crushing. What is the function of the molars? Notice that they are inserted right back near the jaw joint. How does this allow them to function very efficiently?

Look at a dog's skull again and write down its dental formula. Compare the skulls of as many carnivores as you can with the skull of the dog. Try to make a collection of pictures of carnivores with their mouths open to show their teeth.

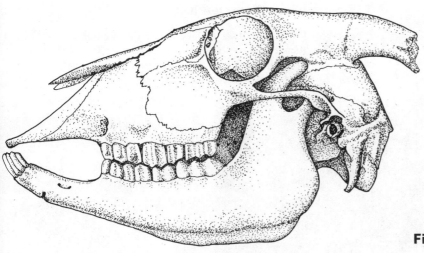

Figure 5.8 A sheep's skull

(*b*) The sheep as a herbivore
Examine the dentition of a sheep, shown in Figure 5.8, and if possible observe a sheep feeding. Try to decide how it uses its teeth.

How is the shape of the grinding teeth related to the way in which the jaws move when the sheep is chewing?

In the lower jaw, you will find eight teeth at the front which are all similar, and which appear to be incisors. In man, the canine teeth are not required for tearing flesh as much as in the carnivores, and they are not nearly so long and pointed. The sheep is completely herbivorous, and the canines have become so modified that they look like incisors. This means that the lower jaw of the sheep has six incisors plus two modified canines. In feeding, the eight lower front teeth chop the grass off by pressing against the horny pad of the upper jaw which carries no incisor teeth. The tongue then sweeps the cut grass to the back of the mouth to be ground up.

Look at the teeth on the side of the sheep's jaw. These are called cheek teeth and there are six in each half jaw. The front three are the premolars, and the back three are molars. The dental formula of the sheep is therefore $\frac{0\ 0\ 3\ 3}{3\ 1\ 3\ 3}$. The W-shaped ridges of the upper cheek teeth fit into the M-shaped ridges of the lower set, so that, when the jaws come together, the only direction in which they can move easily is from side to side.

In a tooth which has just pushed through the gum of a young sheep, the M's and W's have sharp peaks, but constant grinding wears away these peaks. The cheek teeth continue to grow to compensate for this wearing away. This means that they need a rich supply of blood to bring in the materials for growth. At the base of the roots into the pulp cavity, there are bigger openings than in human teeth, allowing the entry of blood vessels.

5.10 Mammals with no teeth

Figure 5.9 shows an anteater. This animal feeds only on ants, and its tongue which is long and sticky is poked into ant heaps to catch the ants in much the same way as flies are caught on sticky fly-paper. The anteater has no teeth.

Figure 5.9 The toothless anteater

The anteater is very large compared to the organisms which it eats. The difference in size between a predator and its prey is even more remarkable in the case of the whalebone whales such as the blue whale. This mammal may measure over 30 m in length yet it feeds on tiny organisms in the water. The mouth parts are modified to form a fine **filter,** and as the whale swims with its mouth open, water containing the organisms flows in. The food is caught in the net-like filter, cleaned off by the tongue and then swallowed. We cannot experiment with blue whales, but we can use a much smaller invertebrate animal which is also a filter feeder to investigate this method of feeding.

5.11 *Mytilus* **as a filter feeder**

1. Lay a specimen of *Mytilus*, the edible mussel, on its side in a dish of sea-water. The front or anterior end is pointed, while the posterior end is rounded. If you leave the mussel undisturbed for a little while, you may see the two **valves** separate along the rounded edge while being held together by a sort of hinge on the straight edge. Any sudden movement nearby results in the valves being pulled together.
2. Look at an empty shell and note the two round marks where muscles were once attached. These are the adductor muscles which are responsible for drawing the valves together when the mussel is disturbed, and they must be cut in order to examine the feeding mechanism.
3. Prise open the two valves with a blunt scalpel, and then insert a sharp blade to slice across the adductor muscles. Try not to damage the rest of the contents of the shell.

4. Pull the two valves apart and return the mussel to the salt water, which should cover it. You have now exposed the large gill flaps.

5. Leave the mussel for two or three minutes to recover, then drop minute mud particles on to the gills and watch what happens, using a lens or a binocular microscope. In what direction do the particles move? How does the action of the gill flaps help in feeding?

6. Cut a small piece out of a gill, mount it in a drop of sea-water, and observe under the low power of your microscope.

What microscopic details help to explain the flow observed over the gill surface?

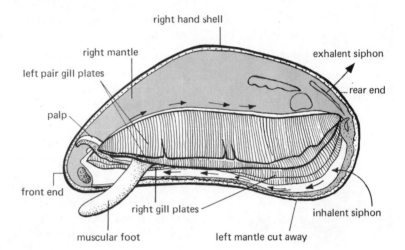

Figure 5.10 *Mytilus* with one valve removed and part of the mantle cut away

Figure 5.10 shows a mussel in which one valve has been removed. Inside is a tent-like flap of tissue, called the mantle, which surrounds the gill flaps. The side of the 'tent' has been cut open to expose the gills. There are four of these, a pair on each side.

In your specimen you may see the orange tip of the foot protruding between the paired gill flaps. The animal is found attached to rocks by a mass of tough threads, and does not move around, hence the small size of the foot compared to that of other molluscs. The mussel does not search for food, but depends on food coming to it. Through the lens you may see small particles of material, which might be food, which get trapped on the gill flaps. They are wafted to the free edge of the gill flap and carried forward in a groove to the anterior. At this end, a pair of finger-like palps scrape off any useful food material and pass it to the mouth, which is hidden between the gill flaps.

Large or unusable particles are rejected and are passed back on the other edge of the gill flaps to the posterior end of the mussel, as if on a conveyor belt. There is a constant current of water which contains particles being drawn in through a tube-like opening between the mantles at the posterior end, while the rejected material passes out through an outflow tube.

The gills also extract oxygen from the water as it passes over them. The current is kept up by the continuous movement of many hair-like structures called **cilia,** on the gills. You should see the cilia quite easily on your microscopic preparation.

5.12 Biting without teeth

Animals with teeth are not the only ones which bite their food, as you will realise from the following observation.

Place a locust in a glass jar with a piece of cabbage leaf and observe it eating. What is the difference between the way it moves its jaws and the way in which a mammal uses its jaws to bite?

Imagine that you were going to take a similar bite. You would have the edge of the cabbage leaf in a horizontal position and would clamp your incisors on either side, one set from above and one from below. When the locust is feeding, the edge of the leaf is in a vertical position in relation to its mouth. It would seem that the cutting edges of the jaws must be placed vertically on either side of the mouth, and come together to cut a leaf from the sides, instead of moving up and down as our jaws do. Look closely again at the locust eating. It is difficult to see the jaws in action because of the large upper lip called the **labrum.** Let us see if our hypothesis about the jaw arrangement is correct by dissecting out the mouth parts of a locust.

1. You are provided with a dead locust, a hand lens or binocular microscope, a pair of forceps and a petri dish lined with cotton wool.
2. Hold the locust on its back between the finger and thumb, grip the labrum with the forceps and exert a steady pull. The labrum should come off quite easily. Lay it upside down on the cotton wool. (This will prevent it being blown away.)
3. You should now be able to see on either side the large jaws with serrated cutting edges. Pull them off carefully. These are called **mandibles.** Notice the grinding surface behind the cutting edges. If you have been careful, you should see two strands of muscles attached to the mandibles. These are the powerful muscles which rock the mandibles from side to side as the locust cuts through the cabbage leaf. The grinding surfaces pulp the cabbage leaf before it is swallowed. Place the mandibles in position on the cotton wool.

4. Remove the lower lip in the same way; it is called the **labium.**
   Notice the pair of small jointed appendages called **palps** attached
   to the labium. Place it in position on the cotton wool.
5. There are still two small jaws to be removed; they are called
   maxillae. (Singular, maxilla.) They are much less powerful than
   the mandibles. Notice the muscle attachments and much larger
   maxillary palps. What is the function of these in eating? Place
   the maxillae in position on the cotton wool and examine the set
   of mouth parts under the binocular microscope. Compare with
   the parts shown in Figure 5.11.

   Is our original hypothesis about the position of the jaws correct?

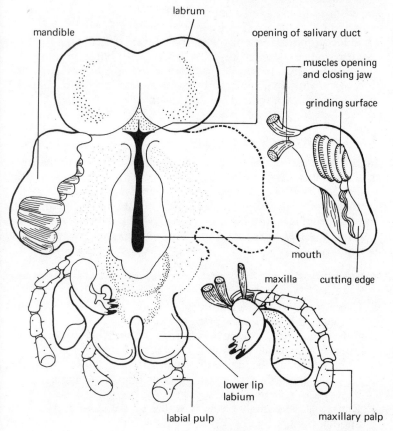

Figure 5.11 The mouth parts of a locust

You will probably agree that a locust is a hungry organism because
it eats its own weight of green plant material every day. It has been
estimated that a swarm may contain as many as one thousand million
locusts. Calculate the amount of food which such a swarm could
consume in one day.

1. Weigh a number of adult locusts and calculate the average weight in grammes.
2. Multiply this weight by 1 000 000 000.
3. Divide by 1 000 to change your answer to kilogrammes.
4. Gather a kilogramme of grass or other green plant material.

You should now realise how deadly an invasion of locusts can be to the crops of farmers in Africa and in the Middle East. Look at the coloured end papers of Book 1 of this series; you will see an individual locust feeding and also a swarm of locusts feeding.

Keep your eyes open for other insects with biting mouth parts and bring them into the laboratory for investigation. If you find them on plants, remember to bring in some of the plant material as well, to ensure a food supply for them.

5.13 Food by sucking

In our investigations of teeth we found various modifications, both in the numbers and in the shapes of the teeth, depending on the feeding habits of the animal concerned. Similarly in the insect world, the mouth parts of various kinds of insects are modified for particular ways of feeding. You are now going to look at a very common insect, a housefly, which we know does not bite, and try to find out how it feeds.

1. Catch some houseflies and keep them without food for 24 hours in a jam jar covered by a piece of muslin.
2. Put a small drop of sugar solution, or syrup, on a petri dish, transfer a fly to the dish and cover with the lid.
3. Observe the fly feeding both from above and from below by inverting the dish. Use a hand lens or binocular microscope to help you to see more detail.
4. Repeat with a small piece of toffee or coloured icing, using another hungry fly.

From your observations, what conclusions can you draw about the way a fly feeds on the solid food?

The fly can take in only liquid food. The labium has become modified to form a tube with a sucking pad at the end, as shown in Figure 5.12. This is called a **proboscis,** and is used to suck up food in liquid form. When not in use, the proboscis is tucked up under the head. The fly has **salivary glands** producing digestive juices, which can be passed down a narrow tube which enters the food canal and then out on to the solid food material such as the toffee or a lump of sugar. The

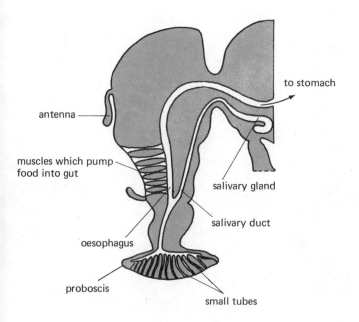

Figure 5.12 Mouth parts of a housefly

breakdown of the food starts immediately, and any dissolved material can be sucked up the proboscis. Digestion is completed in the gut. Some of the saliva is bound to remain as tiny drops on the food material, and, depending on where the fly had its last meal, may well contain millions of disease-spreading bacteria.

What illness may be caused by houseflies? What other parts of the body of a fly might also spread bacteria?

5.14 Other sucking insects

Some other insects are much more selective than the housefly in their choice of food, and their adaptations are even more remarkable. Have you ever been bitten by a mosquito? You probably know that it is 'after your blood', but that it does not really bite. Its proboscis is like a whole set of tools, which pierce the skin, inject a fluid to stop the blood clotting, and then suck some of it up. Only the female mosquito feeds on blood, and in tropical countries the female of certain species is responsible for spreading, when she feeds, the organism causing **malaria.** Look at the drawings in Figure 5.13 and try to recognise and name the mouth parts comparable to those which you found in the locust.

What other insects can you think of which have sucking mouth parts? What are their particular food preferences?

5.15 Animal relationships

So far we have chosen only a few well-known animals to show different methods of obtaining food. The position of the animal in a community in relation to other members, especially in connection with its method of feeding, is termed its **niche.** We should not confuse the term niche with habitat. The habitat is the place where the

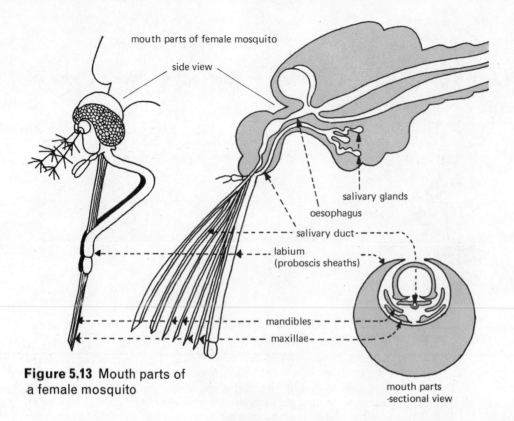

mouth parts of female mosquito

side view

salivary glands

oesophagus

salivary duct

labium
(proboscis sheaths)

mandibles

maxillae

Figure 5.13 Mouth parts of
a female mosquito

mouth parts
-sectional view

organism lives, while its niche describes its way of life in the habitat, especially with regard to its feeding habits. Ladybirds and caterpillars may live in the same tree. The caterpillar is a herbivore feeding on the leaves, while the ladybird is a carnivorous beetle which feeds on small insects such as greenfly. Although they share the same habitat, why could they be described as occupying different niches?

Let us consider the niche of a hill sheep. In Scotland, much hill land attached to farms and crofts is unsuitable for cultivation, and sheep are allowed to roam and feed on the poor land. Rabbits may share the habitat, consuming a considerable amount of the available grass and thus competing with the sheep for food. In some of the crofting counties the disease **myxomatosis** almost wiped out the rabbit population. The sheep no longer had to compete with rabbits, and the numbers able to be grazed on the land increased enormously. The surviving rabbits, however, seemed to be immune to the disease, and the numbers are now increasing again to compete with the sheep.

In this example the fate of the rabbit is just one of the factors to be considered when investigating the niche of the hill sheep. The contour of the land, the climate, predators, parasites, and disease, are some of the other factors. Try to think of more.

Let us now investigate the niches of some of the organisms to be found in one of the freshwater tank ecosystems which were set up earlier in the course.

Table 5.2

	Flatworm	Snail	Hydra
Where found in tank			
Response to light			
Food material			
Enemies			
Method of fighting or avoiding enemy			

Choose any small animals which may be found in the tanks. Make up a table similar to Table 5.2 in which to record your observations. Try to add to the table other factors which have a bearing on the way of life of the organism.

You may prefer to investigate organisms other than the ones suggested; for example, litter organisms, or those found in rock pools.

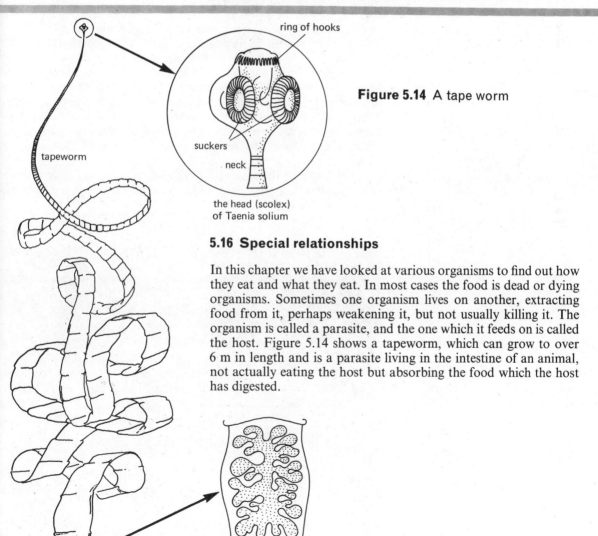

Figure 5.14 A tape worm

ring of hooks

suckers

neck

tapeworm

the head (scolex) of Taenia solium

ripe segment with uterus full of eggs

5.16 Special relationships

In this chapter we have looked at various organisms to find out how they eat and what they eat. In most cases the food is dead or dying organisms. Sometimes one organism lives on another, extracting food from it, perhaps weakening it, but not usually killing it. The organism is called a parasite, and the one which it feeds on is called the host. Figure 5.14 shows a tapeworm, which can grow to over 6 m in length and is a parasite living in the intestine of an animal, not actually eating the host but absorbing the food which the host has digested.

Make a list of other parasites which have animal hosts. You may recall a number of parasites of plants which you investigated previously. Can you think of any parasite which lives on both plants and animals?

In rock pools at the seashore there are often hermit crabs with sea anemones clinging to their shells. A relationship like this where the anemone obtains transport and scraps of food from the crab without giving much in return, and apparently doing no harm, is called **commensalism.** This word means 'eating at the same table'.

Sometimes organisms of different species form an association which is beneficial to both. This relationship is termed **mutualism.** (You may see the term symbiosis, meaning living together, used in some text books. This term is now used generally for any relationship between two organisms of different species.) A good example of mutualism is to be seen in lichen. Species of lichens can be found on bare rocks, on the tops of mountains, on dry stone walls and on trunks of trees, on rocky outcrops in the burning desert, and even near the north and south poles. In fact, lichens grow in many places where no other plants seem able to survive. Part of the lichen is composed of clusters of small simple green plants called algae. The algae are able to photosynthesise and thus they are the producers. They are surrounded by a mass of fungus which supplies water and dissolved salts for the algae and prevents desiccation. Lichens produce acids which eat into some of the rocks on which they grow, helping to break them up. The broken rock eventually becomes one of the constituents of soil. Small animals can shelter amongst the lichens, and miniature ecosystems are formed. The lichens can be looked on as colonisers, often allowing the introduction of life into places where none existed before. Figure 5.15 shows a lichen colony on an oak tree.

Make a list of the different places where you find lichens are growing. Do not confuse them with mosses and *Pleurococcus*, which you saw earlier in the course.

Figure 5.15 Lichens on a tree trunk

5.17 The dead and the left-overs

Not all animals catch and kill their own food. Some just wait for old or injured animals to die, or they depend on getting the remains of the kill of other carnivores such as the lion. These animals are often called **scavengers,** and the illustration in Figure 5.16 shows one of the best known of all scavengers, the vulture.

Figure 5.16 Vultures

What other scavenging animals can you name? In making your list, think of some of the smaller organisms you found previously in the tree and pond ecosystems, and also of the scavengers which congregate wherever man lives to feed on his left-overs. We have already mentioned the fungal part of the lichen as being a plant without green colouring, and hence unable to make its own food. Figure 5.17 shows a large group of Ink-cap fungi growing on the roots of a dead elm tree. The elm had already been killed by the dreaded Dutch elm disease, caused by another fungus, *Ceratostomella ulmi*. This

Figure 5.17 Ink-cap fungi growing on the roots of a dead elm

disease was accidently introduced into America in imported timber just after the First World War, and has wiped out large numbers of elms in the United States. Would you regard the Ink-cap as useful or as a pest?

Fungi live on organic material, in most cases dead plant remains, when they are known as **saprophytes.** Although the idea of scavengers may be a little repulsive, these organisms perform an important role in keeping organic matter circulating, and perhaps preventing the spread of disease. Similarly, the saprophytes hasten the breakdown of plant material, like dead trees, which otherwise might take a long time to return their chemicals to the food cycle. What type of nutrition is found in a fungus?

In this chapter we have looked at some of the ways in which organisms obtain food. In the next chapter we shall try to find out something about food, especially food needed by the human body.

Looking Back at Chapter 5

1. Organisms which consume food are called heterotrophs, and include herbivores, carnivores and omnivores.
2. These all depend on the producers, the green plants, which are called autotrophs.
3. Most mammals develop teeth to help them obtain food. The basic structure is the same in all teeth, but the shapes of teeth are modified to perform different functions in feeding.
4. Different shapes of teeth are given different names depending on their functions: the dental formula is a shorthand way of describing the arrangement of the teeth in the animal's jaw.
5. Bacteria in the mouth cause tooth decay, but regular brushing helps to prevent decay by removing bacteria. One way of achieving control of bacteria is by fluoridation of drinking water.
6. Certain animals have methods of catching food other than by the use of teeth; for example, they may feed by means of sucking fluid or by filtering food out of water.
7. The feeding habits of one organism can affect the lives of others, as in spreading disease or in competing for the same food. Availability of food is one of the main factors to be considered when investigating the niche of an organism.
8. A symbiotic association can be formed between organisms of different species. Examples of such an association are mutualism, commensalism and parasitism.
9. Scavenging by animals like vultures, rats, seagulls and beetles, and the breaking down of dead organic material by saprophytes and bacteria are important in the recycling of chemicals in nature.

FOOD AND MAN

6.1 Nutrients, starvation and malnutrition

You already know that, in every living cell of plants and animals, food is used up in order to obtain energy. Living organisms could be described as machines doing work, the fuel being food. In addition, like machines, our bodies must be built up and have worn-out parts replaced. Of the three foodstuffs—carbohydrates, fats and proteins —which two are especially important in supplying energy? Which is the main source of materials for new growth and replacement of tissues?

Our body processes require to be regulated and controlled. **Vitamins** and **mineral salts** are very important constituents of food, because they help to keep processes functioning correctly and often protect against disease.

Figure 6.1 shows the three main functions of food. The five

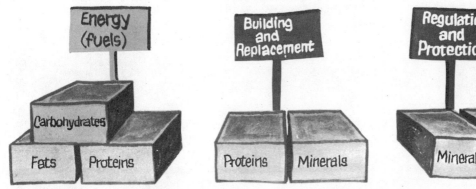

Figure 6.1 Functions of nutrients

components of food which are shown are said to be **nutrients.** Food will meet all our requirements only if our diet contains all the nutrients named.

Although not a nutrient, water is also an essential constituent of food. What are some of its functions in the body? Another substance essential for life is oxygen. What part does it play, along with food, in the metabolism of an organism?

Our food should contain an adequate total amount of nutrients. If it does not, then we suffer from **under-nutrition,** or perhaps **starvation.** Our diets should contain the correct amount of each nutrient, but if they do not, we suffer from **malnutrition.** The person who becomes fat because of eating more carbohydrates in the form

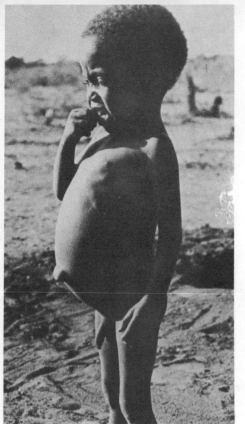

Figure 6.2 A boy suffering from kwashiorkor

of sweets and cakes than are needed by the body suffers from malnutrition, but not from starvation.

In certain parts of the world the population suffers from under-nutrition: in other parts, although there may be just enough food, particular nutrients are not present in adequate amounts. For example, the boy in Figure 6.2 is suffering from kwashiork — a malnutrition disease caused by insufficient protein in his diet. A diet including groundnuts, or other food containing proteins, would have prevented this disease.

6.2 What are the energy requirements of the human body?

A living organism releases energy in the form of heat, as you have already found. Hence, the energy expended can be found by measuring the heat put out by the organism. The units by which heat is measured are either the joule or the calorie, and in Biology it is a form of the latter, the Calorie (kilogramme calorie, 1 000 calories) which is used. 1 Calorie is the amount of heat required to raise the temperature of 1 000 g (1 kilogramme) of water through 1 Celsius degree. We can say that if X Calories of heat are put out, X Calories of energy have been expended and hence X Calories of food have been used as fuel to produce that heat. (1 calorie is equivalent to 4·19 joules. How many joules will be equivalent to 1 Calorie?)

Experiments indicate that, if completely at rest, a man expends about 1 700 Calories per 24 hours in basic metabolic processes. Every time he moves he will expend additional energy. Clearly, 1 700 Calories from energy foods are needed merely to keep alive, and in addition fuel is needed to provide energy for exercise and work.

Figure 6.3 Energy expended in different activities, in addition

The Calories expended while awake depend on a number of factors which we shall now consider.

(*a*) *Activity*

Look at the histograms shown in Figure 6.3. What general conclusions can be made about the relationship between energy-expenditure and work? Why are you more hungry after going for a walk than after writing a letter?

(*b*) *Occupation*

Table 6.1

Occupation	typist	tailor	mechanic	bricklayer	forestry worker
Approximate Calorie requirements per day	2 300	2 800	3 200	4 400	5 200

The data given in Table 6.1 show the approximate total number of Calories expended, and hence the calorific requirement, in certain occupations. Draw histograms in order to present the data visually. What differences would you expect to find in the diets of those in the different occupations?

(*c*) *Age and sex*

Figure 6.4 Calorific requirements in relation to age and sex

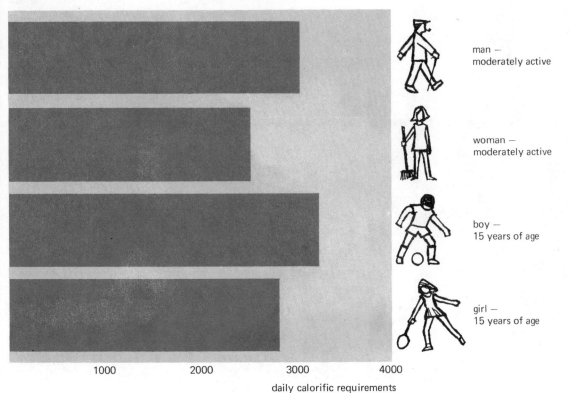

man —
moderately active

woman —
moderately active

boy —
15 years of age

girl —
15 years of age

1000   2000   3000   4000

daily calorific requirements

Consider the information given in Figure 6.4 and assume that the results are typical for men, women, boys and girls. What comparison can be made between the calorific requirements of males and females? Why do human beings require less food as they grow older?

We now know something about the calorific requirements of the body in relation to activity, occupation, age and sex. Each individual, of course, has his or her own particular and individual needs. In addition, the requirements will differ in relation to climate and altitude. In what ways do you think environment will alter calorific requirements?

In the early experiments on calorific requirements, measurements were made by determining the heat expended by the body. Now, however, when calculating energy used, it is more usual to measure oxygen consumed. What is the connection between intake of oxygen and expenditure of energy?

6.3 Foods and their values as fuel

So far we have considered only the energy requirements of the body without dealing with the energy provided by particular foods. You are now going to measure this and find some **calorific values.**

Set up the apparatus shown in Figure 6.5. What is the function of the oxygen supply, and what is the purpose of bubbling the oxygen through the liquid?

1. Place exactly 40 cm³ of water in the boiling tube. What weight of water is now in the tube?

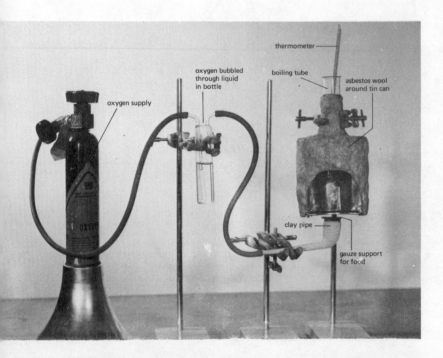

Figure 6.5 Apparatus for determining calorific values of food

thermometer

oxygen bubbled through liquid in bottle

boiling tube

asbestos wool around tin can

oxygen supply

clay pipe

gauze support for food

2. Weigh out exactly 0·5 g of a food such as thoroughly toasted bread crumbled into small pieces. In this case, which class of foodstuff is being investigated?
3. Place the toast on the gauze support and warm the bowl of the pipe and its contents with a moderate Bunsen burner flame.
4. Turn on the oxygen supply and control the flow to a steady stream.
5. Read and note the temperature of the water in the boiling tube.
6. Use a hotter flame and set fire to a little of the toast.
7. When the toast starts to burn, remove the flame immediately and place the bowl of the clay pipe under the bottom of the boiling tube.
8. Keep the water stirred by means of the thermometer.
9. Allow the toast to burn out completely by increasing the oxygen supply as necessary.
10. When the toast has burned out, stir the water for a further minute or two and then read and note the temperature.

Use olive oil instead of toast and repeat the experiment. Soak up the oil into a small piece of asbestos wool, which can be made into a cone before putting it on the gauze support.

In which of these two experiments was the rise in temperature of the water greater? Therefore, of the two substances, carbohydrate and oil, which gives out the more heat and must have a higher calorific value than the other?

You can determine the calorific value very roughly from the rise in temperature obtained in your experiment, although more complicated apparatus would be needed to give accurate results.

Calculating the calorific value
On the assumption that no heat is lost from the apparatus:

heat given out by 0·5 g food = heat taken in by 40 g water
= (40 × rise in temperature) calories

Now, calculate the heat given out by 1·0 g of the food and change the answer from calories to Calories. Use the relationship given in Section 6.2 to express your answer in joules.

Some examples of calorific values
Figure 6.6 shows the energy values of foodstuffs, the figures being based on the weight of the food absorbed and 'burned' to produce energy.

Apart from the value of fat in heat insulation, why is a diet rich in fatty foods of benefit to a person living within the Arctic Circle? Table 6.2 shows the percentage composition of certain items in our diet. Name the substance which will compose most of the remaining

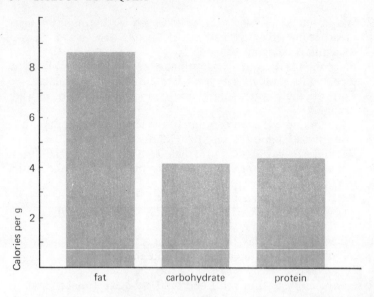

Figure 6.6 Energy value of foodstuffs

Table 6.2
Percentage composition of certain foods

Food	Carbohydrate	Fat	Protein
bread	50·0	2·0	10·0
butter	0·0	85·0	1·0
cheese	2·0	30·0	25·0
boiled potatoes	22·0	0·0	2·0
cabbage	5·0	0·2	1·0
beef	0·0	20·0	18·0

percentage of each of the foods listed. What other nutrients may also be present in these foods?

(*a*) Use the data given in Figure 6.6 and Table 6.2 to calculate the calorific value of a cheese sandwich, and a meat and vegetable course in a lunch. In each case
  (1) weigh the items approximately, before you eat them
  (2) calculate the weights of carbohydrate, fat and protein present in each
  (3) determine the calorific value of the carbohydrate, fat and protein present, and finally
  (4) obtain the total energy intake in Calories and in joules.

(*b*) Prepare pie charts to give a pictorial presentation of the composition of the foods listed in Table 6.2. The Figure 6.7 shows such a diagram for bread.

Figure 6.7 The composition of bread

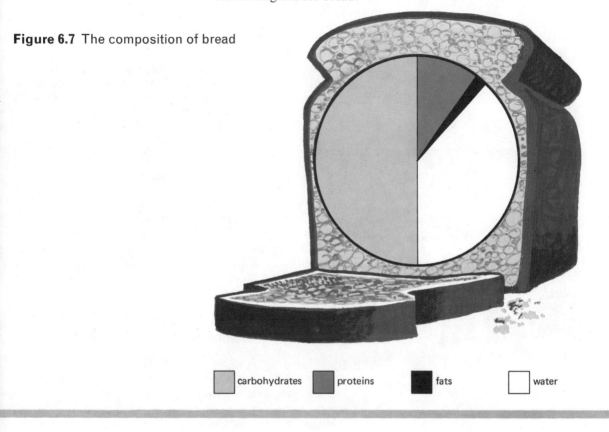

| | carbohydrates | | proteins | | fats | | water |

6.4 Vitamins

In various foods which we eat there are substances which are essential for health, although they are required in only small amounts. Such substances are known as vitamins. Different vitamins are referred to by the use of letters of the alphabet; for example, vitamin A is derived from substances in carrots, and its presence

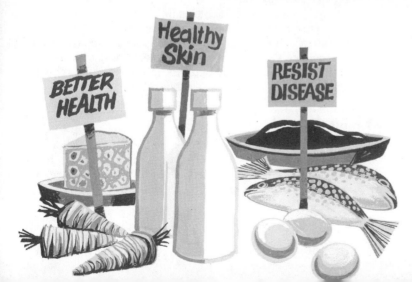

helps to resist disease and maintain our skin in a healthy condition.

Vitamins are complex compounds synthesised by plants and bacteria, and it is from these organisms, directly or indirectly, that animals obtain the vitamins they need. Many vitamins are involved in reactions with enzymes which effect important life processes. For example, vitamin B_1 plays a part in the release of energy from carbohydrates.

Another vitamin of importance is vitamin C, known also as ascorbic acid. You are now going to investigate this substance, using a test reagent by the name of dichlorophenol-indophenol. This name is usually abbreviated to DCPIP.

(a) 1. Pour 1 cm³ of DCPIP solution into a test tube.
    2. Add a few drops of ascorbic acid solution, by means of a pipette, until a colour change is observed.

What change in colour occurred? This provides a test for ascorbic acid.

(b) Test a wide range of foods in your diet, including raw vegetables and fruit, in order to find if they contain ascorbic acid. The food material must be ground to a pulp and shaken up with water and the resulting solution then tested, as above.

From your class results, compile a list of foods which (i) have ascorbic acid and (ii) do not have ascorbic acid in them.

(c) 1. Make an extract from fresh, raw cabbage, and test it for the presence of ascorbic acid.
    2. Boil the cabbage until it is tender. Test the water in which it was boiled, and also test an extract made from the boiled cabbage ground down in water.

What has happened to the ascorbic acid as a result of boiling? What evidence is there that raw vegetables and fruit may be of greater benefit in our diet than cooked ones?

Little was known about vitamins until about 1910, but many have now been analysed and their effects are well known.

(a) Find out about the vitamins A, B_1, B_2, C, D, E and K. For each, make lists such as

   (1) foods which are good sources of the vitamin,
   (2) the effects of deficiency of the vitamin.

(b) Find out which vitamins are frequently added to commercially prepared foods such as breakfast cereals, margarine and dried or evaporated milk. Manufacturers' labels generally show if the nutrient value has been increased by adding vitamins.

6.5 Minerals

The fact that certain minerals are needed for good health has been known for thousands of years. Like vitamins, different mineral elements have different functions and they form only a very small percentage of the constituents of food.

1 Weigh a
porcelain
crucible

2 Reweigh the
crucible containing
chopped up food

3 Obtain the dry
weight, as in
Section 4.1

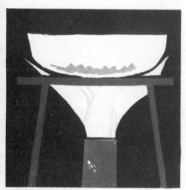

4 Heat gently,
then very strongly over
a Bunsen burner

5 Cool and
weigh

6 Reheat and cool;
then weigh and repeat
to constant weight

Figure 6.8 Finding the mineral
ash content of food

Obtain the mineral ash of a food material such as bread, by following
the method outlined in Figure 6.8. What can be derived from the
weights obtained at stages 1 and 2? What can be calculated from the
further weight obtained at 3?

The strong heat burns off the organic component of the food and
leaves the minerals as an ash. What two facts can be derived from
the final weight at stage 6?

(i) Calculate the percentages of water, organic material, and
mineral ash, present in the original sample.
(ii) Draw histograms to provide a visual comparison of the weights
of the components of the particular food.

In your class, you may try to identify some of the mineral elements present in various foods. These mineral, or inorganic elements, all have a common origin, the soil. What removes them from the soil? How do they eventually reach us? You have already investigated photosynthesis, but now you can appreciate that green plants are also important because they are the source of vitamins and minerals in the food of animals. However, one inorganic substance, common salt, reaches us in only small amounts via a food chain from plants and the soil. What are two of the sources of salt for use by man?

We shall now consider a few of the important inorganic elements in our food. Figure 6.9 gives the data for the amounts of calcium and phosphorus in cheese.

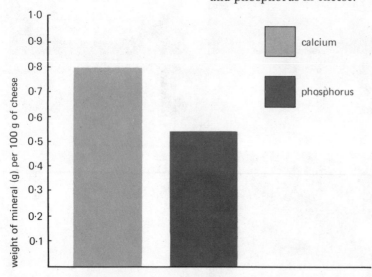

Figure 6.9 The calcium and phosphorus content of cheese

Construct graphs similar to the type shown in Figure 6.9 to show the calcium and phosphorus content of (i) milk, and (ii) egg. The following data, Table 6.3, give the weights of calcium and phosphorus present in 100 g of the food.

Table 6.3

	calcium	phosphorus
milk	0·12 g	0·09 g
egg	0·06 g	0·21 g

Calcium is vital for the formation of strong bones and teeth, and it also plays an important part in the clotting of the blood and in the action of muscles. In the United Kingdom, before the Second

World War, shortage of calcium in the diet caused many children to suffer from a disease called rickets. Even if the diet includes enough calcium, vitamin D must be present for the mineral to be absorbed and utilised adequately. From this it can be seen that the inter-relationships of different nutrients may be very complicated.

Phosphorus is also important in the formation of strong bones and teeth, and it plays an important part in the release of energy from food. What is the function of adenosine triphosphate, ATP, in the energy supply of an organism? Recall what you found out about ATP earlier in the course.

Phosphorus must be present in the diet if the body is to be able to absorb calcium from food. This is a further case in which there is a complex interaction of different nutrients.

Iron is a mineral which is essential for the formation of a substance in the blood. You will learn more about this in Chapters 7 and 8; meantime, note that the iron is obtained from foods such as liver and other meat, flour, potatoes and green vegetables.

Deficiency of iron is one of the causes of anaemia. Absorption of iron from food normally occurs only when we need the mineral: this is an example of the many self-regulating mechanisms in operation in the human body.

6.6 Food, the right kinds and the right amounts

We have discussed individual items of nutrition which are necessary to keep us active and healthy; we shall now consider the over-all requirements. In 1950 the United Nations Food and Agricultural Organisation experts stated that for an 'average person' the daily food intake should include the following:

(*a*) 2 800 Calories from energy-yielding nutrients
(*b*) 70 g of protein, and at least half of the protein intake should be from animal food sources while the remaining Calories should be obtained from carbohydrates and fats
(*c*) 1·0 g of calcium and 12 mg of iron, both in compounds which the body can utilise
(*d*) specified amounts of vitamin A, the various forms of vitamin B and vitamin C.

The vitamin and mineral requirements must be taken into account when deciding on the particular sources of carbohydrates and fats to be included in the diet.

We shall now consider nutrition as a problem facing the human race.

6.7 Food, a world problem

It has been estimated that about 15 per cent of the world population are undernourished. In many countries, even where the people do not suffer from famine and war, the total intake per day is only about 2 000 Calories per person. Further, probably about 50 per cent of the people of the world suffer from malnutrition due to the lack of particular nutrients in their diets. You have already seen in Figure 6.2 a photograph of a boy suffering from protein deficiency. In adults, in underprivileged countries, protein malnutrition can lead to whole communities becoming lethargic, with physical and mental powers reduced. Figure 6.10 shows data for protein intake in several parts of the world. To increase the amount of available

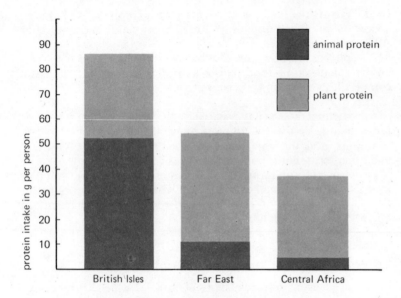

Figure 6.10 Examples of daily protein intake

protein is one of the great problems of many countries, especially in the Tropics.

What do you think are the reasons for the lack of food in the world and the deficiency of essential nutrients? One cause is the rate at which the population of the world is increasing.

Draw a graph from the following data, to show the rate of growth of the population of the world.

Year	Population
Birth of Christ	250 million
1650	500 million
1850	1 000 million
1950	2 500 million
1965	3 300 million
2000	7 000 million (estimated)

What do you think the total population of the world might be in the year 2050?

The rate of increase in population tends to be greatest in the countries economically less well developed; hence the greatest efforts must be made to improve the supply of food in those countries. The problem is often increased, too, by the drift of population away from rural areas to the towns. This not only reduces the number of people involved in food production, but increases the social problems in the towns, where many people may be unemployed.

6.8 Man's efforts to produce food

(*a*) Use of the land

In Canada, almost all the land available for agriculture is fully used, and it is managed in order to give maximum yields. For example, notice the large economic units being cultivated and the mechanical grain elevators shown in Figure 6.11.

In contrast, it is estimated that, of the total land surface of the world, only 10 per cent is under cultivation although a total of 34

Figure 6.11 Cereal production in part of Canada

Figure 6.12 Cow dung being prepared for burning

per cent could be cultivated. What do you think are some of the reasons why land is not fully used in food production?

In many parts of the world where the need to produce more is greatest, the methods of cultivating the land are little different from the primitive methods used for thousands of years. In some areas the soil is poor because it has little organic material in it, and hence it raises very inadequate crops. If the faeces of animals were returned to the land, what improvement would be made to the soil? Figure 6.12 shows cow dung being dried for use as fuel, but artificial fertilisers are seldom used to compensate for this loss of natural fertiliser because the farmers cannot afford to buy them. Why might an Indian farmer still have to use dung as a fuel, even though he realised its use on the land would improve the soil? This is the sort of dilemma which faces the people in many countries of the world.

Even desert soil can be utilised for growing crops if it can be first stabilised to keep the particles of sand from being blown away by the wind. It may then be watered by a system of irrigation channels and eventually produce regular crops. Figure 6.13 shows how a desert

Figure 6.13 Stabilising desert soil

area in Libya is being reclaimed by planting rows of long-rooted grasses which help to keep the sandy soil in place.

(*b*) Plant and animal stocks

In several parts of the world there is need to introduce better varieties of crop plants and better breeds of animals. For example, many of the rice and wheat varieties which are traditionally grown are poor yielding, are often tall and fall over easily and shade each other. In Mexico, however, the use of new varieties of wheat has increased the yield by $2\frac{1}{2}$ times in the last 20 years. Similar successes have been achieved in other countries by the research work of biologists who have developed new varieties of wheat, maize and rice.

During the last 20 years, poultry breeders and nutrition experts in Great Britain have been able to cut down from 14 to 6 weeks the time for a table chicken to reach a weight of about 1·35 kg, and the amount of food required by the growing chickens has been halved. In what ways are these achievements a contribution to the problem of our food supply?

(*c*) Wastage and prejudice

A great amount of wastage occurs, both of crops growing in fields and crops in storage after harvesting. Figure 6.14 shows the loss of grain in India. What proportions of the potential food supply are (i) harvested, and (ii) actually used for food?

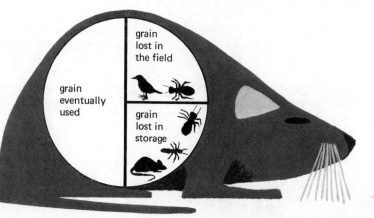

grain lost in the field

grain eventually used

grain lost in storage

Figure 6.14 Wastage of grain in India due to pests

This huge wastage unfortunately is not at all uncommon in many other countries. There is obviously a great need to develop and use herbicides and pesticides to prevent this loss during growth and storage. Try to find the names of some organisms which are likely to be involved in the losses which occur in the fields and in the stores.

In many of the developing countries the problem of eating enough food is increased by taboos and prejudices, and the restrictions often relate to valuable protein foods. Some African tribes do not allow a pregnant woman to eat chicken or fish, lest her baby be born with feathers or fins, and in Ethiopia a pregnant woman is forbidden to eat liver because it is said to cause infants to be born bald. These taboos of course leave more protein for the men! In the Far East, there are Hindus and Buddhists who forbid the killing of animals, and even eggs may be excluded from the diet.

In Great Britain, too of course, there are prejudices. For example, many housewives do not buy a variety of potato called Record because its flesh is yellow and thus different from more traditional varieties.

(d) Increasing supplies of protein

On land, the selection and the maintenance of animals which are efficient food converters and which are also suitable for the environment, are being encouraged. It is also thought that the farming of wild game, such as antelope, could increase meat supplies.

It has been estimated that in the seas and fresh waters of the world the catch of some fish could be increased by 50 per cent without reducing stocks to a dangerously low level. Figure 6.15 shows fishermen in Kenya using modern equipment to catch enough fish for their own food and a surplus for sale.

Over-fishing of coastal waters must be prevented, but it may be possible to increase the rate of turn-over by the addition of artificial fertilisers to the sea. For example, in one experiment it has been found that flounders and plaice had an increased rate of growth when introduced into a loch the waters of which had been treated with fertilisers. What organisms in the sea-water would probably increase first of all? Why would the chances of success of such an experiment be greater in a limited area like a loch than in the open sea?

Protein is so important in our diet that biologists and chemists are investigating new sources of the foodstuff. For example,

Figure 6.15 Fishing: newer methods improve the economy

protein can be obtained from yeasts and plankton, and from leaves of plants not normally thought of as food plants, and efforts are even being made to obtain it from oil and from wool.

(e) Artificial enrichment of foods

In Great Britain there are various laws designed to ensure that people who buy cheaper foods do not suffer from malnutrition. Basic foods like margarine and bread have vitamins and minerals added; for example, calcium in the form of calcium carbonate is added to all flour except wholemeal flour. Why does wholemeal flour not need this enrichment?

In India, enriched food is being produced in various forms, such as 'nutro biscuits', which contain 17 per cent protein from groundnut and wheaten flours, along with added vitamins.

In this section we have outlined a few of the ways in which biologists and other experts are applying their knowledge to help to increase the food supply for the world's population. We have also seen that the difficulties may sometimes be sociological, involving attitudes and ways of life. The problems are being tackled by international organisations, by the governments of individual countries and by voluntary charitable organisations.

Looking Back at Chapter 6

1. The essential nutrients in our diet are proteins, carbohydrates, fats, vitamins and minerals.
2. Proteins, carbohydrates and fats, supply the growth and energy requirements of our bodies: vitamins and minerals are needed for good health and for the control of body processes.
3. The calorific requirements of a person depend on such things as activity, occupation, age and sex.
4. Under-nutrition and malnutrition are world problems caused by increasing population, inadequate production of food because of unsatisfactory agricultural methods, and ignorance.
5. Efforts are being made to produce more and better food as a result of the research being done by biologists and other experts working with various organisations which are often international.

WHAT HAPPENS TO FOOD

7.1 Food within but still outside the body

The heading of this section may seem to be a contradiction, but you will appreciate its meaning from the following model.

Consider the apparatus shown in Figure 7.1. If you pour a little water into the end of the narrow tube at X, and allow it to flow down, in what sense could it be described as still outside the apparatus when it reaches point A?

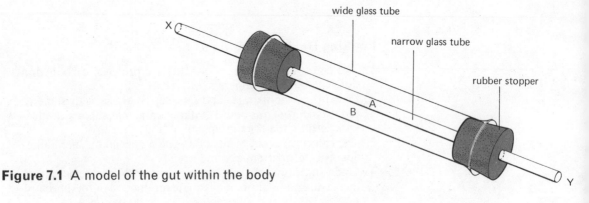

Figure 7.1 A model of the gut within the body

In the model, the tube from X to Y represents the **gut,** from mouth to anus. What is represented by the region B? Here we have what has been called the 'problem of digestion'—the fact that food may be within the gut but still outside the body, because it is separated by the gut wall from the body tissues where it is needed.

Clearly, in order to be of any nutritional value, food must be able to pass through the boundary wall from the cavity of the gut tube into the tissues of the body. In what state should food be in order to do this? The following experiment will help you to answer this question.

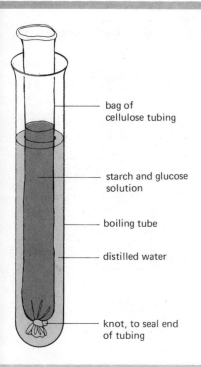

bag of
cellulose tubing

starch and glucose
solution

boiling tube

distilled water

knot, to seal end
of tubing

1. Prepare a 5 per cent starch solution by making a smooth paste of starch in cold water, and then pouring this into a larger volume of boiling water, with constant stirring. Allow to cool.
2. Dissolve 15 g of glucose in this solution.
3. Make a bag from cellulose tubing 15 cm long, tying a knot at one end as you did in experiments in Chapter 4.
4. Pour the mixture of starch and glucose into the bag. Rinse off any drips which are present on the outside.
5. Place the filled bag in distilled water in a boiling tube, as shown in Figure 7.2.
6. Immediately the bag is immersed, remove two samples of the water from the boiling tube by means of a pipette. Test one for the presence of starch, and the other for glucose.
7. Withdraw further samples and test in the same way after 5, 10 and 15 minutes.

Figure 7.2 Apparatus to investigate the passage of foods through a membrane

If there is glucose or starch or a mixture of the two present in the samples tested, how has this happened? If only one of the substances has passed through, what do you think is the essential difference between them which produces this different result?

If a food substance is insoluble, it will not pass through a cellulose membrane, whereas a soluble one will pass through. Of two soluble substances, the one with the larger molecules will pass more slowly than that with smaller molecules. What is true for a membrane of cellulose is also true for the lining of the gut, or **alimentary canal.** To be of nutritional value, therefore, food must either be in a soluble form on entering the body, or be changed into a soluble form within the alimentary canal. The process of converting the food into smaller, simpler molecules, is called digestion. The digestive system of the body will be considered in Sections 7.4 and 7.5, but you are now going to investigate one example of digestion.

7.2 An example of digestion

1. Test a piece of oatcake, or cream cracker, or other starchy food to check that the brand used has no reducing sugar in its composition.
2. Grind down and crush the oatcake and then separate it into two

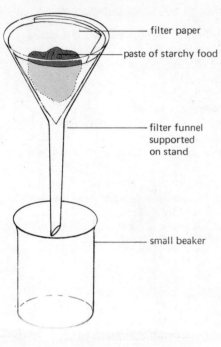

- filter paper
- paste of starchy food
- filter funnel supported on stand
- small beaker

portions. Mix one lot into a paste with distilled water and mix the other lot into a paste with fresh saliva.

3. Place the two lots of material on separate filter papers in filter funnels, as shown in Figure 7.3.

4. After 10–15 minutes pour a little distilled water over the starchy paste, wetting it just enough to allow several drops to flow steadily into the beaker beneath.

5. Test the two filtrates, separately, for reducing sugar.

In which lot was reducing sugar present? What must have brought about the change from insoluble starch to soluble sugar? What process had taken place?

Figure 7.3 Digestion of a starchy food

You have now investigated one example of digestion and seen that saliva, or a substance in saliva, is capable of breaking down the

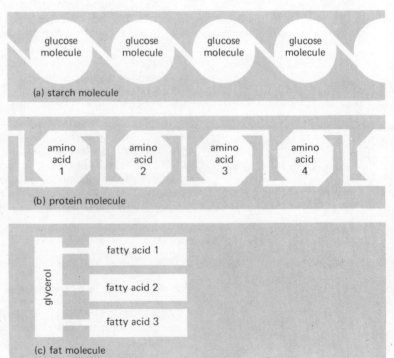

(a) starch molecule

(b) protein molecule

(c) fat molecule

Figure 7.4 Diagrams showing the composition of a molecule of (a) starch, (b) protein, (c) fat

starch into soluble sugar which can pass through a filter paper. A molecule of starch is made up of a very large number of glucose molecules linked together; see Figure 7.4(*a*). Digestion involves the splitting of the large starch molecule into separate glucose molecules, water being required for this process. Such a breaking down of starch can be achieved in the laboratory by heating starch solution with acid, but clearly this method cannot be employed in a living organism such as the human body. Instead, we find that digestion is carried out by enzymes, complex chemicals which you have already heard about in Chapter 3. The general name given to an enzyme which digests, or splits starch, is **amylase**: the particular amylase in saliva is sometimes called ptyalin.

Proteins and fats are also insoluble. What change must occur if protein or fatty food is going to benefit the body? Proteins are large molecules made up of many smaller units known as **amino acids,** see Figure 7.4(*b*). Amino acids are soluble and more than twenty different ones are known. Enzymes known as **proteases** are able to digest, or split up, a protein into the separate amino acids of which it is composed. In the same way, enzymes called **lipases** are able to split large fat molecules into the smaller molecules of **glycerol** and **fatty acids** from which they are made, as shown in Figure 7.4(*c*).

7.3 Investigating digestion *in vitro*

Most essential life processes take place within an organism, and therefore it is not always easy to find out about them. However, digestive functions were amongst the earliest to be understood because, as you have seen in Section 7.1, the contents of the alimentary canal are not really inside the body. In the eighteenth century, for example, a French scientist, Réaumur, found out about digestion in a bird by dropping material tied to a string down the animal's throat and hence into the alimentary tract. After leaving test materials for various lengths of time he pulled them out to study the changes which had taken place.

Réaumur's experiment could be called *in vivo*, because it was conducted in an environment of intact living tissue. You are now going to make a further study of the digestive activity of amylase by carrying out an experiment *in vitro* (which means, 'in glass'), and thus outside the body. Why would it be unwise simply to assume that the result of an *in vitro* experiment will explain what happens *in vivo*?

Set up 7 test tubes, and put 2 cm³ of 1 per cent starch solution into each tube. Then treat the tubes as shown in Figure 7.5.
After you have maintained the tubes for 15 minutes at the stated temperatures, remove drops from each tube and test with iodine solution on a tile. If you extract drops for testing by means of a pipette, what precautions must you take?

Remove further drops for testing at intervals of 5 minutes thereafter. When no further changes occur, test the contents of each

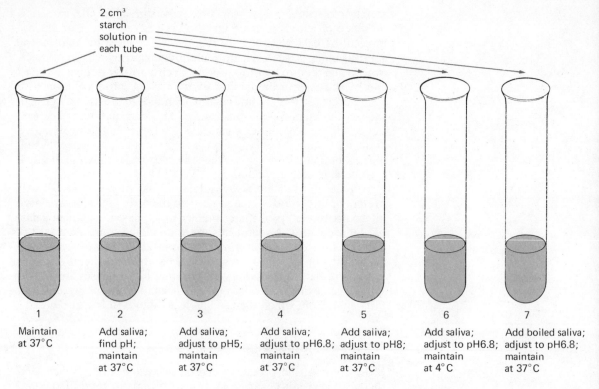

2 cm³ starch solution in each tube

1	2	3	4	5	6	7
Maintain at 37°C	Add saliva; find pH; maintain at 37°C	Add saliva; adjust to pH5; maintain at 37°C	Add saliva; adjust to pH6.8; maintain at 37°C	Add saliva; adjust to pH8; maintain at 37°C	Add saliva; adjust to pH6.8; maintain at 4°C	Add boiled saliva; adjust to pH6.8; maintain at 37°C

Figure 7.5 Investigating the action of amylase

tube for the presence of reducing sugar.

If starch disappears and reducing sugar appears, what process must have taken place? What evidence is there that a substance in saliva, amylase, can effect digestion? What appears to destroy amylase? Does amylase work better in acidic or alkaline conditions? What conclusions can you draw from comparing the results from tubes 4 and 6?

You have already found out something about enzymes in Chapter 3, and now you have investigated the conditions for activity of a particular digestive enzyme. Amylase is most active when in a slightly acid or neutral medium and at body temperature. It is generally true that each enzyme reacts best at a particular value of pH. In Chapter 3 you investigated the action of the enzyme phosphorylase. How does the action of phosphorylase differ from that of amylase?

Find out the pH of your saliva by means of test papers, and collect the results for the whole class. Is there any connection between these results in general and a particular condition for the activity of salivary amylase?

7.4 The digestive system

The digestive system is the alimentary canal along which food is passed, together with special organs such as glands connected with it. Digestion of the food takes place owing to the action of parts of the canal itself, or of the special organs. Different kinds of animals have different digestive systems, but the examination of the inside of a rat will give a good idea of the layout of the digestive system in a mammal. Figure 7.6 shows a rat dissected to display organs of the digestive system. Use this Figure to identify the parts of the rat dissected in the laboratory.

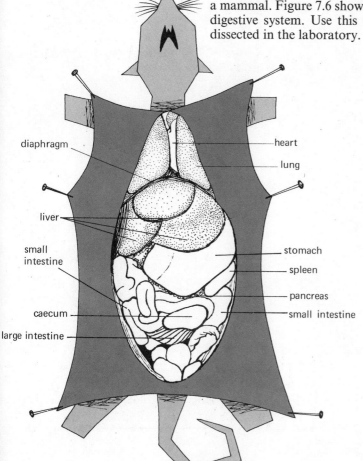

Figure 7.6 Digestive organs in a rat

If a fresh rat has been used, observe the moist film over all the organs. What is the function of this?

Unravel the alimentary canal and trace it through from the **oesophagus** to the **anus.** What do you think is the significance of such a large total length? Observe the fan-like array of blood vessels in the thin tissue known as the **mesentery.** What is the function of these vessels?

Observe and feel the **stomach, small intestine** and **large intestine.** Are the walls of these parts thick or thin? How do the diameters of these parts compare with each other? What evidence is there that the contents of the canal become drier as they pass towards the anus?

7.5 What processes occur in digestion?

We shall now consider the digestive processes which occur along the alimentary canal of our own bodies. Figure 7.7 illustrates the main organs but you will appreciate from your study of the rat that the diagram shows the layout in a very simplified form.

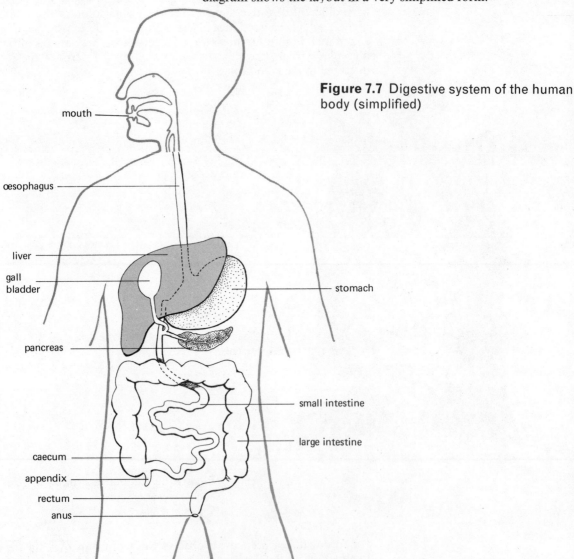

Figure 7.7 Digestive system of the human body (simplified)

mouth
œsophagus
liver
gall bladder
pancreas
stomach
small intestine
large intestine
caecum
appendix
rectum
anus

Preliminary stages of digestion

One of the first things which happens to food is that it is selected because of its taste, smell, or texture. If it is accepted, it is acted upon by the teeth. What are the functions of the different types of teeth mentioned in Chapter 5? What are the advantages of breaking down a solid mass of food into small particles?

You have already found that saliva contains an enzyme which begins the breakdown of starch. You are now going to find another function of saliva.

Swallow all the saliva in your mouth and then try to swallow again immediately afterwards. What happens, compared with swallowing mouthfuls of water in quick succession?

What is the particular function of saliva investigated in this experiment?

Food which is swallowed moves quickly down the oesophagus, or gullet, into the stomach. It is then passed along the different regions of the alimentary canal by a process called **peristalsis.** The gut wall relaxes and widens in front of the food: behind the food, the gut wall contracts and pushes the food onward. This movement occurs as a series of waves, and it can be understood easily by making a simple model.

Select a 20 cm length of rubber tubing and a marble or dried pea which can just be squeezed into the cavity of the tube. Move the marble along as shown in Figure 7.8.

1 stretch the tubing, and insert the marble

2 squeeze the marble along inside the tube, by pressing, as shown

squeeze

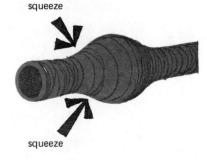

squeeze

Figure 7.8 Demonstrating peristalsis

In the stomach, digestion of proteins begins as a result of the secretion of the enzyme pepsin in the **gastric juice.** As this juice also contains hydrochloric acid, the pH is acid, and most suitable for pepsin activity. The acid also helps to kill bacteria. Look at the photograph of a section of stomach shown in Figure 7.9. What is the possible significance of the cavity being very irregular in outline?

What is the function of the strong muscular walls of the stomach? What happens as a result of the churning of the food?

After this preliminary treatment, food is passed on to the intestines.

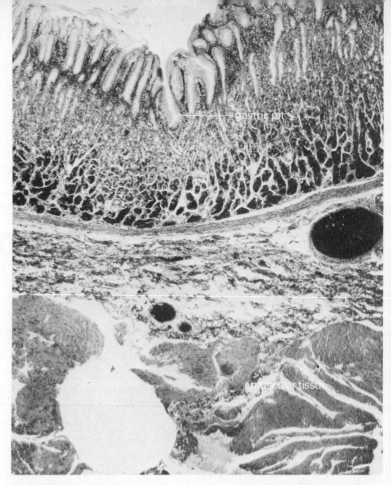

gastric pit

muscular tissue

Figure 7.9 A section of the wall of a human stomach (low power magnification)

Main stages of digestion

As soon as the food is passed from the stomach to the small intestine, it is acted on by digestive juices from the **pancreas.** This pancreatic juice contains amylases, proteases and lipases. The walls of the small intestine also produce enzymes which act on all three classes of foodstuffs. The digestion of carbohydrates and proteins involves several different enzymes, each of which acts in a specific way to produce small molecules suitable for absorption.

This first part of the small intestine which is clearly a region of active digestion is known as the **duodenum.** Compare the structure of the part of the duodenum shown in Figure 7.10 with that of the

Figure 7.10 Section of the duodenum of a pig (low power magnification)

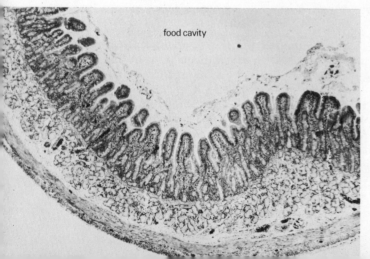

food cavity

stomach, Figure 7.9. In what ways do they differ? Try to relate the differences to the various functions performed.

The **liver** produces **bile** which contains salts to aid digestion, by emulsifying fats and oils. The bile is stored in the **gall bladder,** and then is passed into the duodenum along with the pancreatic juices.

Find out about the emulsification of an oil as follows.
1. Set up three test tubes and add 3–4 cm³ of olive oil to each.
2. To the first tube add water; to the second tube add dilute caustic soda solution; to the third tube add bile salts in powdered form.
3. Shake up the three tubes vigorously and leave aside for a few minutes before examining carefully.

In which tubes has an emulsion formed? In what form is the oil present (i) where no emulsion has formed, and (ii) where an emulsion has formed? What evidence is there that bile salts might be alkaline?

Bile salts do not contain enzymes, but they do help to break up the fats into small globules. What will happen to the total surface area of the fat as a result of this? How may this affect the action of lipase?

7.6 Absorption of nutrients

What are the end products of the digestion of carbohydrates, proteins and fats? What substances in the diet do not require to be digested?

All these nutrients are now absorbed by the cells lining the cavity of the small intestine. They are then passed into the transport system of the body, which you will investigate further in Chapter 8. The volume of food to be absorbed is considerable.

Look at the photograph of a section of part of the small intestine, Figure 7.11.

Figure 7.11 A section of the absorptive part of the small intestine of a mouse (low power magnification)

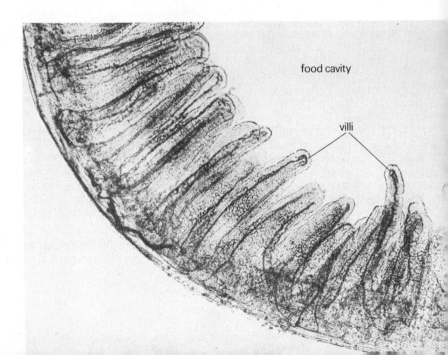

The part shown is mainly concerned with absorption of nutrients. What adaptation of the inner surface allows efficient absorption? The little finger-shaped processes, called **villi,** greatly increase the total absorptive surface, and they also move, contracting and expanding in the digested food.

The material which passes on into the large intestine is mainly food which cannot be digested readily, such as the cellulose of the cell walls of vegetables. Such material, however, serves a useful function in that it provides **roughage** in the form of bulky material. This stimulates the muscles producing the peristaltic waves which push food along the alimentary canal. This undigested solid forms part of the faeces which are got rid of when the muscular anus relaxes. Other components of the faeces are cells from the gut wall and bacteria. However, before the faeces are voided, a very large amount of water is removed by the large intestine. What is the importance of the large amount of water being left in the alimentary canal until the digestion and absorption of nutrients are complete?

We have now traced the process of digestion throughout the alimentary canal. Look back at Figure 7.7 and write a summary of the part played in digestion by each of the following (*a*) the mouth, (*b*) the stomach, (*c*) the small intestine and (*d*) the large intestine.

7.7 Beneficial bacteria

The large intestine has many bacteria present which synthesise vitamins B and K. These important vitamins are then absorbed into the body through the intestinal wall, through which water is also absorbed. In those mammals which have a diet consisting of a great deal of plant material, bacteria play an important part in breaking down substances, often carbohydrates, which are difficult to digest. For example, sheep and cows have large numbers of bacteria in their stomachs and large intestines. Rats, and herbivores such as rabbits, have a large structure called the caecum (see Figure 7.6), in which plant material is digested mainly by the action of bacteria which produce enzymes able to break down cellulose.

7.8 How is digestion controlled?

The production of enzymes at various points along the alimentary tract is not continuous, but takes place only when food is present. The prevention of unnecessary and wasteful production of enzymes is controlled in various ways: we shall consider only one example. The presence of food, or even of a weak acid, in the first part of the small intestine causes cells lining the canal to produce a substance called **secretin.** This substance is carried all over the body in the bloodstream, but it specifically stimulates the pancreas to produce enzymes. Chemicals like secretin which are carried in the blood and which affect other organs are known as **hormones.**

7.9 The products of digestion and their fate

The products of digestion are required for various purposes by the body. We shall now discuss what happens to the end products of the digestion of carbohydrates, proteins and fats.

(*a*) End products of digestion—glucose

1. Centrifuge a sample of ox or sheep blood for 5 minutes, or allow it to stand for 2 days.
2. Test a sample of the clear fluid, the **plasma,** with Benedict's reagent.

Is glucose present in the plasma? What is the origin of the glucose?

Glucose is carried by the blood, and is available to every cell in the body. It is a source of potential energy owing to the chemical composition of its molecule.

Glucose does not release its energy directly to cells. Instead, it is broken down stage by stage as a result of enzyme action, in order to build up the compound ATP, adenosine triphosphate. ATP is formed by ADP, adenosine diphosphate, combining with phosphate, thus:

$$ADP + P + \text{energy from glucose} \rightarrow ATP$$

The ATP molecule can be moved within the cell and, if it is broken down to give ADP again, it will yield energy. Energy is released by

products of respiration of glucose

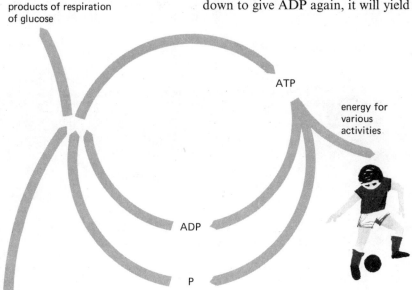

ATP

energy for various activities

ADP

P

glucose
(chemical
energy)

Figure 7.12 Energy release in living cells

the breaking of the chemical bond linking ADP and P. Breaking this bond releases a large supply of energy, which can be used for heat, movement, synthesis of chemical compounds, electrical work and for other vital processes.

Figure 7.12 summarises the role of glucose and ATP in energy release. What is the origin of energy in glucose? Why could ATP be compared to money and called energy currency? Which of the substances shown in the diagram must be replaced continuously in the cell?

When energy is required by almost any cell in any living plant or animal, it is obtained from ATP which is present in the cell.

In your body, the amount of glucose present in the blood is kept fairly constant. This control of blood sugar concentration is complex, and it involves the activity of several organs of the body, such as the liver and the pancreas.

Liver. This organ maintains the concentration of glucose in the blood at about 0·1 per cent. If blood reaching the liver is rich in the end-products of carbohydrate digestion, the latter are removed and stored as **glycogen,** a substance often called 'animal starch'. As a result of, say, muscle activity, the blood sugar concentration will fall, but enzymes convert enough of the glycogen into glucose, which then enters the bloodstream to maintain the normal concentration. This reconversion of glycogen back to glucose is under the control of the hormone **adrenalin,** produced by **adrenal glands** situated close to the kidneys.

Pancreas. You have already found that the pancreas is involved in the digestive processes. However, in 1889, it was found that the removal of the pancreas from a dog caused sugar to appear in the urine. This clearly indicated that the pancreas also functions in controlling sugar in the body. Figure 7.13 shows part of the pancreas as seen through a microscope. The outer cells of the lobes produce digestive enzymes which flow via ducts into the alimentary canal.

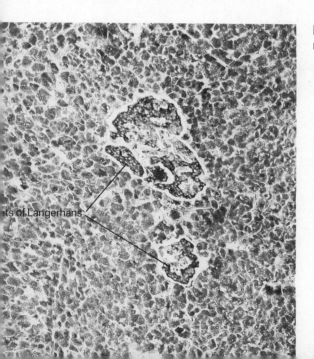

Figure 7.13 Pancreatic tissue (high power magnification)

ts of Langerhans

The inner cells, the **Islets of Langerhans** produce a hormone called **insulin.** Why would you expect blood vessels to be especially associated with hormone-producing tissue? The insulin determines the amount of glucose which should be stored as glycogen. If too little of the hormone is produced, a disease called diabetes occurs. This is a condition in which the glucose content of the blood is too high, and can result in loss of weight and tiredness. A diabetic person may control the glucose concentration in the blood by obtaining specific amounts of insulin at regular intervals.

We shall now discuss more briefly what happens to the other end products of digestion.

(b) End products of digestion—amino acids

Amino acids absorbed through the walls of the small intestine are carried by the bloodstream. They enter into the cells of the body and are rebuilt into proteins, from which body material is made.

Unlike carbohydrates, excess protein cannot be stored in the body. However, the liver breaks up surplus amino acids in the blood, resulting in the formation of carbohydrate material and the waste product **urea.** Details of the excretion of waste products are given in Chapter 10. The action of the liver, described above, is known as **deamination.**

The liver is also important in the formation of red blood cells, in that it is able to store and supply iron needed for their formation. Further, it is able to store vitamins A and D, which is the reason for taking cod or halibut liver oil even though your body may not be lacking these vitamins at the time.

It will be obvious to you now that the liver has many important functions. Make a summary of the life processes of the body in which the liver plays a part. Look at the photograph showing liver tissue, Figure 7.14. Note the arrangement of cells into spongy lobes, with

Figure 7.14 Liver tissue (low power magnification)

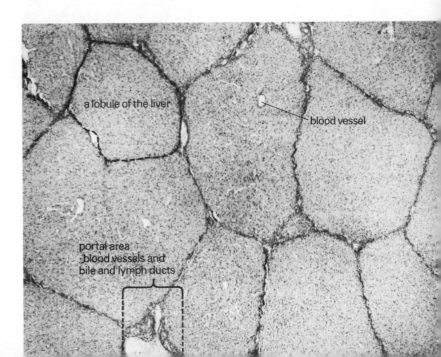

blood spaces between. What is the significance of the blood being in direct contact with the liver cells?

(*c*) End products of digestion—fatty acids and glycerol

After absorption, fatty acids and glycerol recombine to form fats, which are generally transported in ducts called **lymphatics** rather than in the bloodstream. This is because the lymphatic system of the body can absorb and transport molecules which may be too large to pass into the bloodstream.

Fat which is not needed for immediate use as a source of energy or heat is deposited under the skin, and at the back of the body cavity. Look for this deposit of fat in a dissected animal, or in a carcass at a butcher's shop. When required, fat is transported to the liver and there it is eventually converted into compounds which can readily be broken down in order to supply energy or heat. Fat may thus be a source of potential energy.

Some fat plays an important part in the structure of cells. For example, the cell membrane includes substances of a fatty nature, as well as proteins and other substances. What vital functions are performed by the cell membranes?

Looking Back at Chapter 7

1. Most foods are insoluble, and, to be of value as nutrients, they must pass through the wall of the alimentary canal and then be carried round the body by the bloodstream.
2. For this to happen, foods must be digested, that is, broken down into simple molecules which are soluble and able to diffuse.
3. Carbohydrate foods are broken down to glucose or other reducing sugars, by enzymes called amylases, proteins to amino acids by proteases, and fats to glycerol and fatty acids by lipases.
4. Digestive enzymes are produced by different regions of the alimentary canal, and by the pancreas. The activity of each enzyme is limited by particular conditions, such as pH.
5. The first part of the alimentary canal is mainly concerned with digestive processes: the remainder is responsible for absorption of nutrients and water.
6. The liver plays an important part in the control and utilising of glucose, protein and fat in the body. Hormones, such as insulin, are also important in controlling blood sugar.

8 TRANSPORTING MATERIALS

8.1 Movement within cells

In Chapters 2 and 3 you investigated cells. Each cell has a complicated set of requirements which must be satisfied before the cell will
function properly. It must, for example, receive raw materials for
growth, an energy supply, an oxygen supply, and it must have waste
materials removed. Even within the cell we would suspect that
materials must be moved from place to place.

You have already seen several one-celled organisms. One of
these, called *Paramecium*, can be used to find if materials are moved
within a single cell. Most of the substances in a cell are in solution
and cannot be seen, but some solid particles are present and so we
can study them.

Look at a drop of water from a pond, or from an aquarium which
has decaying plant material in it, to find if *Paramecium* is present.

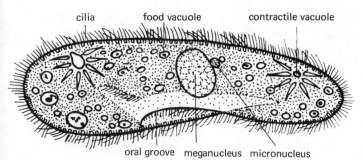

cilia   food vacuole   contractile vacuole

oral groove   meganucleus   micronucleus

Figure 8.1 A species of *Paramecium*

10 µm

Because of their rapid movement, these cells are difficult to study,
but you can slow them down by adding a drop of Polycell to the
water.
1. Place on a microscope slide one drop of a culture of *Paramecium*,
   with one drop of a suspension of yeast cells stained with congo
   red.
2. After 2 minutes add one drop of Polycell.
3. Place a cover slip over the liquid.

4. Find a stationary animal and observe the cell contents under the high power of the microscope (Figure 8.1).

Have any of the yeast cells passed into the animal? By means of a series of drawings, trace the position of the coloured cells to find out if their position within the cell changes.

The congo red used to stain the yeast works rather like Bicarbonate Indicator solution, in that it changes colour according to the pH. Congo red goes blue if the conditions become more acid.

What changes can you see in the colour of the yeast cells within the *Paramecium* compared with the yeast cells in the water? What must have been produced within the *Paramecium* cell to bring about the change in pH? As the yeast cells pass round the *Paramecium* they are slowly digested.

In the leaf of *Elodea* we do not have to introduce coloured particles to find out if movement takes place, as the cells contain chloroplasts.

1. Mount a leaf of *Elodea* on a slide as you did earlier in the course.
2. Under the high power of the microscope observe cells near the centre line of the leaf.
3. Describe any movement of the chloroplasts, noting whether they remain within one cell or pass from cell to cell.
4. Focus carefully and try to see if there is any movement or streaming of the cytoplasm in the cell. If you do not see movement, it does not mean that it is not there; the cytoplasm is transparent and is very difficult to see. Observe any of the other material that you are given, to see if there is any streaming of the cytoplasm.

Remember that most of the materials in the cell are in solution and that we cannot expect to see oxygen, dissolved food or waste materials being moved about.

8.2 Movement from cell to cell

While movement of materials within the cell is very important, movement from cell to cell is vital for the life of an organism. Food would be of little use to us if it were not carried from the intestine to every cell of the body. It would seem from this, therefore, that all large multicellular living organisms are likely to have a transport system, and we can investigate a few to see if this hypothesis is correct.

Some animals have a skin which is more or less transparent. We shall now look at such animals to see if materials are moved about.

1. Place a small aquatic crustacean such as *Gammarus* or *Daphnia* in a little water on a microscope slide.
2. Look at the animal under the low power of the microscope.
3. Describe any movements of the fluids within the body. Do not consider movements of the limbs or other appendages. Where does most of the flow within the body take place? Is the movement continuous, or is it periodic? What is responsible for moving the fluid?

Place a tadpole of frog or *Xenopus*, or a trout alevin, in a drop of water on a microscope slide.

The animal can be held in place for observation by placing a small piece of soaked paper towel over half the body as shown in Figure 8.2.

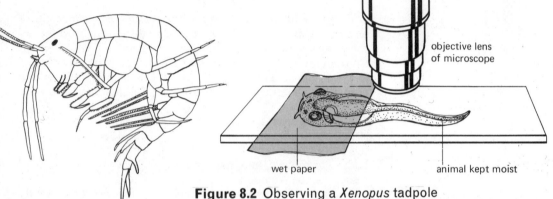

Figure 8.2 Observing a *Xenopus* tadpole

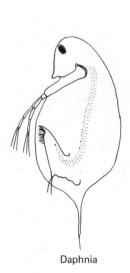

Gammarus

Daphnia

Use the low power of the microscope to observe any movement within the body. How does this movement differ from that within the body of *Gammarus* or *Daphnia*? In *Xenopus* you will see that the fluid which is moving is orange coloured; this is the **blood** of the animal. Materials in most animals are moved from cell to cell by the blood.

Use this animal to find out more about the way in which a blood system functions. Does the blood fill the spaces between the parts of the body, or is it enclosed in tubes? If tubes or vessels are present, are they all of the same size? Try to estimate the size of any vessels relative to the size of the blood cells, which are about 30 microns across in the case of the *Xenopus* and about 20 microns across for the trout.

Observe the blood in the vessels of the tail for a few minutes. Choose two of the larger vessels which are close together and study the blood flow in each. Is the blood flowing in the same direction in each vessel, towards or away from the end of the tail? Why is the blood flowing smoothly in one vessel and in spurts in the other? A further examination of the animal will help you to answer this question. Examine the **heart** which is situated near the middle of the body. What evidence is there that the heart is the pump that keeps the blood moving? Observe the flow of blood in the vessels leaving the heart. Is the flow smooth or in spurts? You should now be able to explain why the flow of blood was jerky in one tail vessel and smooth in the other.

Vessels carrying blood from the heart to all parts of the body are called **arteries,** and vessels with blood flowing smoothly back to the heart are called **veins.**

Use a stopclock to find out how many times the heart beats in a minute.

Perhaps this rate can be altered by changes in the animal's environment. The habitat of the *Xenopus* tadpole is near the surface of the water of lakes in Africa. What environmental changes will occur in this habitat which will affect the animal? Try to reproduce these changes in the laboratory. Factors such as temperature, vibration and light intensity are all worth investigating.

This type of investigation is only possible when the skin of the animal is transparent. Other ways have been developed for tracing the path of the blood within the bodies of animals. Radioactive isotopes are injected into an animal's bloodstream. As small doses of this kind do not harm the body, this technique is used for a number of investigations of disorders of human and other animal bodies.

Radiation from the radioactive isotopes can be detected by using a Geiger tube or photographic film. The isotopes are injected into the bloodstream and the detecting device placed over part of the body. The movement of the isotopes and hence the pattern of blood vessels can be recorded.

A system of tubes through which the blood can flow rapidly has been evolved in higher animals and makes possible the efficient transport of materials. Figure 8.3 shows a diagram of the arrangement of tubes in the human body.

As you saw in the crustaceans, not all animals have their blood flowing in tubes. When the blood flow is in tubes it is called a **closed blood system,** but when the blood moves in a large space round the organs it is called an **open blood system.** Both these systems require a pump, a heart, to keep the blood moving round the body.

If you trace the pattern of blood vessels in Figure 8.3, you will see that man really has two overlapping circulations. One set of vessels goes from the heart to all parts of the body and back again. The other set links the heart and the lungs. This double pattern is found in all birds and mammals, and these animals are said to have a **double circulation.** Figure 8.4 shows a diagram of a double circulatory system.

Notice that the blood passes round each 'circulation' alternately and goes back to the heart between each 'circulation'.

8.3 The work of William Harvey (1578–1657)

How much do you know about your own heart and the blood vessels through which your blood flows? Before 1600 it was believed that our blood ebbed and flowed like the tides of the sea. About that time a scientist called William Harvey carried out experiments on

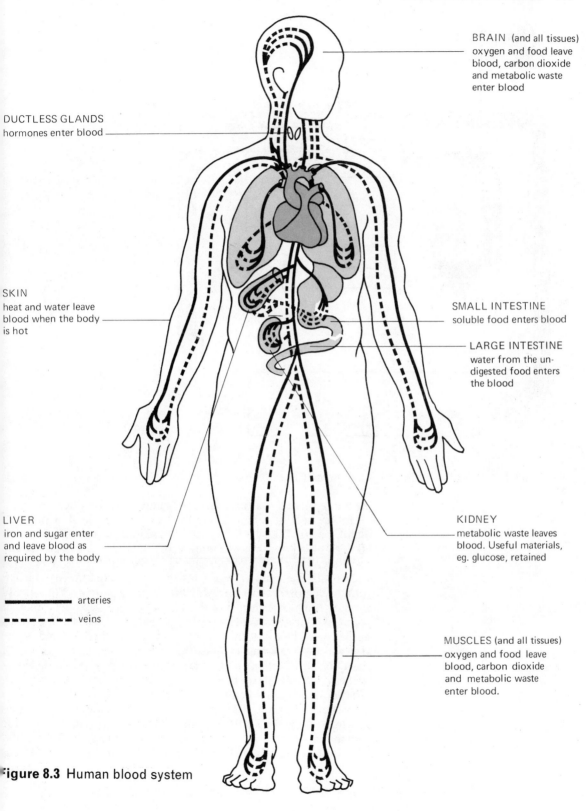

BRAIN (and all tissues)
oxygen and food leave
blood, carbon dioxide
and metabolic waste
enter blood

DUCTLESS GLANDS
hormones enter blood

SKIN
heat and water leave
blood when the body
is hot

SMALL INTESTINE
soluble food enters blood

LARGE INTESTINE
water from the un-
digested food enters
the blood

LIVER
iron and sugar enter
and leave blood as
required by the body

KIDNEY
metabolic waste leaves
blood. Useful materials,
eg. glucose, retained

————— arteries

- - - - - - veins

MUSCLES (and all tissues)
oxygen and food leave
blood, carbon dioxide
and metabolic waste
enter blood.

Figure 8.3 Human blood system

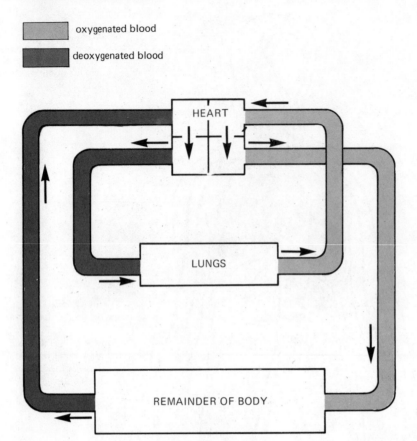

oxygenated blood

deoxygenated blood

HEART

LUNGS

REMAINDER OF BODY

Figure 8.4 Diagram of double circulation

the human blood system. Figure 8.5 shows you what he did.

Harvey tied the arm as in Figure 8.5 to restrict the flow of blood out of the arm. This had the effect of making the veins near the skin fill with blood and become more prominent. These vessels are not easily seen in young people or in women because of the layer of fat underneath the skin. If you want to try this experiment yourself, your father or grandfather will be the best patient. You should never attempt experiments of this type, using a tourniquet, on other pupils of your own age. Harvey found that if he placed a finger on a raised vessel, he could empty it by pushing the blood out and up the arm with another finger. When he released the finger nearest the heart, the blood did not fill up the vessel. When he released the finger farthest from the heart he found that the blood did fill the vessel. What does this tell you about the direction of flow of the blood in the vessel? By this and other demonstrations, Harvey was able to convince many of his fellow scientists and doctors that blood in the human body flowed in one direction inside a vessel, and not to and fro. Nowadays we talk about the circulation of the blood. How is

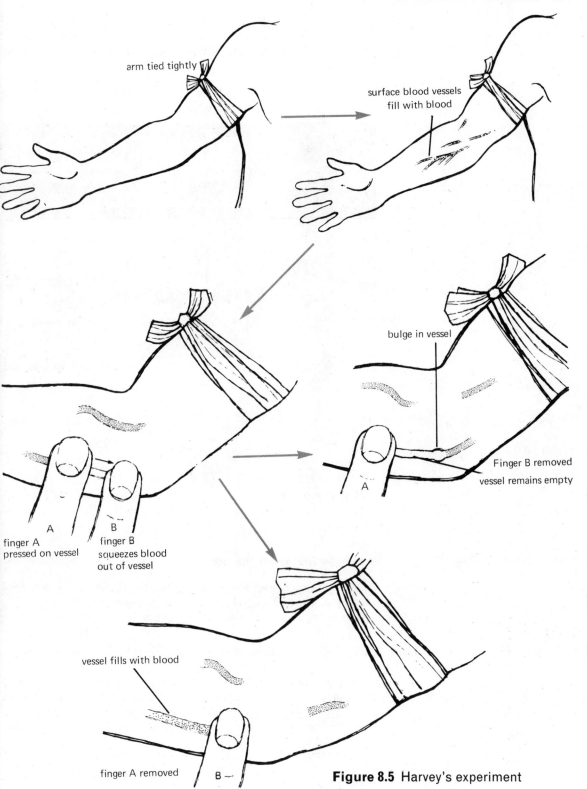

Figure 8.5 Harvey's experiment

arm tied tightly

surface blood vessels fill with blood

bulge in vessel

Finger B removed vessel remains empty

finger A pressed on vessel

finger B squeezes blood out of vessel

A

B

vessel fills with blood

finger A removed

B

the back-flow of blood prevented in the veins? You can check your suggestions by looking inside the vessels. The walls of these vessels have flaps of tissue called **valves** which work as shown in Figure 8.6.

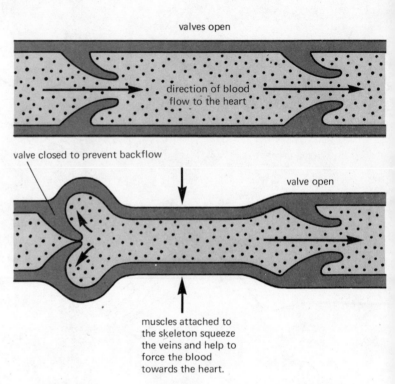

Figure 8.6 A vein with valves

If you watch Harvey's experiment being carried out on a person with very little fat under the skin, you will see the valves as bumps in the veins.

8.4 Your finger on the pulse

We have found some information about our blood vessels, but how much can we find out about our hearts? We can investigate the action of the heart in a number of ways.

In certain parts of the body large arteries come near the surface of the skin, and you can feel the beat of the heart at these points. By placing your fingers over your partner's wrist, as shown in Figure 8.7, you can count the rate at which his heart is beating. You are, of course, taking his **pulse.**

Count the number of beats for fifteen seconds. Repeat this three times and obtain an average value. Calculate how many times per minute your partner's heart is beating.

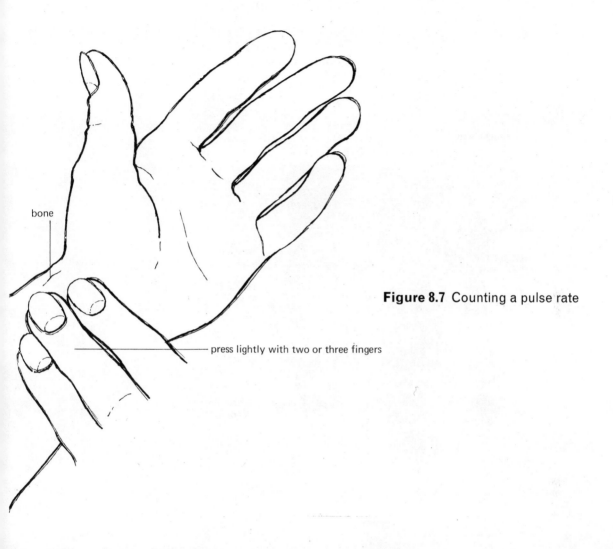

bone

press lightly with two or three fingers

Figure 8.7 Counting a pulse rate

The normal rate for a human is said to be 72 beats per minute. How many people in your class are 'normal'? The difference in your case is probably due to the fact that you are younger than the normal adult, but even if you counted the rate for several adults, you would probably find that only some of them had a rate of 72 beats per minute. To be scientifically accurate the statement above should have said that the rate of heart beat, averaged for a large number of human beings, is 72 beats per minute. A good way of expressing results of this type is to plot all the results as a histogram. From the class results you will see the range of values found and the approximate average figure for your class.

8.5 The human heart

Figure 8.8 shows a diagram of the human heart. How does this vital organ work? As all mammal hearts are very similar, we can look at the heart of a cow, pig or sheep to investigate its functioning.

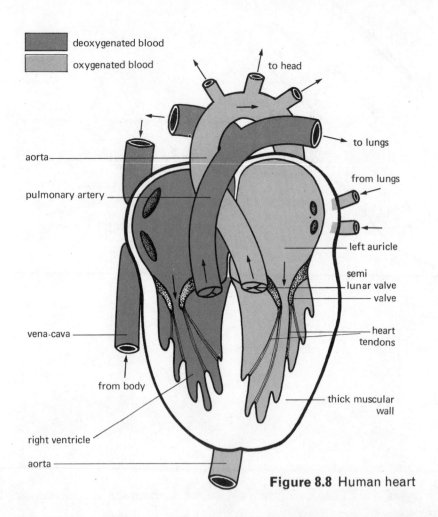

deoxygenated blood
oxygenated blood

to head
to lungs
from lungs
aorta
pulmonary artery
left auricle
semi lunar valve
valve
vena-cava
heart tendons
from body
thick muscular wall
right ventricle
aorta

Figure 8.8 Human heart

How does the lower part of the heart, which is responsible for pumping blood round the body, differ from the top half, which collects blood?

With a sharp scalpel cut open the top half of the two auricles and the bottom half of the two ventricles and look inside. At this stage try to avoid cutting the walls between the auricles and ventricles.

Using a pencil or blunt instrument, find the openings of the vessels which enter and leave the four chambers. Investigate each of the entrances to see how the back-flow of the blood is prevented. You can check your observations in the following way.

1. Hold the heart upright and pour water into the auricles.

2. Hold the heart upside down and pour water into the ventricles. What can you tell about the direction of flow of blood through the heart by observing the different ways in which water ran through it?

Cut the heart completely open and use Figure 8.8 to identify the different parts.

Why are the walls of the ventricles much thicker than those of the auricles? What is the function of the white, tough, heart-tendons?

8.6 Blood vessels

The human heart is a very powerful pump because it can force the blood through miles of fine tubes so that the entire 5 litres of blood circulates completely round the body once per minute.

The veins near the skin which we investigated earlier have valves to prevent the back-flow of the blood. Blood returns to the heart via the veins, and by the time it reaches these vessels the pressure has been greatly reduced. Figure 8.9 shows a nurse taking the **blood pressure** of a patient. Will blood pressure be given as a reading from the arteries or veins?

Since the blood pressure in the vessels coming from the heart is very great, what properties must the walls of the arteries have? As you will see from Figure 8.10, the walls of arteries are much thicker than those of veins. Near the heart the thick artery walls

Figure 8.9 Taking blood pressure

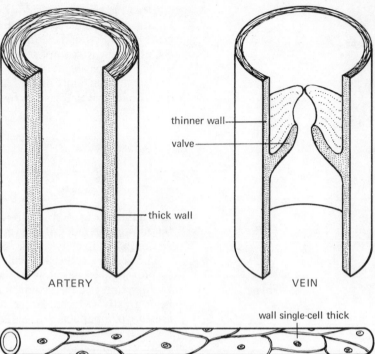

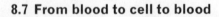

Figure 8.10 Blood vessels

consist mostly of **elastic fibres** but in other parts of the body they are composed of **muscle fibres.**

The elastic walls of the **aorta** expand when the heart beats. When the ventricles relax and the aorta valves close, the elastic fibres in the walls of the vessel return to their original shape, and the blood is thus forced along the artery. The muscle cells in the walls are contracted or expanded to control the amount of blood passing to any part of the body. Although the entrance to the aorta has valves, there are no valves present in the arteries throughout the body.

When we get a fright, the walls of the arteries going to the stomach are tightened so cutting down the flow of blood to this region. The 'butterflies' which we have in our stomach at this time are an indication that the supply to the gut is being cut down, and that the blood is being sent to places where it is most likely to be needed, muscle, brain and nerve tissue.

8.7 From blood to cell to blood

When the arteries reach the tissues, the materials dissolved in the blood must be able to diffuse into the cells. This is possible because the arteries divide up into a network of very narrow tubes called **capillaries.** Figure 8.10 shows that capillaries have very thin walls, usually one cell thick. Dissolved materials in solution can pass in and out of the blood through the walls of the capillaries.

You probably saw that the capillaries in the trout alevin or the *Xenopus* tadpole were so narrow that the blood cells could pass through them only in single file.

There is a continual two-way passage of materials; from the blood to the cells and from the cells to the blood. The dissolved materials pass from the capillaries to the cells and the waste material passes into the blood. Fine tubes join up to form the veins in which the blood is then carried back to the heart.

The vital materials necessary for the life of the cells enter the blood at different parts of the body. Oxygen is collected in the lungs and food material and water enter from the intestine.

Waste materials produced in the tissues are removed and passed out of the body through the lungs, the skin and the kidneys.

You will also remember that one of the advantages that mammals and birds have over the rest of living things is that each cell in the body is maintained at a constant temperature.

If you have not done so before, find out the body temperature of the members of your class. Use a clinical thermometer to work out the range of temperatures and the average temperature, and compare this with the average adult body temperature of 37°C. The temperature of all parts of your body is very similar, and your blood is responsible for spreading heat evenly throughout the tissues.

8.8 Blood

You have now examined a number of hypotheses about blood systems. In Chapter 2 you studied the cells of different tissues. We will now go on to investigate blood, which is a fluid tissue.

By jabbing your finger with a fine needle called a lancet, you will be able to squeeze a drop of your own blood on to a microscope slide. In this way you will be able to study the detailed structure of blood.

Figure 8.11 shows how to prepare a slide of your blood. As you found earlier in the course, it is often useful to add stain when preparing a microscope slide. In this case Leishman's stain is added, to show up the nuclei of the cells.

Smear preparations are the only types you are allowed to view under the high power without using a cover slip.

Look at the slide. Try to estimate the number of red blood cells in the slide. You will find this a very difficult task from your preparation, but blood cells can be counted using a specially marked slide called a haemocytometer. This slide has a grid marked on it, and when the cover slip is slid into place a known volume of blood is trapped over the grid. The cells on the grid are counted and, by multiplication, the number in each cubic millimetre (mm^3) can be calculated.

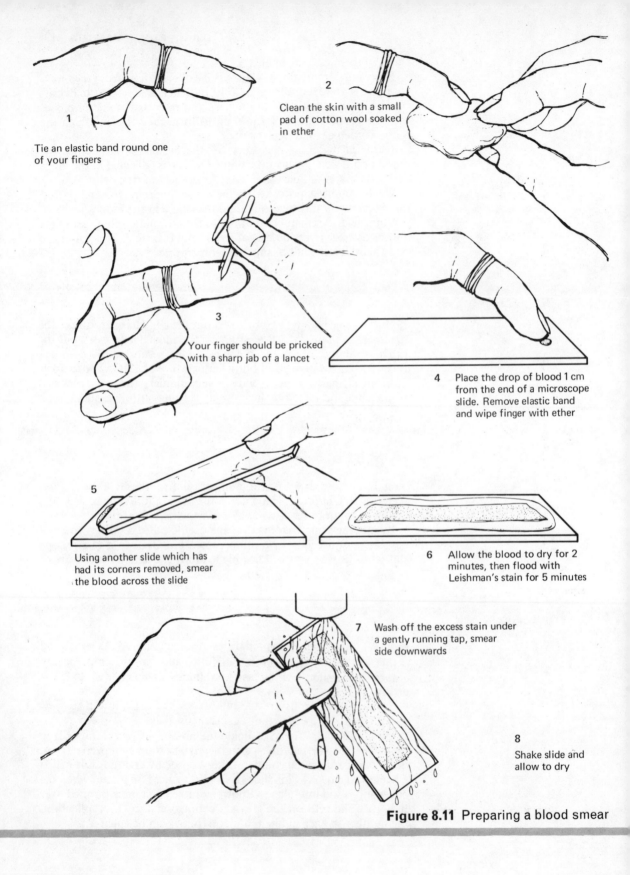

1 Tie an elastic band round one of your fingers

2 Clean the skin with a small pad of cotton wool soaked in ether

3 Your finger should be pricked with a sharp jab of a lancet

4 Place the drop of blood 1 cm from the end of a microscope slide. Remove elastic band and wipe finger with ether

5 Using another slide which has had its corners removed, smear the blood across the slide

6 Allow the blood to dry for 2 minutes, then flood with Leishman's stain for 5 minutes

7 Wash off the excess stain under a gently running tap, smear side downwards

8 Shake slide and allow to dry

Figure 8.11 Preparing a blood smear

A man has about 5 million red blood cells or corpuscles in a mm^3 of his blood and a woman has about 4·5 million. Each red blood corpuscle is about 7·5 microns in diameter and this makes them almost the smallest cells in the human body. Red blood corpuscles are the only living cells in the body which do not have a nucleus when mature. They are just tiny bags containing cytoplasm and the red pigment called **haemoglobin.** You will see that Leishman's stain has coloured the nuclei of certain cells. When unstained, these blood cells are colourless and are called white corpuscles. How does the number of white corpuscles in your blood compare with that of the red? In a human adult the proportion is about 1 white to 600 red cells.

8.9 Platelets

The other solid particles which you may see in your blood are tiny pieces of cytoplasm called **platelets.** When any part of the body is damaged, the platelets help to form a network of **fibrin,** from fibrinogen, which is one of the blood proteins. Each network of fibrin is called a **clot** of blood, or a **thrombus,** and it seals a cut or wound in the skin or in internal organs. You may have heard of an older person suffering from thrombosis. What do you think has happened to some of the blood in this person? Thrombosis is sometimes very serious, because the supply of blood is cut off to a certain part of the body when the thrombus blocks an artery. If the clot passes into the coronary arteries that supply the heart, the whole body will be affected because the heart muscle cannot function without an adequate blood supply.

Only the solid parts of the blood are visible on your slide. What fraction of the volume of the blood do these solid parts make up?

You can measure the proportion of solid to liquid by using cattle blood, which is very similar to human blood. This blood can be prevented from clotting by adding a chemical called sodium citrate. The citrate has been added to the blood before you are supplied with it.

1. Fill two centrifuge tubes with blood.
2. Centrifuge for 5 minutes. When the tubes are spun round in a centrifuge the heavier solid particles are forced to the bottom of the tube.
3. Observe the tubes, and record the fraction of the blood that is liquid **plasma** and the fraction that is solid.

About 90 per cent of the plasma is water. What percentage of water is present in blood?

8.10 Haemoglobin

While you have a sample of cattle blood, you can investigate some of the other functions of the blood. We know that blood carries oxygen and carbon dioxide round the body, but can we find out how this is brought about?

The first thing to do is to find out what happens to blood in the presence of these gases.

1. Pour 10 cm³ of blood into each of three test tubes labelled A, B and C.
2. Bubble oxygen through the blood in A.
3. Bubble carbon dioxide through the blood in B.
4. Leave C untouched. What is the purpose of this sample of blood? What differences can you now see between the blood samples? What conclusions can you draw from these differences?
5. Now check your observations and explanations by reversing the bubbling, that is, by passing oxygen through B and carbon dioxide through A.

A change of colour indicates that the blood reacts differently in the presence of either gas. From this we might conclude that haemoglobin could be responsible for carrying these gases round the body.

It is always very important not to conclude more from an experiment than it actually tells us. Often an experiment does not prove what we set out to find, but it may suggest a further hypothesis. In this experiment all that we have really found is that haemoglobin may have something to do with the transport of gases in the blood. We cannot be sure, because we have not determined exactly what is the reaction between the blood and the gases. Also, we are not investigating blood in arteries and veins but in test tubes, where the concentration of oxygen and carbon dioxide is much higher than it would ever be in the blood vessels.

To find the exact explanation we have to study the work of research biologists. They have discovered that oxygen molecules become attached to the haemoglobin to form what is called **oxyhaemoglobin.** When blood is exposed to a high concentration of carbon dioxide, this gas replaces oxygen from the blood, changing the oxyhaemoglobin into haemoglobin. As you saw, this darkens the colour of the blood. Carbon dioxide does not become attached to the haemoglobin, but is carried in the blood as sodium bicarbonate. About 30 per cent of the bicarbonate is carried in the red blood corpuscles. Without haemoglobin present, 100 cm³ of human blood would be able to carry 0·5 cm³ of oxygen, but by forming oxyhaemoglobin 100 cm³ of blood can carry 20 cm³ of oxygen.

Assuming that 5 litres is the normal volume of your blood, calculate the maximum amount of oxygen your blood could carry at any one moment. In fact the blood never carries this amount of oxygen because of the presence of carbon dioxide.

8.11 White blood cells

The function of the white blood corpuscles is much more difficult to investigate, but you do have a clue in the fact that a large number of them collect when part of the body is infected. A pimple or spot in your skin is due to the multiplication of the bacterium *Staphylococcus* which has entered the body at that point. The white matter in the spot consists mostly of the remains of white blood cells. Figure 8.12 shows the work of the white blood corpuscles in the body.

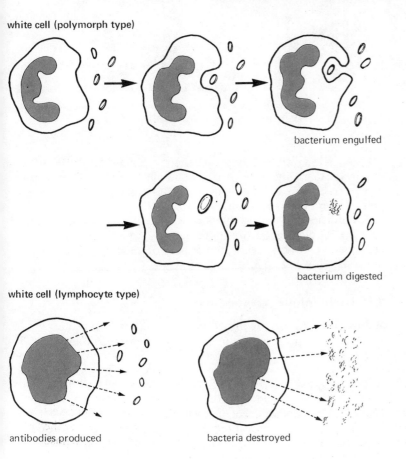

Figure 8.12 The function of white blood corpuscles. Two different types of white cells are shown

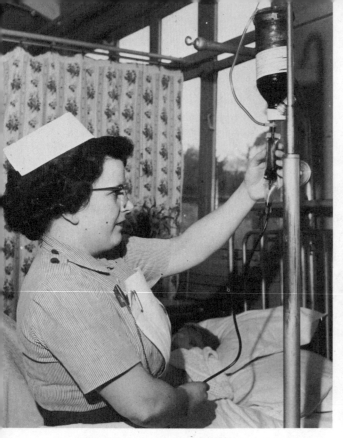

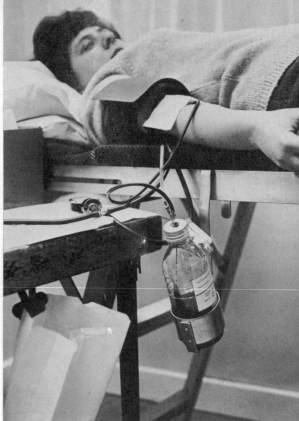

Figure 8.13 A blood transfusion

Figure 8.14 A blood donor

Blood is one of the body's defences against disease. It is very important to maintain the quantity and quality of the blood when a person is injured or ill. Figure 8.13 shows a patient receiving a pint of blood by transfusion.

There is no substitute for human blood, and doctors keep a supply or 'bank' of blood ready for immediate use. The blood for the bank comes from donors, who give a pint of their blood at regular intervals, as in Figure 8.14.

8.12 Unwelcome passengers

As you have found, the blood is responsible for the transport of many different materials round the body. The materials are normally useful to the cells, but occasionally harmful material can also be carried by the blood; you can think about this aspect of blood transport by considering any of the common complaints from which you may have suffered. What happens when you catch 'measles'? How does the doctor recognise that you have the disease? If you have had measles, you will remember that you had a sore throat, a headache, and that your skin became covered in spots. How did the measles germs spread through your body from your mouth and nose where they entered?

Measles germs are tiny particles called **viruses.** They are about

0·05 microns in diameter, which is smaller than bacteria. Diseases such as measles, chickenpox, mumps, polio, influenza, common cold and several others are caused by viruses. Other diseases, such as tuberculosis (T.B.), scarlet fever and diphtheria are caused by bacteria.

These viruses and bacteria are easily transported by the blood, and, once in the body, they spread quickly to all parts. These organisms which cause disease are known as **pathogens.** How does blood react to the presence of pathogens?

8.13 Transport in plants

In these investigations into the transport of materials to living cells, we have considered only animal tissue. It is a reasonable hypothesis to suggest that plants also require a transport system to ensure that each cell has the basic requirements for life.

When a plant is cut, a watery solution may flow from the cut surface, but blood certainly does not appear. This suggests that water may be used by the plant in the same way that the animal uses blood. Unfortunately water is colourless and usually we cannot see if it is moving in a plant. By the addition of a red dye we can see the position of the dye solution in the plant. In this way we can test our hypothesis.

1. Place the roots or cut ends of leeks, asparagus or other plants into water dyed red.
2. Observe the white parts of the plant after 30 minutes.
3. Cut one shoot along its length to see where the solution has gone in the plant.
4. Cut across at different points up another stem and look at the cut surfaces. What do the red dots indicate?

What evidence is there that plants have tubes or vessels in which water and dissolved materials can travel? If you look at the plants after two days you will see that the water has passed from the roots through the stem and into the leaves. This shows that the transport system extends throughout the plant.

Another way of investigating the movement of materials within a plant is to use radioactive isotopes as tracers, in the same way as mentioned in Section 8.2. The movement of the soluble substances taken in by the plant can be followed, as shown in Figure 8.15. The roots of the tomato plant were placed in water which contained radioactive phosphorus (^{32}P). After a short time the plant was laid on a large photographic film and Figure 8.15 was produced when this was developed. The ^{32}P appears white in the photograph and shows the way in which water and dissolved materials have passed up the plant.

Figure 8.15 Autoradiograph of a plant

glucose with radio active carbon →

1 hour later

24 hours later

Geiger counter used

None | High

Low | High

High | Low

to record radio active source

Figure 8.16 The movement of sugar

From the results of your experiment, and from Figure 8.15, it would appear that the theory that the plant has a transport system is correct. The very narrow tubes in which water and minerals flow up the plant are called **xylem vessels.** You have seen some of these in work on cells in Chapter 2.

8.14 The food distribution system of plants

Transport within the plant is not just upward, as most of our investigations have tended to indicate so far. There must also be conduction downwards within the plant. What must happen to the sugars produced in the leaves during photosynthesis if the entire plant is to have a source of energy? Figure 8.16 shows an experiment which may support your explanation.

Glucose containing radioactive carbon (^{14}C) was placed on an upper leaf of a tomato plant after removal of the waxy cuticle. The radiations from the carbon in the glucose were detected by a Geiger counter as shown in Figure 8.16. When the leaves are newly treated, the Geiger tube reading shows them to be highly radioactive. After 1 hour, a high level of radiation was detected in the stem below the treated leaf. After 24 hours the highest level of radiation was in the

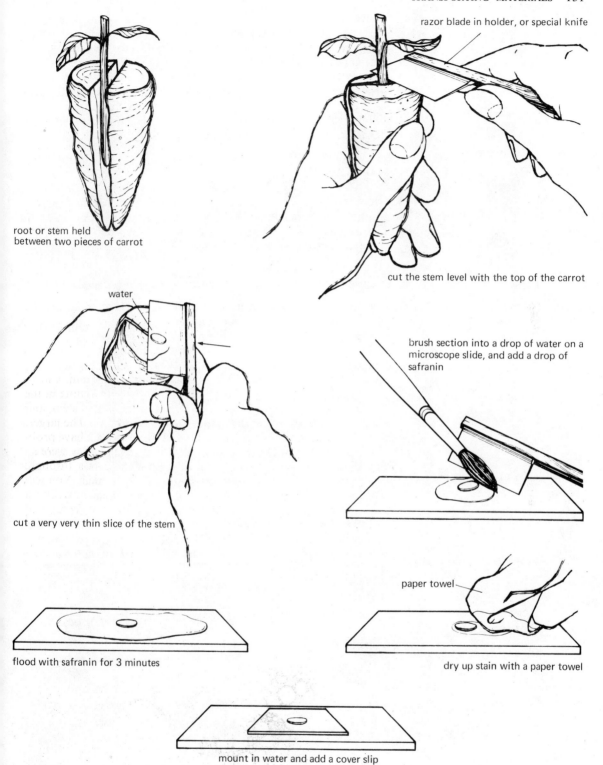

root or stem held between two pieces of carrot

razor blade in holder, or special knife

cut the stem level with the top of the carrot

water

cut a very very thin slice of the stem

brush section into a drop of water on a microscope slide, and add a drop of safranin

flood with safranin for 3 minutes

paper towel

dry up stain with a paper towel

mount in water and add a cover slip

Figure 8.17 Cutting plant sections

fruits. What does this tell you about the direction of flow of sugars in this experiment? In this plant what use has been made of the sugar from the leaves? When a potato tuber is formed underground, it gradually enlarges with deposition of starch, which must have been formed from sugar carried from the rest of the plant above the ground. Sugars in solution do not move in the xylem vessels which are responsible for the upward flow of water and mineral salts. Other cells, in **phloem** tissue, are present for this conduction of sugars in solution.

8.15 Plant anatomy

More information about the vessels within plants can be found by examination under the microscope. The method used by botanists to study plant tissue is to cut thin slices of each part and observe them under the microscope.

Use a special knife, or a razor blade in a holder, to cut as thin slices as possible from the root and from the stem of a plant, as in Figure 8.17.

The addition of a drop of dye helps to distinguish between the different types of cells. The red dye safranin stains lignin, which, as you discovered in Chapter 1, is often found as thickening in the walls of cells. Look at the slices, sections, of the root and stem, and try to draw a diagram of the arrangement of the parts. The larger, more open spaces within the tissues are the vessels. You have probably found that, although you cut very thin sections, they were so thick under the microscope that little light could pass through, and the section was too dark to distinguish many details. You will be given slides with sections on them cut by a machine like a miniature bacon slicer, which is called a **microtome.** What will be the approximate thickness of the sections? Remember that each is rather less than one cell thick. After observation of your own slides, the prepared sections, and Figure 8.18, perhaps you can now appreciate that plants have a transport system of narrow tubes arranged in a set pattern.

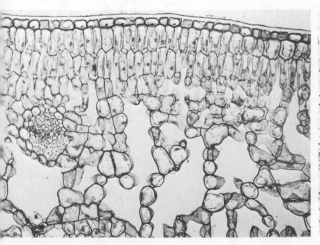

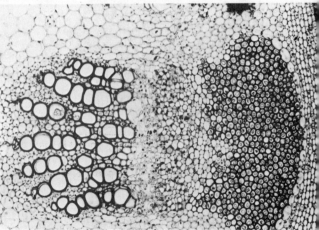

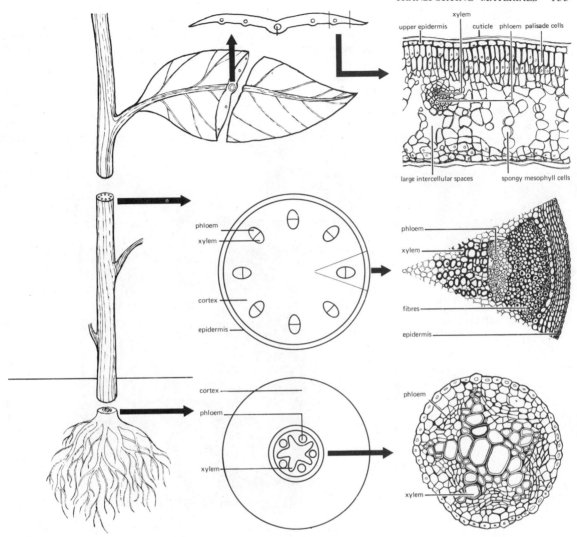

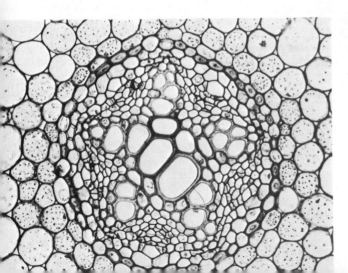

Figure 8.18 Plant anatomy. The photographs, left to right, show sections of a leaf, a stem and a root. (Relate to line drawings above)

The position of the veins, which are bundles of tubes, can be seen easily from the outside of leaves. Look at prepared slides of a section of a leaf and at Figure 8.18 to see the arrangement of the vessels inside a leaf.

Look carefully at all the slides once more, paying special attention to where red staining is to be found. This shows the position of lignin thickening in the plant. Is it scattered over the entire section or concentrated in particular parts? Remember that the vessels are very long tubes. What is the significance of the position of the lignin in the sections?

If you look at Figure 8.19 you will see some of the types of vessels and other cells which you studied in Chapter 2. In this

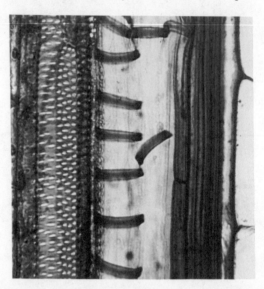

Figure 8.19 Vessels and fibres

photograph you can see the cells in their natural position within the stem. Which parts of the vessels and fibres are thickened? These fibres which support the plant are often taken out and used by man. Paper, linen and jute are all made from plant fibres.

The sections shown in Figure 8.18 were of very young root and stem. If you look at a section of a twig, and at the Christmas tree which you cut earlier in the course, you will see that it consists almost entirely of woody xylem tissue. Where is the phloem in a woody stem? The only possible area for cells transporting sugar down the trunk would appear to be round the edge, just within the bark. Carry out the following experiment to check this hypothesis.

1. Carefully cut into the bark of 30 cm long twigs, as shown in Figure 8.20.
2. Place the twigs in water and each week observe closely any changes that occur.

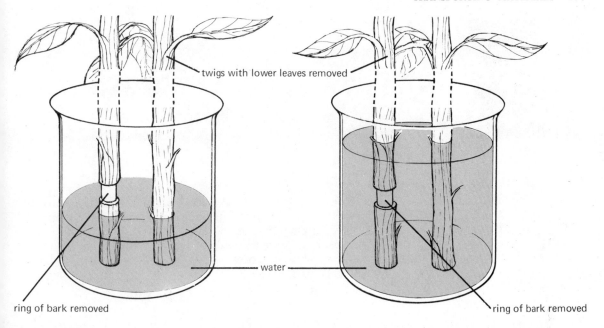

twigs with lower leaves removed

water

ring of bark removed

ring of bark removed

Figure 8.20
A ringing experiment

3. What difference is there between the cut and the untreated twigs?
4. What has happened to the part of the twig above and below the cut?
5. What does this tell you about the position of the phloem in these twigs?

Looking Back at Chapter 8

1. Conduction of foods and gases takes place within cells.
2. Larger organisms also have transport of substances from cell to cell.
3. In many animals, blood carries the substances round the body in open or in closed blood systems.
4. The heart is the pump which forces the blood through the vessels and round the body.
5. Blood vessels have their structure related to their function. Arteries are thick-walled, while veins are thin-walled with valves.
6. Blood is also responsible for sealing wounds by clotting and for destroying pathogens.
7. Plants have a system of tubes filled with watery sap for the conduction of materials. Unlike animals, the vascular system of plants does not provide the transport system for gases.
8. In plants, supporting tissue is closely associated with conducting tissue.

9 EXCHANGE OF GASES

9.1 Using oxygen

Earlier in the course you have investigated the way in which the body uses oxygen. Why do our bodies require this gas? Which gas is produced during respiration?

The results of your analyses of changes in gases taken in and given out may not have been exactly the same as the average figures for adults quoted in Table 9.1.

Table 9.1

Gas	Inhaled air	Exhaled air
oxygen	21 per cent	17 per cent
nitrogen	79 per cent	79 per cent
carbon dioxide	less than 0·1 per cent	4 per cent

The exchange of gases which takes place between living things and the air is a very important aspect of Biology. Before we go on to consider plants, and other animals, we shall carry out a more detailed and quantitative study of gas exchange in man. What information is required in order to find the quantities of oxygen and carbon dioxide passing into and out of our bodies? You will certainly need to know how much air is taken in when breathing normally.

Devise an experiment to find out how much this is for your own body. The method which you used to collect exhaled air in previous experiments could be modified for use here; but we can assume that the volume of air breathed out is the same as the volume taken in.

To calculate the amount of oxygen taken into the body you will also have to know how often the volume of air you measured is taken in per minute.

136

Watch the person next to you closely, and count how many times he breathes in one minute. Make at least three counts and calculate an average figure. An average for your class will make the figure more typical of people of your age and sex.

You should now be able to work out the rate at which oxygen is used by the human body.

$$\begin{array}{l}\text{Rate of oxygen} \\ \text{use by the body}\end{array} = \begin{array}{l}\text{Volume of air} \\ \text{per breath}\end{array} \times \begin{array}{l}\text{Percentage of} \\ \text{oxygen used} \\ \text{from the air}\end{array} \times \begin{array}{l}\text{Rate of} \\ \text{breathing} \\ \text{per minute}\end{array}$$

This is of course the rate at rest. Find out the effect of exercise on the rate of oxygen used by the body. To do this you will have to remeasure each of the three figures used in the calculation, if you do not have results from your previous work.

An active man during exercise can use up to 8 litres of oxygen per minute. From this it would seem that one of the factors which we must consider when finding the rate of respiration of other organisms will be their activity.

9.2 Gas exchange in ecosystems

You can go on to study other organisms now that you have an understanding of gas exchange in your own body. A direct measurement of the rate of uptake of oxygen is difficult to carry out experimentally with smaller living organisms. The rate of oxygen uptake or of carbon dioxide production which is easier to measure, is taken as an indication of the amount of energy released in living tissue, as was mentioned in Section 6.2. Carbon dioxide gas is produced at almost the same rate as oxygen is used up.

Earlier in your Biology course you studied the interplay between organisms in a number of ecosystems. The rate of gas exchange and release of energy of each organism has an effect on all the others. We cannot easily study the gas exchange of animals and plants in their natural habitat, but we can check the rate under controlled conditions in the laboratory.

Use the apparatus shown in Figure 9.1 to compare the rate of production of carbon dioxide from a variety of organisms which live in an ecosystem. To obtain an accurate comparison, you should use exactly the same amount of each animal or plant. As you cannot use halves or parts of living things, it is easier to work out the rate per gramme for each organism. The method is as follows.

1. Select a number of different plants and animals from a particular ecosystem. If the ecosystem is the aquarium tank which you studied earlier, you might choose *Elodea*, duckweed, flatworms, snails, water boatmen, shrimps, or water slaters as organisms worth investigating. Slaters, millipedes, beetles, flies, spiders, leaves or moss tufts are materials that you might choose to study from a tree ecosystem.

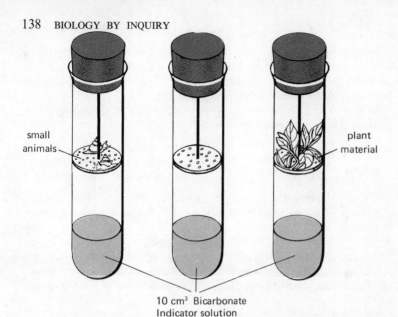

Figure 9.1 Comparing respiration rates

small animals

plant material

10 cm³ Bicarbonate Indicator solution

This comparison is based on measurements of carbon dioxide produced. What precautions should you take when using green plant material, and why?

2. Place 20 cm³ of Bicarbonate Indicator solution in each of several boiling tubes.
3. Weigh the living organisms and place approximately equal weights of different organisms in separate tubes.
4. Add drops of dilute acid to 10 cm³ of Bicarbonate Indicator solution in a boiling tube, until the orange colour just changes to yellow. Keep this as the standard yellow colour.
5. Note the time that each of the tubes with living material takes to change to this standard yellow colour.

Work out a comparison of the rates of carbon dioxide production by finding how long a gramme of each organism takes to change the Bicarbonate Indicator solution to yellow.

If the time taken to turn yellow=3 minutes

and the weight of the organism=6 g

then the time for 1 g to turn the Bicarbonate Indicator to yellow=6×3=18 minutes.

Estimate the numbers of each organism in the ecosystem, or look back at the results you obtained if you have already done this. From these figures and the results of this experiment you can calculate which organisms in the ecosystem are using up most oxygen. What would happen in the ecosystem if the numbers of this animal changed suddenly? Which organisms used the least oxygen? The individual bacteria present in the ecosystem probably use the least oxygen, but we cannot test them in this apparatus. What would happen to the amount of oxygen available if the number of bacteria greatly increased? This is what happens when a pond or river becomes heavily polluted with sewage. The number of bacteria increases at a tremendous rate. Why do many of the animals present, including fish, die?

When you tested the green plant material from the ecosystem, you kept it in darkness in order to stop photosynthesis complicating the situation by causing carbon dioxide to be taken in. Under natural conditions, the green plant material is able to respire and photosynthesise during daytime when carbon dioxide uptake is very much greater than the carbon dioxide output. This means that in bright light the carbon dioxide which is produced by respiration never leaves the plant, but is immediately used up to make carbohydrates. Under these circumstances the plant gives off only water vapour and oxygen.

Although every organism in an ecosystem must take in oxygen and give out carbon dioxide, the approximate proportions of these two gases remains reasonably constant. An aquarium is a suitable ecosystem to study this aspect of gas exchange. What two sources provide the oxygen necessary for life in the aquarium? If our explanations of gas exchange are correct, when should the level of carbon dioxide in the water be highest, and when should it be lowest?

Remove samples of the water and test with Bicarbonate Indicator solution to check your predictions. If you wish to keep the aquarium in darkness until you are ready to perform the test, it can be covered with a black cloth.

The number of animals and plants which can exist in an ecosystem depends partly on the amount of oxygen available in the air, and partly on the amount of oxygen which the plants can produce. Light and the amount of carbon dioxide present, affect the amount of oxygen produced. There is therefore a balance in the ecosystem between the plants and the animals, dependent on the amount of light entering. If the ecosystem is a woodland and a tree is blown or cut down, as in Figure 9.2, the balance is upset and a new set of relationships develops.

Figure 9.2(a) **and** (b) Changes in a woodland ecosystem

You can investigate the balance in the small ecosystem shown in Figure 9.3.

This is really a miniature pond in which the light conditions can be easily altered.

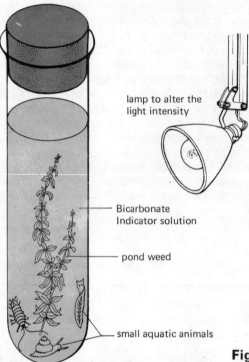

lamp to alter the light intensity

Bicarbonate Indicator solution

pond weed

small aquatic animals

Figure 9.3 A miniature pond

Set up a tube with four small animals and a piece of pond weed in Bicarbonate Indicator solution, and observe in laboratory conditions. What can you conclude about the gas exchange if the Bicarbonate Indicator turns

(a) yellow or

(b) darker red?

If our theory about the balance between the gas exchange of plants and animals is correct, then, by altering the amount of light energy entering the system, we should be able to alter the balance of the gases. Investigate this theory by altering the intensity of light falling on the tube. Remember that the Bicarbonate Indicator will change colour very slowly as the amounts of gases involved are very small.

Watch closely to find if a change in light intensity alters the activity of the animals. Why might this affect the amounts of gases in the tube?

In your field work you may need to know more accurately the amounts of gases in a water sample, and other more complicated methods are available for their determination.

In all these experiments you did not measure the actual amount of carbon dioxide but only made a comparison for different organisms. If you wish to know the exact amount of carbon dioxide, you must use apparatus of the type shown in Figure 9.4.

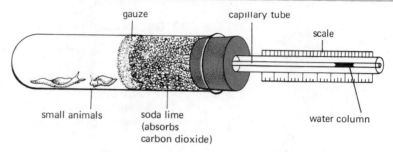

gauze   capillary tube   scale

small animals   soda lime (absorbs carbon dioxide)   water column

Figure 9.4 Measuring carbon dioxide production

When small animals or plants respire in the tube, oxygen in the air is replaced by carbon dioxide. This carbon dioxide is absorbed by the soda lime, causing air to be drawn in from the capillary tube. A drop of water is placed at the end of the capillary tube, and the rate at which the drop moves along the tube is a measure of the rate of uptake of oxygen by the organisms. The volume of carbon dioxide produced, and hence the amount of oxygen used up, is found by multiplying the bore of the capillary tube by the distance that the water drop has moved.

A rough comparison of the gas exchange of larger organisms can be made using the apparatus shown in Figure 9.5.

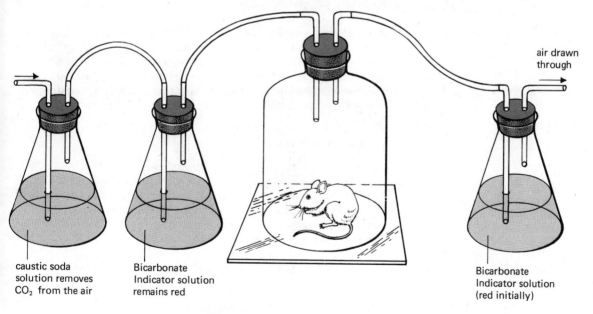

air drawn through

caustic soda solution removes CO_2 from the air

Bicarbonate Indicator solution remains red

Bicarbonate Indicator solution (red initially)

Figure 9.5 Comparing respiration of larger organisms

In this experiment, a current of air is pumped or drawn through the flasks and belljar. The air passes first through a solution of sodium hydroxide which removes any carbon dioxide present. The second flask is to check that the air passing into the belljar contains no carbon dioxide. The time taken for the liquid in the third flask to show the presence of carbon dioxide is taken as an indication of the rate of respiration of the organism in the belljar.

9.3 Gas exchange surfaces

In all our investigations of respiration and gas exchange in animals and plants, we have not yet considered one of the most important factors affecting the life of the organism. Gases must enter and leave plants through a surface either inside or outside their bodies.

From your knowledge of the chemistry of the gases which we are considering, what would you expect to be the properties of these surfaces?

You can possibly think of a number of requirements, of which two are listed below.

1. The surface must be extensive enough to allow large volumes of gases to pass through.
2. The surface must be moist, as gases can diffuse into living cells in solution only.

If you start by investigating these hypotheses, you may find that several other factors must also be considered before you can come to a general theory about the nature of surfaces involved in gas exchange.

At this stage the surface area to volume ratios which you worked out earlier in the course are important. In what ways will the problems of gas exchange differ in larger and in smaller living things? In *Euglena*, and in most very small organisms, there is an adequate body surface area for all the gas exchange necessary for life. In a larger animal, the surface area of the body is small, relative to its volume. This means that, as organisms increase in size, the surface area available for gas exchange becomes proportionally less. This problem has been overcome in higher animals by the development of special respiratory surfaces.

9.4 Large surfaces

Our skin is a waterproof layer through which gases cannot pass. How do oxygen and carbon dioxide pass in and out of the body? The respiratory surface is internal in most higher animals, and in the human body it is the inner surface of the **lungs.** We cannot cut up a human lung to investigate our first hypothesis, but we can dissect the lung of a cow or a sheep.

Observe a lung of a cow or sheep. Estimate roughly the outer surface area. Would this be adequate for the gas exchange required by such a large and active animal? The conclusion from this is that the inner surface must be greatly extended in some way.

Cut off a piece of the lung and observe its structure. How has the internal surface area been increased? Figure 9.6 shows you that the spaces you see are further subdivided down to a microscopic level. Each of these tiny spaces is called an **air sac,** and each pocket in the air sac is called an **alveolus**. By this arrangement the respiratory surface in our bodies is increased to about 100 m², approximately the surface area of twenty rolls of wall paper.

Figures 9.6(a) **and** (b) Alveoli and blood vessels

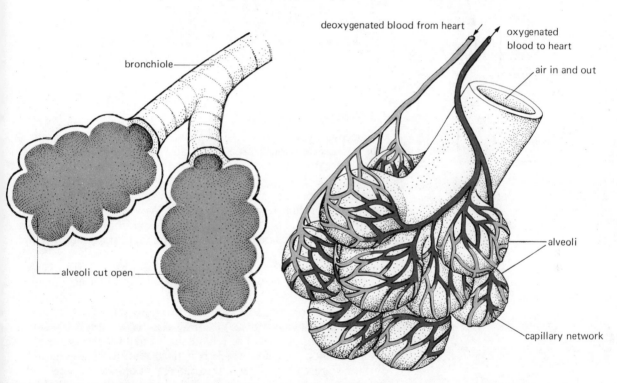

Gills are another type of respiratory surface found in certain large animals. The gills of fish consist of numerous gill arches, which have tiny filaments attached as in Figure 9.7. The filaments are thin-walled and have extensive capillary networks. In this way a very large surface of the body and of the blood system is exposed to the water. This extensive area is necessary in all gill-breathing organisms, because there is less oxygen available in water than in air.

From all this evidence it appears that the first of our hypotheses

gill cover removed

about respiratory surfaces, namely, that a large organism requires a large respiratory surface, is correct.

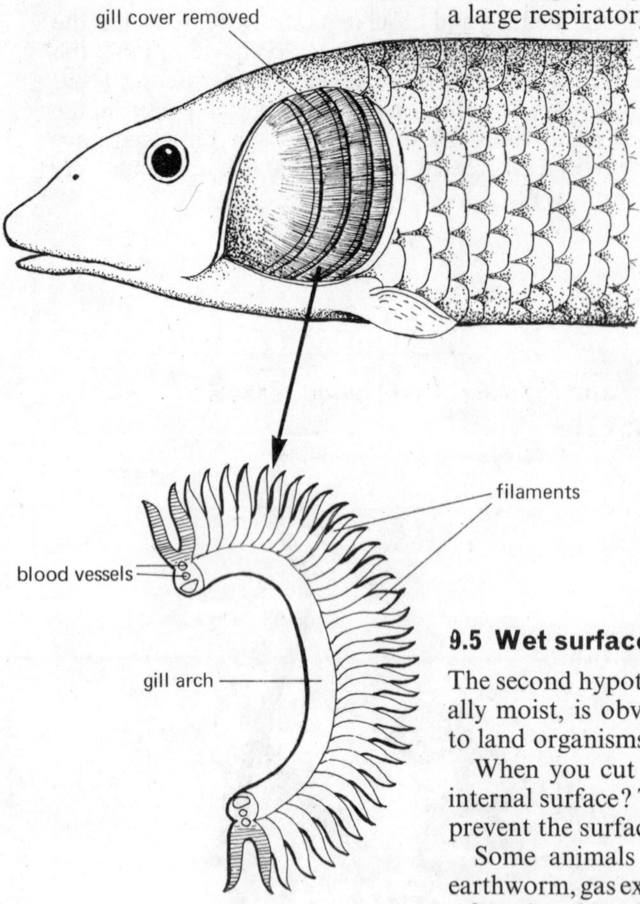

Figure 9.7 Gill arch and filament

filaments

blood vessels

gill arch

9.5 Wet surfaces

The second hypothesis, that gas exchange surfaces must be continually moist, is obviously true of aquatic animals, but does it apply to land organisms?

When you cut open the lungs, what was the appearance of the internal surface? The slime or mucus which you probably saw helps prevent the surface from drying up.

Some animals use their skins as a respiratory surface. In an earthworm, gas exchange occurs only through the skin, and, although a frog does have lungs, its skin also is used for gas exchange. Study the skin of earthworms and frogs to see if our second hypothesis is correct. If their skins were to dry up, what would happen to these animals?

The respiratory surfaces you have examined have a large surface area and are always moist. You may also have noticed that lungs and gills are bright red. The red colour is due to the presence of an extensive blood supply, which is a third feature of a respiratory surface. Figure 9.6(*b*) shows the arrangement of blood vessels round the alveoli of the lungs. You will see that a large volume of the blood is exposed to the air in the alveoli. Diffusion of gases takes place from the damp surface of the alveoli into the blood.

9.6 Breathing mechanisms

Earlier you calculated the rate at which oxygen was taken into your body. By what means does the oxygen enter? Did you observe muscle tissues between the spaces of the lungs? If there are no muscles, contraction of the lungs to draw in air will not be possible. How, then, does air enter our lungs? You can make a number of observations before you try to explain this mechanism.

Figure 9.8 Measuring chest expansion

Place a hand at the bottom of your breast-bone and breathe deeply in and out. What happens to that part of your body when you breathe? Place a measuring tape round your chest as in Figure 9.8. Breathe deeply. What happens to your chest measurement when you breathe in and out? Record the different sizes of your chest when air has been inhaled and exhaled.

From these observations, you should now be able to suggest a hypothesis to explain the way in which air is forced into and out of the lungs.

Figure 9.9 shows the same evidence presented in a different way.

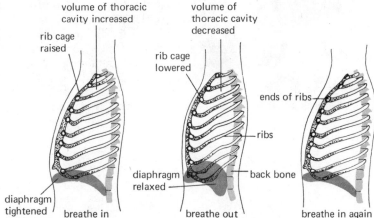

Figure 9.9 Breathing mechanism in man

Air is forced into the lungs from the atmosphere when the volume of the thoracic cavity increases. When the volume of the thoracic cavity decreases, the pressure on the lungs increases and air is forced out.

9.7 Bronchitis and cancer

If you look once again at the lungs, you will see two tubes at the top called **bronchi,** which carry the air into each lung. These tubes join to form the **trachea,** or **windpipe,** which carries air to the back of the throat. Why do these tubes stay open when air passes through them? What part of your body will be affected when you suffer from **bronchitis?** The ending *-itis* means inflammation. What is an inflammation of the voice-box, the **larynx,** called?

Bronchitis is a very common complaint in Scotland because this bacterial disease is more active in a damp atmosphere. A dangerous complication with bronchitis is that the infection may spread down into the lungs and breathing then becomes very difficult. Every

year many old people die from bronchitis, which is aggravated by the fumes present in city fog. This is one of the reasons why most cities are trying to cut down the smoke and dust in the atmosphere by declaring certain areas to be 'smokeless zones'.

Cancer of the lung is a disease which kills many people every year, as you will see from Table 9.2. This disease is caused by irritation of the lung tissue due to the effects of cigarette smoking. Products of the combustion of tobacco, and also perhaps fumes from diesel and petrol engines and other atmospheric pollution, cause the cells of the lungs to behave abnormally. Once this abnormal behaviour, or cancer, of the cells has started, it must be checked, as otherwise the whole body will be affected eventually, and death will result. In its early stages cancer can be cured by drugs, but in an advanced state the diseased parts of the lungs must be removed by surgery.

Table 9.2 lists the deaths due to bronchitis and lung cancer in Scotland for the years 1961 to 1968. Although fewer people died from bronchitis than from lung cancer, bronchitis is a very much commoner condition. It has been estimated that 3 million man-hours are lost each year in Scotland because of bronchitis.

What reasons can you advance to explain why the death rate due to one of these conditions is increasing?

Table 9.2

Year	Lung cancer		Bronchitis	
	number of deaths	rate per 100 000 of population	number of deaths	rate per 100 000 of population
1961	2 478	48	2 516	48
1962	2 604	50	2 474	48
1963	2 772	52	3 052	59
1964	2 904	56	2 666	51
1965	2 979	57	2 854	56
1966	3 145	61	2 877	56
1967	3 218	63	2 242	44
1968	3 289	64	2 726	53

9.8 Gas exchange in plants

Gas exchange in plants would appear to be less of a problem than in animals, because plants generally have a very large surface area relative to their volume, and they are less active. However, if you look back at Figure 8.18, you will see that the surface of the leaf is covered by an almost impervious layer called the **cuticle**. Gas exchange is thus impossible over the entire surface. Instead, it takes place through pores called **stomata** (singular, stoma), which are on the leaves and stems. Gases pass in and out of the plant when the stomata are open, but, when they are closed, gaseous exchange with the atmosphere is reduced almost to nothing. To understand how these pores function, we must first study their structure. Most stomata are found on the leaves, and, although they can be seen in a transverse section of a leaf as in Figure 8.18, they are more easily studied in surface view.

1. Peel a piece of lower and upper epidermis from each of the leaves you are given.
2. Mount these thin layers in water on a microscope slide under a cover slip.
3. Observe and draw the epidermal cells and stomata.

The two cells round the pore are called **guard cells.** How do they differ from other epidermal cells?

You will remember from Chapter 4 that, when the maximum amount of water is present in a cell it is firm and is then said to be turgid. This turgid state is found in leaf epidermal cells, and we can investigate the effect of turgidity of the guard cells as a possible means whereby the stoma opens.

Figure 9.10 shows a model which represents the guard cells of a stoma, and we can use this to investigate one aspect of stomatal action.

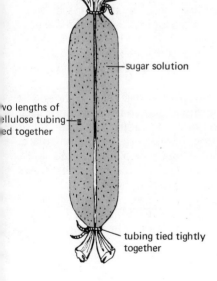

sugar solution

two lengths of cellulose tubing tied together

tubing tied tightly together

Figure 9.10 A model of a stoma

1. Fill two 20 cm lengths of cellulose tubing with sugar solution.
2. Bind the two tubes tightly together at the top and bottom as in Figure 9.10.
3. Place the model in a container full of water. Each tube represents a guard cell in a non-turgid state. The tubes gain water, just as the guard cells do under certain circumstances.
4. Observe the model after an hour when the tubes are turgid. What has happened to the space between the tubes?

5. Place the model in a very strong sugar solution.
Which way will the water now move? What happens to the space when the tubes lose water?

This model shows that the space opens when water enters the tubes and they become turgid. When water leaves the tubes they lose turgor, and the space closes. The stomatal pores open and shut by a similar mechanism, but the way in which the cell walls are thickened is also related to the movement.

There are complicated reasons why the guard cells should at times gain and at other times lose water. Part of the explanation is that the guard cells are the only epidermal cells that have chloroplasts, and they can thus manufacture sugars. Sugars may also be produced in the guard cells by the action of enzymes on starch which is already present. How will an increase in sugar content affect the flow of water into the guard cells? What effect will this have on the pore? The pore will close when sugars in the cells are removed or changed into starch. Usually the pores are open during the day and closed at night. The factors which affect stomatal opening and closing are not yet fully understood, in spite of considerable research on the problem.

Once inside the leaf, gases dissolve in water in the walls of the mesophyll cells. What part of the leaf is responsible for the conduction of water to these cells? Reference to Figure 8.18 will help you to answer this question. In plants, the stomata and the damp walls of the mesophyll cells are adequate for all gas exchanges, because of the very large external and internal surface area of the leaves.

From Figure 8.18 you will see that there are air spaces between the cells. Gases can diffuse through the air spaces between the cells from leaves to stem and root tissues. Oxygen which is dissolved in soil water can also be used by the roots. In the same way, some of the carbon dioxide produced by root tissues can diffuse out into the soil.

In darkness, the gas exchanges of plants are similar to those that take place in animals all the time. Some oxygen from the air is used up in respiration, and the carbon dioxide produced diffuses out of the cells. In sunlight, however, when photosynthesis is taking place, carbon dioxide produced by respiration in the plant is immediately used to make sugars. Additional carbon dioxide at this time diffuses in from the air, and excess oxygen diffuses out of the plant.

In our studies of gas exchanges we have not considered the release of water vapour from organisms. Both plants and animals give out large quantities of this gas, and we will investigate this gas exchange later in the course.

9.9 Gas exchange in insects

Insects are a group of animals in which gas exchange mechanisms are worth investigating. We can study these animals to test some of our theories about the movement of materials, especially gases, inside the body.

Place a large insect, such as a locust or a cockroach in a boiling tube and close the end with a loose plug of cotton wool. Observe closely the movements of the abdomen. If this is the animal breathing, the movements will be regular. Check this by finding the rate of movement of the abdomen for several 15-second intervals.

Add a small amount of carbon dioxide to the tube. Count the rate once again.

What is the effect on the movement of the abdomen of adding carbon dioxide?

From your observations you will probably agree that the pulsing of the abdomen in an insect is part of the mechanism of breathing of the animal.

You can now carry this investigation further by opening up a dead insect to find out if it has a respiratory surface, and if the blood system is responsible for carrying gases round the body.

1. Fix the ventral surface of a dead locust or cockroach into heated wax, as shown in Figure 9.11.

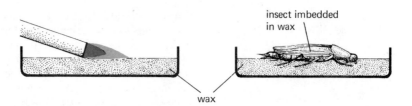

insect imbedded in wax

wax

Figure 9.11 Preparing an insect for dissection

2. Cut off the wings.
3. Remove the upper plates of the outer skeleton, starting about the middle of the abdomen.
4. Cut away the entire upper part of the hard exoskeleton carefully, in order to expose the internal organs, as in Figure 9.12.
5. Flood the dissection with water.

Did you see any red blood as you cut open the insect? Can you see any blood vessels? Does the insect have lungs or other obvious large respiratory organs? You have probably seen numerous very thin white tubes within the body.

6. Remove some of the white tubes.
7. Observe and draw a piece of such a tube under the low and the high powers of the microscope.

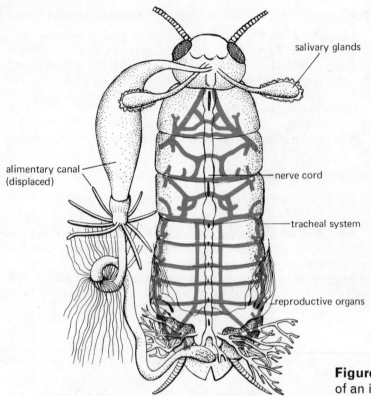

salivary glands

alimentary canal
(displaced)

nerve cord

tracheal system

reproductive organs

Figure 9.12 The internal organs
of an insect

These tubes are not blood vessels but are called **tracheae,** and they
have rings of strengthening material to keep them open.

In insects air diffuses from openings on the skin, called **spiracles,**
through the tracheae and into the cells of various tissues: waste
gases pass out by diffusing in the opposite direction. The blood of
an insect does not carry oxygen. How may this be related to the
colourless appearance of the blood?

The tracheae divide in the tissues into very fine tubes called
tracheoles, which are about 50 times thinner than human blood
capillaries. These narrow vessels contain a fluid in which gases
dissolve. Oxygen can diffuse through the thin walls of the tracheoles
into the cells, and carbon dioxide passes out of the cells into the
tracheoles. Diffusion of air through the tracheae is assisted by the
pulsing of the abdomen, which produces pressure changes in the
tracheae that help to force the gases to and from the cells. These
pulses were the breathing movements which you studied earlier.

9.10 Gas exchange and circulation

In Chapter 8 you investigated the transport systems of living
organisms, and in this chapter you have studied gas exchange. The
gases taken in must be carried round the body, and in most cases

this is done by the transport system. From the study of athletics, where the human body is forced to the extremes of performance, we can investigate human gas exchange in relation to the blood system.

As you will remember from your earlier work, energy is released in living cells by the oxidation of glucose. When this release of energy takes place, what happens to the glucose? What is the name of the energy-rich compound that is formed within the cell?

It has been calculated that in muscle cells a quarter of the available energy is used for mechanical movement. In what form of energy is the rest released?

The release of energy in the cells depends on an adequate supply of glucose and oxygen, and on the removal of waste materials by the blood. We can carry out an experiment on muscle action in order to find more about what happens when energy is released in the tissues.

This experiment uses muscles to change energy from one form to another.

1. Place the back of your hand on the edge of the bench as shown in Figure 9.13.
2. Hang a weight of 200 g from your finger over the edge of the bench.
3. Try to raise and lower the weight each time the metronome clicks, which is about twice every second.

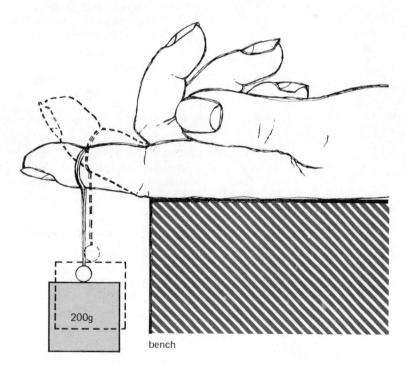

Figure 9.13 Lifting a weight

200g

bench

4. Raise and lower for three consecutive minutes. You will require a timekeeper and another person to count the raising and lowering.
5. Count the number of times the weight is raised in each minute.
6. Repeat the experiment after a 5-minute rest, allowing yourself a 30-second rest between each minute of activity.
7. Record the rate as before.
8. Repeat, after resting for 5 minutes, but allow a 1-minute rest each time between activity.

Why were you unable to raise the weight at the same rate for each of the 1-minute periods?

In what way did the rest periods alter the rate? Did longer rest periods alter your performance?

Although you can say what happened to your muscles, this experiment does not tell you what is causing the muscle fatigue. To find out this you would have to test samples of the blood in your finger during the course of the experiment.

While the muscles of your finger were rapidly using up energy, a substance called **lactic acid** was built up in your muscle. During the rest periods, the lactic acid concentration fell. Where did the lactic acid come from?

When a large supply of energy is required quickly by the cells, the oxidation of glucose does not provide a sufficient amount of energy. Under these circumstances the cells can release energy from the glucose without the addition of oxygen.

What organism that you have studied releases most of its energy without oxygen being present?

When this **anaerobic respiration** takes place, glucose in the cells is changed into lactic acid. If the concentration of lactic acid reaches a certain level, it poisons the cells. At what point in the experiment did the concentration of lactic acid start to affect your muscles?

By using this method of respiration, the body can release a great deal of energy in the absence of oxygen. Oxygen is required later to make energy available to change the lactic acid back to glucose. When the tissues release energy in this anaerobic way, the body is said to have built up an **oxygen debt.** For the body to continue to function, this oxygen debt must be repaid.

A runner in the 100 m race gets most of his energy for the race without using oxygen, but he has to gasp in air after the race to pay back his oxygen debt.

9.11 Altitude and athletes

In 1968 about 8 000 athletes took part in the Olympic Games in Mexico City. Biologically, these were very interesting Games: because Mexico City is 2 242 m above sea level, atmospheric pressure is lower and the air has less oxygen in it than at sea level.

Most athletic performances depend on the runner's ability to withstand a large oxygen debt, and so we would expect that a reduction in the amount of oxygen in the air would have an effect

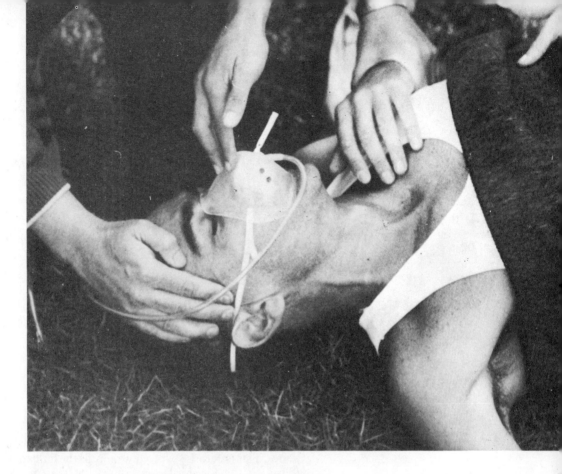

Figure 9.14 A runner receiving oxygen after competing in a race

on the performances. The technique of running a race is to move at a pace which does not allow the lactic acid to reach a level which causes muscle fatigue during the race. Thus, a sprinter can cover 100 metres in under ten seconds, but if he continued at this pace his muscles would fatigue before he reached the 400 metre mark.

In the 'thinner air' of Mexico City, the athletes were unable to draw in as much oxygen as usual during the race, and thus their oxygen debt built up more quickly. Many athletes collapsed after their races, and had to be supplied with oxygen gas to enable them to repay their oxygen debts. Figure 9.14 shows Ron Clarke, of Australia, one of the greatest runners of all time, receiving oxygen at the end of the 10 000 metres race.

Look at Table 9.3 showing winning times and compare the performances of the athletes at five different places where the Olympic Games have been held. What effect did altitude have on the performances? Why do you think that not all the winning times were affected in the same way?

Table 9.3

Race	Melbourne 34 m above sea level	Rome 49 m above sea level	Tokyo 200 m above sea level	Mexico 2 242 m above sea level	Munich 52 m above sea level
	1956	1960	1964	1968	1972
100 m	10·5 s	10·2 s	10·0 s	9·9 s	10·2 s
200 m	20·6 s	20·5 s	20·3 s	19·8 s	20·0 s
400 m	46·7 s	44·9 s	45·1 s	43·8 s	44·7 s
800 m	1 min 47·7 s	1 min 46·3 s	1 min 45·1 s	1 min 44·3 s	1 min 45·9 s
1 500 m	3 min 41·2 s	3 min 35·6 s	3 min 38·1 s	3 min 34·9 s	3 min 36·3 s
5 000 m	13 min 39·6 s	13 min 43·4 s	13 min 48·8 s	14 min 28·4 s	13 min 26·4 s
10 000 m	28 min 45·6 s	28 min 32·2 s	28 min 24·4 s	29 min 27·4 s	27 min 38·4 s

Many of the athletes trained at high altitudes for the Mexico Games. This is because over a few months the human body gradually adjusts to the lower oxygen content of the air. A person who normally lives at a height of over 1 000 m differs from a person who lives below 300 m in the following ways.

1. His breathing is deeper.

2. The volume of his blood increases from about 5 to about 6·5 litres.

3. The number of red cells in his blood increases from about 5 million per mm^3 to about 7 million per mm^3.

What effect will these features have on the amount of oxygen that the blood can carry and hold at any one moment? Compare the value that you can calculate from these figures with the value you obtained for yourself.

It is suggested that athletes who are born at, and live at, high altitudes, become better adjusted to the lack of oxygen in the air than others who live in these conditions for periods of up to a year.

What evidence is there in Tables 9.4 and 9.5 that this theory might be correct?

Table 9.4
400m race results

Mexico 1968
1. L. Evans, U.S.A.
2. L. James, U.S.A.
3. R. Freeman, U.S.A.
4. A. Gakou, Senegal
5. M. Jellingshaus,
   West Germany
6. T. Bezabeth, Ethiopia*
7. A. Badenski, Poland
8. A. Omoio, Uganda*

Tokyo 1964
1. M. Larrabee, U.S.A.
2. W. Mottley, Trinidad
3. A. Badenski, Poland
4. R. Brightwell, U.K.
5. W. Williams, U.S.A.
6. T. Graham, U.K.
7. P. Vassella, Australia
8. E. Skinner, Trinidad

Table 9.5
10 000m race results

Mexico 1968
1. N. Temu, Kenya*
2. M. Wolde, Ethiopia*
3. M. Gammoudi, Tunisia*
4. J. Martinez, Mexico*
5. N. Sviridov, Russia†
6. R. Clarke, Australia
7. R. Hill, U.K.
8. W. Masresha, Ethiopia*

Tokyo 1964
1. M. Mills, U.S.A.
2. M. Gammoudi,
   Tunisia*
3. R. Clarke, Australia
4. M. Wolde, Ethiopia*
5. L. Ivanov, Russia
6. K. Tsuburaya, Japan
7. M. Halberg,
   New Zealand
8. A. Cook, Australia

* Athletes who lived most of their lives at high altitudes.
† Athletes who had trained at high altitude for one year prior to the games.

The end of a race

Looking Back at Chapter 9

1. The human body uses large quantities of oxygen for energy release.
2. The rate of oxygen uptake is affected by the activity of organisms.
3. The volume of oxygen used up is approximately the same as the volume of carbon dioxide produced during respiration. The volume of carbon dioxide produced can thus be used as an indication of the rate of energy release in living tissue.
4. In all ecosystems there is a complicated relationship involving the amount of light energy entering, the rate of photosynthesis, and the rate of respiration.

5. Gases enter and leave living cells only in solution.
6. Surfaces for gas exchange must be moist and extensive, and have a close contact with the transport system.
7. Most higher animals have an internal surface for gas exchange, usually lungs or gills.
8. Animals with internal gas exchange surfaces must have a method of taking air into the body.
9. Human breathing is effected by the muscles of the rib cage and the diaphragm.
10. Insects have no internal gas exchange organs; gases diffuse through tracheae between the tissues and the air.
11. Gases enter and leave plants mostly through the stomata on the leaves. These pores open and close due to changes of turgor in the guard cells.
12. Plants have no special gas exchange organs, because they have an extensive external and internal surface and they require only small quantities of oxygen from the air.
13. Gases move to and from all parts of the plant by diffusion in the intercellular spaces, and by diffusion from cell to cell.
14. Much useful information about human physiology can be obtained from the study of athletic performances.

10 CO-ORDINATION AND CONTROL

10.1 The internal environment

We are all familiar with the sensation of thirst, and the urge to drink which accompanies it. But just what is thirst? It is not merely a dry throat, for that is remedied by the first swallow. We go on drinking until we feel satisfied. From this it seems clear that we respond to a shortage of water within ourselves by some action to remedy the shortage. This is also true for other organisms.

There are many other internal changes which an organism must detect and act upon. You learned in Chapter 7 of the digestion of food by a succession of enzymes as it moves through the gut. It would clearly be wasteful if these enzymes were continuously secreted, yet they must be released on to the food at the appropriate stages in digestion. In Chapter 8 you learned about the movement of glucose in the blood. For what purpose is this carbohydrate constantly being used up? As it is used in the body, more glucose is added to the blood, and the concentration of blood sugar is kept constant at 80–180 mg per 100 cm^3 of blood.

In these and other ways, the body responds to changes in its **internal environment**; that is, the conditions that exist within it. These adjustments are as vital to survival as are the responses made to stimuli from the outside world. Every living cell of an organism is a complex and delicate mechanism, and, to carry out its metabolism effectively, the conditions in which it exists must be carefully and accurately controlled. The maintenance of steady conditions in a system, in this case the internal environment, is known as **homeostasis,** and it is an important aspect of an organism's responses to internal stimuli.

10.2 Control of water content

It will be convenient to consider first the control of water content as an aspect of homeostasis. Through what structures in the leaves of plants is water lost? How do you think these structures might respond if the plant were losing more water through its leaves than it was taking in through its roots?

The following experiment allows us to compare the stomata in leaves with a plentiful water supply with those in leaves with a water shortage.

1. You are provided with two similar leafy shoots. One has been kept in water; the other has had no water for 24 hours.
2. Remove a leaf from both shoots.
3. Paint about 1 cm² of the under surface of both leaves with a thin layer of nail varnish, and leave to dry.
4. Using a mounted needle and forceps, peel the dry varnish off the leaves.
5. Mount the two peels in water on a microscope slide, add a cover slip and examine under the microscope.
6. Make careful drawings of the shapes of the stomata and guard cells of both leaves, as revealed by the peels.

How has the leaf responded to a shortage of water? In what way is this an example of homeostasis?

A more complex example of homeostasis is seen in water balance in man. In what ways does your body gain water? How is water lost from your body? The following table shows the average daily water gain and loss in an adult.

Table 10.1

Water gain in		Water loss in	
drink	1 450 cm³	urine	1 500 cm³
food	800 cm³	sweat	600 cm³
water released in chemical reactions	350 cm³	lung evaporation	400 cm³
		faeces	100 cm³

How many of the items in this table vary from day to day? Which of the items will be adjusted so that the water content of the body remains constant?

The **kidneys** produce **urine,** and by varying its composition and quantity they help to maintain a steady state of water and salts within the body.

Examine the kidneys and associated structures of a dissected mammal. What shape are the kidneys, and where are they situated? Trace out the structures by which urine is removed from them and passed to the outside. These structures together form the **urinary system.** With what other system of the body is the urinary system associated? Is this association different in the two sexes? In what part of the system is urine stored before being passed to the outside? What must be a property of the walls of this structure? What must be present at the point where the urethra leaves the bladder, so that the excretion of urine can be controlled?

What structures in your dissection suggest the source of the materials from which the kidneys produce urine? Locate the renal arteries from which each kidney receives an abundant supply of blood. The kidney is often spoken of as 'purifying' the blood which passes through it. The materials for the formation of urine are extracted from the blood as it passes through the kidney. Although only a proportion of the blood passing along the aorta goes through the kidneys, circulation in a mammal is rapid, and in man 1 litre of blood passes through the kidneys every minute. This means that a volume equivalent to that of all the blood in the body will be dealt with by the kidneys every 4 or 5 minutes.

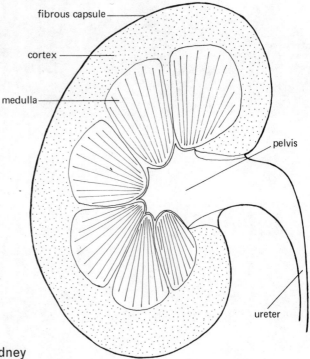

Figure 10.1 Section through mammalian kidney

Examine Figure 10.1 and the cut surface of a bisected kidney. Notice the thin tough covering tissue and the two distinct zones of kidney tissue, the outer **cortex** and the inner **medulla.** What is the difference in colour between these zones? What does this indicate is the distribution of blood in the kidney? What evidence can you see of the way in which urine is collected and passed to the ureter?

This investigation however does not tell us much about how the kidney functions. The structures which extract materials from the blood and produce urine from them are known as **nephrons,** or kidney tubules. They are extremely small, and each kidney contains about a million of them. Their structures can be revealed only by delicate dissection technique and microscopic examination. Figure 10.2 shows portions of nephrons seen in microscopic section and Figure 10.3 shows the structure and arrangement of a single nephron diagrammatically.

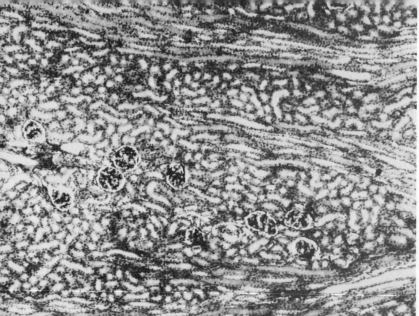

Figure 10.2 Photomicrograph of kidney tissues

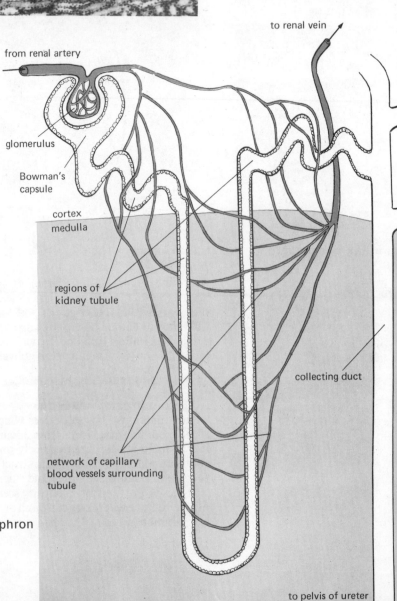

to renal vein

from renal artery

glomerulus

Bowman's capsule

cortex
medulla

regions of kidney tubule

collecting duct

network of capillary blood vessels surrounding tubule

Figure 10.3 Structure and arrangement of a single nephron

to pelvis of ureter

At what point do the blood supply and the nephron first come close together?

The exit vessel from the glomerulus has a narrower bore than the vessel delivering the blood. What effect will this have on the pressure of the blood in the glomerulus? The pressure in the Bowman's capsule is much lower. The blood and the hollow centre of the capsule are separated from one another by only the thin walls of the blood vessel and the single-celled walls of the Bowman's capsule. As a result, a process of **ultra-filtration** or **pressure filtration** occurs, by which a proportion of water and substances in true solution are pushed out of the blood into the tubule. The resulting **glomerular filtrate,** as it is called, will vary in composition according to the state of the blood, but would normally include glucose, salts and urea in the same proportions as in the blood. In fact its composition is similar to that of blood plasma, but without the proteins. How do you think that these various components of the glomerular filtrate originally entered the blood?

We must now compare urine and the glomerular filtrate in respect of composition and rate of production.

Consider the data in Table 10.2.

Table 10.2

Urine		Glomerular filtrate	
Rate of production	1 500 cm³ per day	Rate of production	130 cm³ per minute
water	96·0 per cent	water	98–99 per cent
urea	2·0 per cent	urea	0·02 per cent
total salts	1·8 per cent	total salts	1·0 per cent
glucose	nil	glucose	0·1 per cent
other substances containing nitrogen	0·2 per cent	other substances containing nitrogen	a trace

How many times faster is the rate of glomerular filtrate extraction than the rate of the body's urine production? What proportion of the water extracted from the blood of the kidneys leaves the body in the urine? What do you think happens to the remainder of the water? The arrangement of the structures shown in Figure 10.3 may help you to answer this question. What other substances from the filtrate are retained by the body? What substance is concentrated in the urine as a result of the action of the kidney?

How do you suppose these adjustments in the composition of the filtrate, resulting in the formation of urine, have been made? Some 99 per cent of the water in the filtrate, the glucose and a proportion of the salts are passed back into the blood flowing through the capillaries surrounding the nephron. For this **selective absorption** to occur, energy is required which is released in the cells of the tubule. In what way is this energy source different from that used for ultra-filtration in the Bowman's capsule?

The urine from all the nephrons passes into a system of collecting channels, as indicated in Figure 10.3, which open on the pyramids of the medulla, and so the urine is passed into the ureter.

Thus, there are three ways in which the kidneys act as homeostatic devices, regulating the internal environment of the body.

1. They remove surplus salts and keep the salt concentration in the blood plasma at a steady level.
2. They remove just enough water to keep the osmotic pressure of the body fluids constant.
3. They remove waste nitrogen compounds, mainly urea produced by the breakdown of surplus amino acids in the liver.

Note that, in removing urea, the kidney is acting as an organ of excretion; that is to say, it is removing harmful waste products resulting from the body's metabolism. The body has no further use for these substances, and they could possibly be toxic, if they were allowed to accumulate. What other excretory material is being removed continuously from the body?

10.3 Control of kidney function

The kidney is remarkable, not only for the way it adjusts the composition of the blood, but also for the accuracy and precision with which the adjustments are carried out. How do you think such precision is obtained?

Some types of engine have a device called a governor, by which the speed of the engine is kept steady. A simple form of governor is shown in Figure 10.4.

The vertical rod is connected to the engine and rotates with it. As its speed increases, the weights will tend to move outwards, so bending the springs and pulling the collar farther down the rod. This collar is linked either to the brake or to the fuel inlet of the engine, in order to counteract the increase in speed which caused the weights to move outwards.

This is an example of **feedback control.** This occurs when any change in a certain feature (in this case the speed of the engine) brings into action a mechanism which automatically counteracts the original change. Kidney function is also regulated by feedback control mechanisms. What sort of mechanisms do you think these will be?

Important in the process is the **pituitary body.** Find its location from Figure 10.5. The pituitary produces a substance called Anti-Diuretic Hormone, ADH. This travels in the blood to the kidney where it stimulates resorption of water from the glomerular filtrate into the blood. The pituitary is sensitive to the osmotic pressure of the blood, and when this is high it secretes an increased amount of ADH. This in turn will increase the rate of resorption of water, and so a smaller volume of more concentrated urine will be produced.

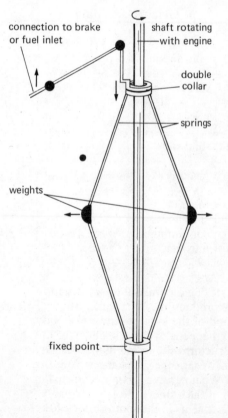

connection to brake or fuel inlet

shaft rotating with engine

double collar

springs

weights

fixed point

Figure 10.4 A simple form of governor

More water will be returned to the blood, bringing its osmotic pressure down again. What could you do to produce a low osmotic pressure in your blood? How would your pituitary and kidneys react? How do you think the sensation of thirst, mentioned earlier in this chapter, is related to the mechanism we have just considered?

ADH does not work alone, but in conjunction with a similar but more complex system for controlling the amount of sodium in the blood.

What other features of your internal environment might be kept steady by feedback mechanisms?

10.4 Chemical co-ordination

The pituitary body is able to detect a stimulus, in this case changes in the osmotic pressure of the blood. The organ which produces the response is the nephron. What provides the link between them?

ADH is one example of a hormone. Various hormones are produced and between them they regulate not only homeostatic processes, but also orderly growth and development of the body. The structures producing hormones are known as ductless glands.

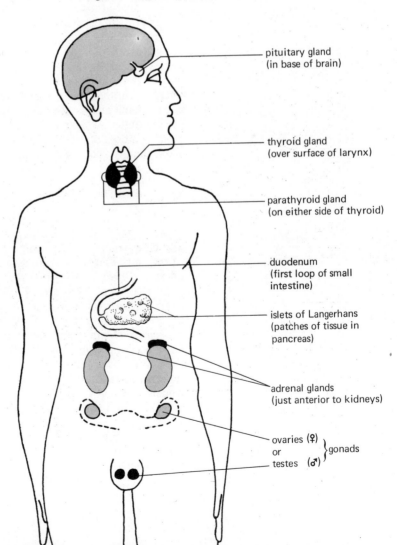

Figure 10.5
The endocrine system

pituitary gland
(in base of brain)

thyroid gland
(over surface of larynx)

parathyroid gland
(on either side of thyroid)

duodenum
(first loop of small
intestine)

islets of Langerhans
(patches of tissue in
pancreas)

adrenal glands
(just anterior to kidneys)

ovaries (♀)
or
testes (♂)
} gonads

Why do you think they have this name? How do ductless glands differ from glands such as salivary glands? Figure 10.5 shows the distribution of the main ductless glands of the body, which together make up the **endocrine system.**

Hormones can exert their effect on a number of widely separated 'target organs' at the same time because the blood system is used to distribute them. Hormones are organic compounds, with molecules much smaller than those of enzymes. They are able to diffuse rapidly from the blood to their target organs. They are unstable compounds, breaking down chemically soon after they have been produced. Why is this property of importance to the body?

In Chapter 7 you learned about insulin and adrenalin. Where are these hormones produced? What is their function in the body? In what ways are their functions homeostatic?

The thyroid gland produces the hormone thyroxine which is involved in control of growth and development. Iodine is necessary for the production of thyroxine, and hence it is important as a mineral component of the diet. Adding thyroxine or even extra iodine to the water in which tadpoles live will hasten their metamorphosis into frogs. On the other hand, if a tadpole's thyroid gland is removed, the tadpole may grow to more than twice its usual size, but it will not develop into a frog.

In man, an incorrect amount of thyroxine is sometimes produced. Thyroxine deficiency in a growing child leads to a condition known as cretinism. A cretin is retarded in both mental and physical development, having a short stunted body and a mental age of not more than about three years. Adults also need a small continuous secretion of thyroxine; if there is a deficiency, a condition known as myxoedema results. A person with myxoedema will be grossly overweight and slow in speech and thought. Happily, both these conditions can now be treated successfully by giving an extract prepared from the thyroid glands of animals.

10.5 Hormones and sex

What do we call the stage in boys and girls when sexual development begins? What features other than the production of sperms and eggs develop at this time? They include, in boys, the breaking of the voice and the growth of hair on parts of the body such as the chest and face, and in girls the development of the breasts. These features are known as secondary sexual characteristics. What other examples can you think of in the animal world? These characteristics are developed under the control of the **sex hormones** which are released from the ovaries in the female and the testes in the male.

As with many hormones concerned in growth and development, the continued secretion of sex hormones following maturity is also important. In the female, the sex hormones interact with **gonadotrophic hormones** from the pituitary gland, to control the oestrous cycle; that is, the regular alternation of ovulation and menstruation, which occurs at intervals of about twenty-eight days .

Following menstruation, the follicle cells which surround the eggs in the ovary secrete the hormone oestrogen. They do this under the influence of FSH (Follicle Stimulating Hormone), which is produced by the pituitary gland. Oestrogen causes the development of a spongy vascular lining in the uterus, but an increase in oestrogen concentration also inhibits the production of FSH. This is an example of negative feedback. On the fourteenth day of the cycle another pituitary hormone, LH (Luteinising Hormone), causes an egg to be shed from its follicle in the ovary. The empty follicle is now also influenced by LH, which is secreted throughout the second half of the cycle.

The follicle cells grow to form a structure called the **corpus luteum,** which in its turn produces yet another hormone, **progesterone.**

If a fertilised egg becomes embedded in the uterus lining, the corpus luteum persists, and the level of progesterone in the blood remains high. This, together with other hormones from the pituitary gland and the placenta, is important in controlling the sequence of events in pregnancy. The progesterone level in the blood is so high during pregnancy that there is always progesterone in the urine. Its detection there provides a simple way of determining whether or not a pregnancy has begun. The high progesterone level inhibits further ovulation throughout pregnancy.

Figure 10.6 The oestrous cycle and its control

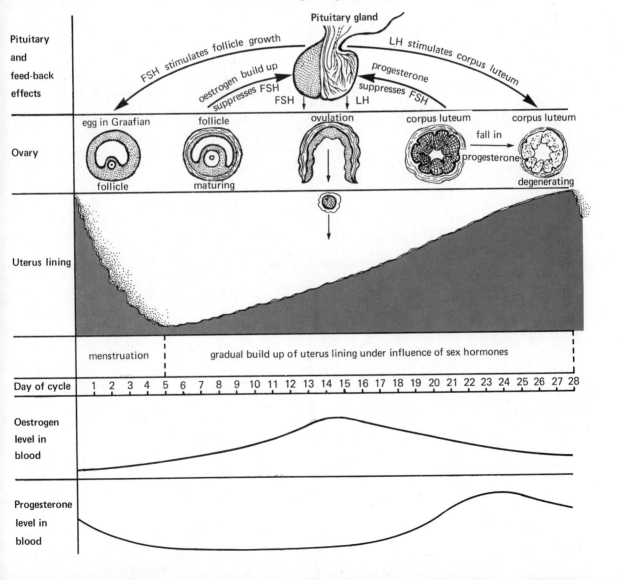

Table 10.3 Hormones and their actions

Gland	Location	Hormone(s) secreted	Action	Remarks
Pituitary	Underside of brain	Growth hormone	Stimulates growth	Deficiency gives dwarfism. Over-production gives giantism
		Gonado-trophic hormones, FSH and LH	Help to control oestrous cycle	Affected by feedback from hormones of ovary
		Thyroid-stimulating hormone TSH	Controls action of thyroid gland	Examples of pituitary hormones which affect the action of other ductless glands
		Anti-diuretic hormone ADH	Controls water balance and salt balance by regula-ting kidney function	Part of homeostatic mechanism

If fertilisation does not occur, the corpus luteum degenerates at about the twenty-eighth day. The resulting drop in progesterone means that the thickened uterus lining can no longer be maintained, and so it breaks down and is shed in menstruation, and the cycle begins again. The cycle and its hormonal control are summarised in Figure 10.6.

The recently developed oral contraceptive, popularly known as 'the pill', contains substances closely related to the sex hormones, which inhibit the release of eggs from the ovary. Other hormone preparations are beginning to be successfully used in the treatment of women who are infertile through failure to ovulate.

There are many other hormones which are not discussed in this book. Some ductless glands, such as the pituitary and adrenal glands, produce several different hormones with a wide variety of effects. Some hormones are well understood, while little is known of the chemistry and action of others, and there may be others which have yet to be discovered. Complete Table 10.3 by filling in details, under the appropriate headings, of the hormones you have studied. Details for hormones from the pituitary gland have already been entered, to show you how to complete the table.

Looking Back at Chapter 10

1. Living organisms show homeostasis in the control of their internal environment.
2. The control of the water content of the body is one example of homeostasis.
3. The kidney is an important homeostatic organ, maintaining water and salt balance and excreting waste nitrogen compounds from the body.
4. Precise control of kidney function is achieved by feedback mechanisms involving ADH and other hormones.
5. Hormones are chemical regulators, co-ordinating growth and development and many other activities of the body, including ovulation.

11 EYES AND EARS

11.1 The world in which we live

Imagine that you can see a leaping pattern of red and yellow shapes, you hear a harsh crackling sound and a smell of burning wood fills your nostrils. What would you do? Depending on the circumstances, you might find yourself fleeing from an advancing forest blaze, or moving in closer to the bonfire for warmth and comfort. In either case, the action would have been determined by the various types of information reaching you from your external environment, or surroundings. Certain parts of your body, such as your eyes, ears and skin, are specially developed in order to be sensitive to information from the external environment. Such parts of the body are known as **receptors,** and any type of information from the environment which brings a receptor into action is called a **stimulus.**

How many types of environmental information can you think of which act as stimuli for the human body? Are there types of information which act as stimuli for some animals but which you cannot perceive? To what environmental information are animals insensitive?

It is essential for every living organism to be sensitive to some kinds of information from the environment and to react by taking the necessary action to ensure its safety and survival.

The reactions which organisms make to the stimuli which they receive are known as **responses,** and the sum total of an organism's responses constitutes its **behaviour.**

11.2 Perceiving the world around us

When it comes to perceiving and reacting to stimuli from the outside world, a set of structures which act in co-operation is involved. The first of these are the receptors, and just as a great variety of stimuli reach us from the environment, so the body has a number of different receptors which are sensitive to these stimuli. Make a list of those receptors that you can think of: include in the list the type of stimulus to which the receptor is sensitive.

All receptors are connected to the **brain** or to the **spinal cord,** and the function of any receptor is always the same: in response to the stimulus it receives, it initiates a nerve impulse which passes into the brain or into the spinal cord.

Some receptors, as we shall see later, are very simple structures, but in others the sensitive cells have become associated with an elaborate arrangement of additional structures which enable them to function with greater precision and accuracy, and thus form special **sense organs.** Examples of these are the eye and the ear, and it is with these that this chapter is concerned.

11.3 The eye as a sense organ

The eye is a sense organ which responds to light. But your eye does much more than perceive whether you are in an illuminated environment or in darkness. By considering certain simple questions and the answers to them, it is possible to reach certain conclusions about the functions of the eye.

Question	Answer	Conclusion
Can you 'see' shapes?	Yes	therefore there must be some mechanism for receiving and recording an image of the object 'seen' by the eye.
Can you determine the distance of the object 'seen'?	Yes	therefore........................ ....
Can you 'see' only black or white, that is, light or no light?	?	therefore........................ ....

Complete the table on a separate piece of paper by adding the answers and conclusions.

Some of the complexity of function of the eye should now be apparent. The complex structure of the eye which we shall now investigate can be related to the complicated functions which it performs.

11.4 The structure of the eye

The eye of the bullock is very similar in structure to that of our own eye. Careful examination and dissection of this animal's eye will help you to understand how the eye of a mammal is constructed and how the various parts function.

Follow the instructions given below, referring constantly to Figures 11.1 and 11.2. Each group is provided with a bullock's eye.

At the back of the eye look for a quantity of yellowish-white fat, which serves to cushion the eye in the hemispherical depression in the skull in which it is contained, the **orbit**. Trim this fat away, using forceps and a pair of scissors. As you remove the fat you will expose a number of strips of pinkish tissue. These are the six muscles which anchor the eye in the orbit, and which move it; they are not always easy to distinguish separately. How are the muscles attached to the outside of the eye? Where would you expect the other ends of the muscles to be found?

Remove the muscles and the fat carefully and expose the **optic nerve.** This is a white cord-like structure about 0·5 cm in diameter which is attached to the back of the eyeball. Its function is to carry nerve impulses from the eye to the brain. Examine the orbit of a sheep's skull to see the hole through which the optic nerve passes.

Now make a circular cut round the eyeball so that a portion can be lifted out with the optic nerve in the centre (Figure 11.2).

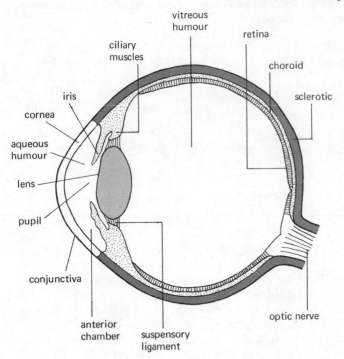

Figure 11.1 Section through human eye

Figure 11.2 Back view of eyeball, showing position of cut

Hold the eyeball steady with the fingers and begin the cut, using a sharp scalpel. Several cuts may be necessary to penetrate the **sclerotic,** which is a tough and fibrous tissue. Notice the colour of the sclerotic as you cut through. This tissue provides a protective outer coat for the eyeball and anchorage for the eye muscles.

Beneath the sclerotic you will see the black colour of the **choroid** layer. Also, the **vitreous humour,** the jelly-like, transparent material which fills the back of the eye, may begin to emerge through the cut you have made. Now insert the blade of a pair of scissors through the incision, and cut round the eyeball as shown in Figure 11.2. Carefully lift off this portion of the eyeball by grasping the optic nerve, and examine it from the inside. What do you think is the function of the black surface of the choroid?

You may just be able to make out the **retina,** which is the light-sensitive region, as a thin transparent layer over the surface of the choroid. The nerve fibres which link up with its receptor cells can

usually be seen converging towards the point where the optic nerve penetrates the eyeball.

Now examine the other half of the eye. Squeeze gently to remove the vitreous humour. Usually when this is done, the **lens** comes out as well; note its shape. Then lay it on a flat surface and compress it slightly with your finger. Notice what happens when you relax the pressure of your finger again. If the eye is fresh enough for the lens to be still transparent, use it to focus an image of a bright object, such as a bench lamp, on to a piece of paper.

You may find that a small quantity of transparent liquid has also emerged from the eyeball. This is the **aqueous humour,** which fills the front chamber of the eye between the lens and the cornea.

Look inside the front of the eye to see the shape and the arrangement of the **ciliary muscle,** to which the lens was attached. The black pigment of the choroid continues forward to cover the back face of the **iris.** The best way to see the iris and the **pupil** is to put your finger into the eyeball and look at it from the front of the eye through the cornea.

How does the shape of the pupil compare with that of your own eye? The size of the pupils of your own eyes is not always the same. Look in a mirror, or examine each other's eyes, in order to compare the size of the pupil in dim and then in bright light. Why do you think this variation occurs? Why does the pupil, which is not itself a structure, but merely a circular hole in the iris, look black? You have probably noticed that on passing from bright to dim light, or vice versa, such as going in or out of doors on a summer's day, it takes your eyes some moments to become accustomed to the different conditions. What does this indicate about the action of the iris?

11.5 Focusing the image

Knowing something about the structure of the eye, the following experiment will help you to understand how images are received on the retina.

1. Hang a sheet of white paper vertically to act as a screen.
2. Move an empty 500 cm³ flask backwards and forwards slowly between the screen and the window of the laboratory. Observe the screen and note any changes in the image thrown on it.
3. Fill the flask with water and move it backwards and forwards as before, again observing the screen.

What conclusions can you draw from this experiment?

The light from the window passes through the empty flask and is not focused on the screen, but, when the flask is filled with water, an image of the window is cast on the screen. By moving the flask backwards and forwards, a point is reached where a clear, upside-down, or inverted image is produced on the screen. The flask acts as a lens. Your eye contains structures that act as both lens and screen. When rays of light pass at an angle from one medium such as air into another such as glass or water, they are bent or **refracted.** The surface of the cornea is rounded, and many of the rays of light reaching it will be refracted. If the source of the rays is at the correct distance away from the cornea, a clear inverted picture will be cast on the screen of the eye, the retina. If the observed object is not at the correct distance from the cornea, the image will be blurred, or out of focus.

The human eye cannot move the retina or the lens forwards or backwards. How then can it focus on objects both near at hand and far away?

1. Replace the 500 cm³ flask from the previous experiment with a thick convex lens, such as a reading glass.
2. Move the lens until you obtain a clear inverted image on the screen.
3. Replace the thick convex lens with a thinner one, and focus again.

Do they both focus at the same distance from the screen, or does the thin lens have to be moved nearer or farther away to obtain a clear image?

You will find that the thicker the lens, the closer it must be moved towards the screen in order to bring the picture into focus. As thinner lenses are used, the screen must be moved farther back, or the lens must be moved forwards.

The light rays are bent as they enter the eye and the lens refracts the rays. If the thickness of the lens is altered, it will act as if a different lens had been added.

We have seen that the ciliary muscles encircle the edge of the lens and are fastened to it by the suspensory ligaments. If the muscle fibres contract, the circle will get smaller and the tension on the ligaments will get less. The lens will get thicker in the middle, as seen in Figure 11.3(a).

If the ciliary muscles relax, the circle gets bigger, tension is increased on the suspensory ligaments and the lens becomes thinner in the middle, as seen in Figure 11.3(b). In this way, blurred images can be focused by changing the shape of the lens, by contracting or relaxing these muscles, without either the lens or the retina having to move backwards or forwards.

The ability to alter the shape of the lens in order to focus is called **accommodation.** If the rays of light are coming from a near object, they diverge considerably and have to be refracted more, as in Figure 11.3(a). If the object is far away, the rays of light are almost parallel, and they do not have to be bent so much; the lens will thus become flatter as in Figure 11.3(b).

Why do you think that focusing for long periods on near objects is more tiring than focusing on distant ones?

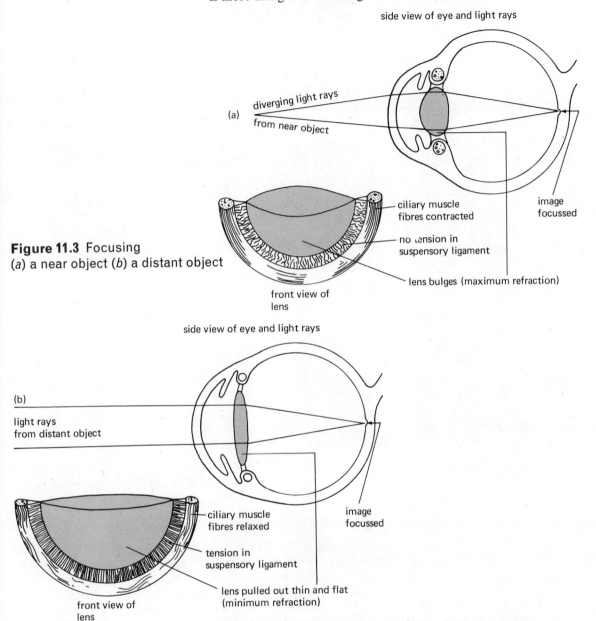

Figure 11.3 Focusing
(*a*) a near object (*b*) a distant object

11.6 Dealing with the light rays; action of the retina

You may have noticed that in very dim light, such as moonlight, you can distinguish light and shade, and pick out the shapes of objects seen against the sky, but it is impossible to distinguish colours. This is because there are two types of light-sensitive cells in the retina, known as **rods** and **cones.** The rods distinguish light and shade and will function in very low illumination, whereas the cones, which are responsible for colour vision, require much stronger illumination before they produce a response. Figure 11.4 shows the arrangement of these special receptors within the retina.

Over most of the retina there is a fairly even dispersal of rods and cones. You are now going to obtain evidence that one of the two types of light-sensitive cells predominates at the front of the retina.

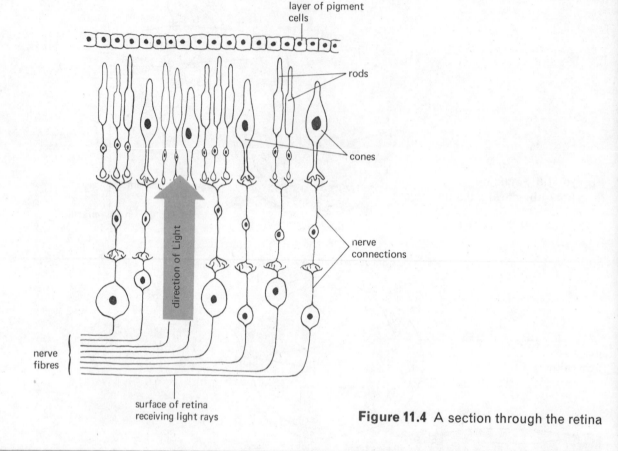

Figure 11.4 A section through the retina

Sit in a chair and look straight ahead. Your partner now stands behind you, about four or five feet to one side, holding up a pencil, which he moves slowly forward until it just enters your field of vision. Stop him at this point, and without moving your head or eyes, try to determine the colour of the pencil.

If the image of the pencil can be seen, but not its colour, which light-sensitive cells must be most frequent near the front of the eye, where the image is focused?

In a small region of the retina, directly behind the lens at the back of the eye, the receptor cells are packed more closely than anywhere else in the retina, and so it is this region which gives the most accurate vision. When we wish to look very carefully at any object in order to make out fine detail, the eye muscles move the eye so that the image of the object falls on this region known as the **yellow spot.** You see this happening if you watch the movements of the eyes of a person who is reading a book. The receptor cells of the yellow spot are cones only.

The optic nerve leaves the eye and interrupts the layers of the eyeball including the retina. What will happen if, when we look at an object, its image falls directly on to the optic nerve?

Hold this book at arm's length, squarely in front of your face, close your right eye, and look at the dot on the right of the page with your left eye. Now slowly move the book towards you, keeping your left eye fixed on the dot. At first, the cross is visible out of the corner of your eye, but as you move the book there will come a point when it disappears. Its image is then falling on the optic nerve, and so you experience no sensation of vision. This position of the image is the **blind spot** of the eye.

In normal vision, the part of the image falling on the blind spot of one eye falls on a perceptive part of the retina of the other eye, so that no gap in vision occurs. In the experiment, you appeared to see plain paper when the cross disappeared. Repeat the experiment with a cross and a dot on coloured paper. What explanation can you suggest for the new results?

11.7 Binocular vision

In man, the eyes are fairly close together in the front of the head, and so their fields of vision have a considerable region of overlap. This means that the two eyes receive slightly different images of an object to the front, each from a slightly different viewpoint. This does not result in our 'seeing double', for, in some way not fully understood, the brain can put the two pictures together into one and at the same time gives us an appreciation of depth and distance. A simple experiment will demonstrate this.

Close one eye and hold a pencil vertically at arm's length so that it obscures some more distant vertical object, such as part of a window frame. Now open your closed eye and close the other eye. Do the pencil and distant object still appear to be aligned?

What sort of animals would you expect to be aided by binocular or **stereoscopic** vision? What advantage is there to an animal like a rabbit in having its eyes at the sides of its head, rather than at the front? If you draw the rabbit's field of vision, this will help you to answer the question.

11.8 Protection of the eye

The eye is a delicate organ and it is protected from damage and injury in a number of ways. It is set well back in the orbit, while the eyelids offer some degree of protection against small objects striking the eye, and the eyebrows and eyelashes help to shade the eyes and keep out liquids such as rain and sweat.

However, the conjunctiva, a delicate layer of living, transparent skin overlying the cornea, is continuously exposed while we are awake. When you try to 'stare someone out' you will know that your eyes feel prickly and uncomfortable if you deliberately refrain from blinking for a few minutes. Watch one of your classmates who does not know that he is being observed, for a few moments, and you will appreciate how often we blink without being aware of it. Every time we blink, a small gland called the **lachrymal gland** or tear gland beneath the upper eyelid is squeezed, and a small drop of lachrymal fluid is washed down over the surface of the conjunctiva in a thin film, rather as the windscreen wiper of a car spreads the water from the windscreen washer. This continuous washing with lachrymal fluid serves three very important purposes.

1. It keeps the conjunctiva moist.
2. It washes away dust particles which fall on the surface of the eye.
3. It is slightly antiseptic and so kills off bacteria which land on the eye.

Once used, the lachrymal fluid drains away down the tear duct into the back of the nose. If you pull down your lower eyelid and examine its inner corner closely in a mirror, you can see the small opening of the tear duct.

11.9 The ear

Only part of the ear is visible from the outside: the internal portions are embedded in the bone of the skull, so it is impossible to carry out a dissection of it as we did with the eye.

Figure 11.5 shows the main structures of the ear, and also summarises how these structures operate in hearing or in the maintenance of balance.

Of course this description of the ear and its functions is a very brief one and highly simplified. Your teacher may ask you to investigate the ear in more detail using other books, and perhaps models.

Figure 11.5 The ear and its functions

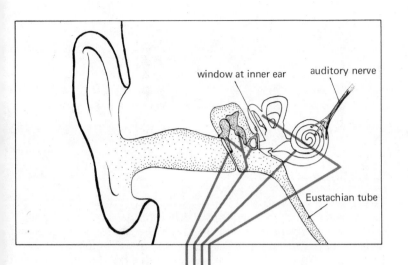

window at inner ear

auditory nerve

Eustachian tube

HEARING

Sound waves travel down ear. Set up vibrations on tympanum, or drum. Tympanum stops vibrating when sound waves cease.

BALANCE

When head moves, or stops moving, fluid movement in semi-circular canals stimulates receptors, and impulses are transmitted to brain.
Note: Other organs detect changes in position such as tilting.

Vibrations amplified and transmitted by movement of hammer, anvil, and stirrup (three small bones) to window at boundary of inner ear.

Vibrations transmitted through fluids filling cochlea, cause vibrations of some sensitive hair cells. High pitched notes detected at base of cochlea, low pitched ones at apex. Nerve impulse is generated and passes out along auditory nerve.

Looking Back at Chapter 11

1. All organisms are constantly bombarded with stimuli from their external environment.
2. These stimuli are perceived by receptors, and the corresponding responses are directed towards the survival of the organism.
3. The eye and the ear are examples of specialised receptors called sense organs, and are adapted to register conditions with great precision.
4. The eye is sensitive to amount and colour of light. Light is focused in the eye and an image is formed.
5. In man, the eyes are able to register the distance of objects and to focus in depth on these.
6. The ear is a complex sense organ sensitive to sound waves. It also plays a part in the maintenance of balance.

12 LINKS: NERVES AND THE BRAIN

12.1 Skin as a receptor

The skin is a very remarkable part of the body because at one and the same time it both isolates the body from its surroundings and also provides a very important link with the environment. It is in fact a sense organ but much simpler in structure than the eye or ear. Figure 12.1 shows nerve endings which enable the skin to function as a sense organ.

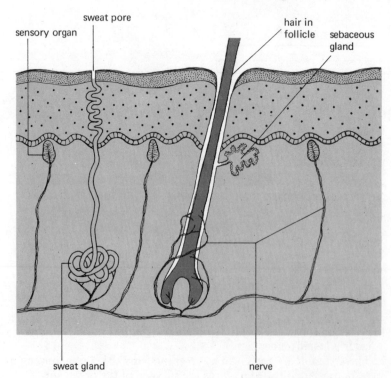

Figure 12.1 Section through skin, showing nerve endings

The nerve endings in skin make up what is known as the **general sensory system.** We are well aware that our skin is sensitive to a variety of different stimuli, giving us various sensations, such as heat, cold, touch and pain. It was thought at one time that each of the different types of nerve endings in the skin was responsible for a particular sensation. We now know that this is not so. For example, some nerve endings will give rise to a sensation of pain when stimulated either by intense heat, by cold or by pressure. Furthermore, you may well have experienced a skin nerve ending giving a

178

'wrong' response: for example, on touching a very cold object, you may at first feel as though your finger has been burned. However, in spite of occasional instances of confusion, skin sensations are distinct, and they convey information to us about our physical environment.

The nerve endings themselves are not evenly distributed all over the body, as we can easily appreciate from this simple experiment.

Carry out the experiment in pairs. The subject is blindfolded, and the experimenter touches his skin lightly with one or both of the points of a pair of dividers. Each time a touch is given, the subject states whether he thinks one or two points of the dividers were used. Start with the points of the dividers wide apart, and gradually bring them closer together as the experiment proceeds. Eventually a stage will be reached where a double touch is reported as one. This shows that the two points are both stimulating the same nerve ending, and the distance between them gives some indication of the distance between the nerve endings in that part of the body. Begin the investigation on the finger tips and extend it to the back of the hand, the upper arm, and the back of the neck.

What can you conclude from this experiment about the distribution of nerve endings in the skin? Are all parts of the skin equally sensitive to different stimuli?

12.2 Environment-behaviour links

The experiment you have just performed tells us something about the distribution of nerve endings in the skin. It also tells us that the stimulus of touch was recorded in the brain, since the subject was 'aware' of being touched. Had he been pricked too hard he would have jumped! That is to say he would have responded by some form of muscular action, and perhaps by a cry of pain. Clearly there must be some link between skin, the receptor, and the brain.

Consider the functions of your eyes, ears and other sense organs when you play football or tennis. In a fast activity, the link between the stimuli received by your receptors, and the responses made to them by the action of your muscles needs to operate rapidly. To bring about the swift, smoothly co-ordinated responses which we are constantly making to the barrage of stimuli reaching us from the outside world, a linking system is needed, the nervous system. The arrangement and main parts of this system are shown in Figure 12.2.

The human nervous system is made up as follows.
1. Nerves: there are many pairs of these which link our receptors with the **effectors** (the structures such as muscles and glands), with the spinal cord and brain. Those nerves joined to the spinal cord are called **spinal nerves,** while those linked to the brain are **cranial nerves.** What examples of cranial nerves have you already learned about?

Figure 12.2 The nervous system in man

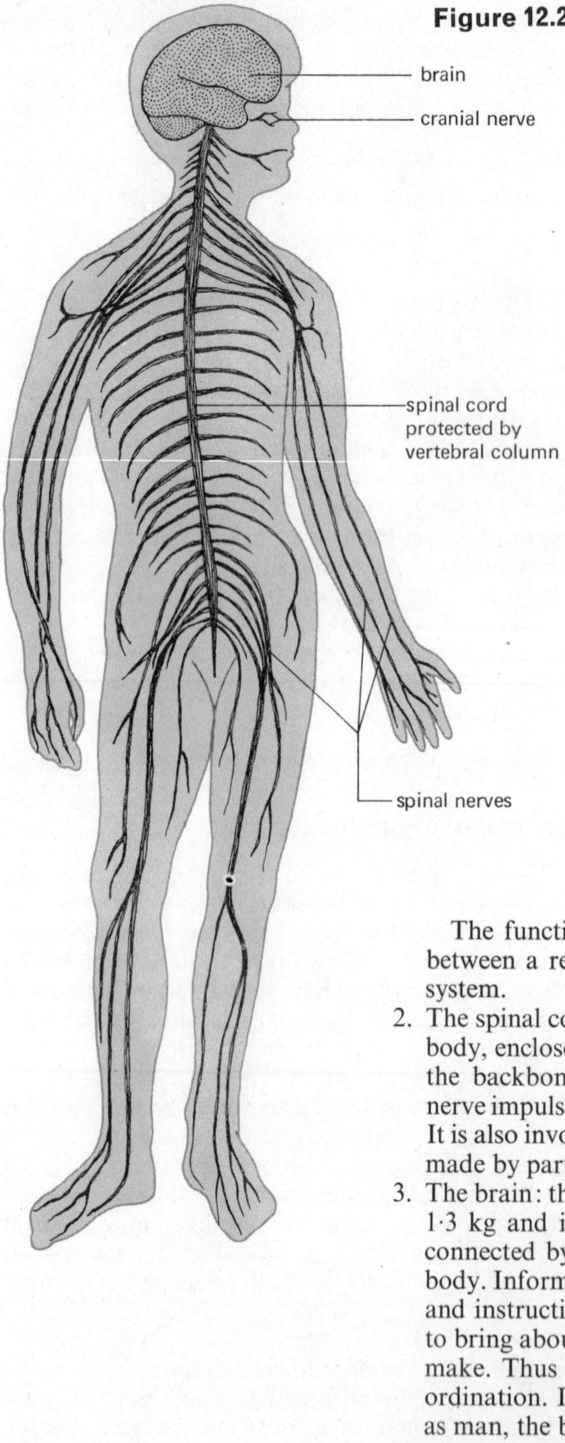

- brain
- cranial nerve

spinal cord
protected by
vertebral column

spinal nerves

The function of a nerve is to conduct a message or **impulse** between a receptor or an effector, and the rest of the nervous system.

2. The spinal cord: this runs from the brain along the length of the body, enclosed in and protected by the vertebrae which make up the backbone. It functions as a communicating link, passing nerve impulses to and fro between the brain and the spinal nerves. It is also involved in direct control of some very simple responses made by parts of our body, as we shall see later.

3. The brain: this is housed within the skull. In man it weighs about 1·3 kg and is composed of many millions of nerve cells. It is connected by the spinal cord and by nerves to all parts of our body. Information from all our sense organs is fed into the brain, and instructions from the brain are sent out to all our effectors to bring about the various responses to stimuli which we need to make. Thus the brain is the body's centre for control and co-ordination. In addition, particularly in the higher animals such as man, the brain is the seat of mental activity, such as learning, memory, thought and imagination.

The brain and spinal cord together constitute the **central nervous system,** or CNS; the cranial and spinal nerves make up the **peripheral nervous system.**

12.3 Nerve cells

Though the nervous system is made up of various parts each with their different functions, only one type of cell is involved, the nerve cell, or **neuron.** All neurons have basically the same structure, though the proportions of their various parts differ according to their function, and the way in which they are located in the nervous system, as shown in Figure 12.3.

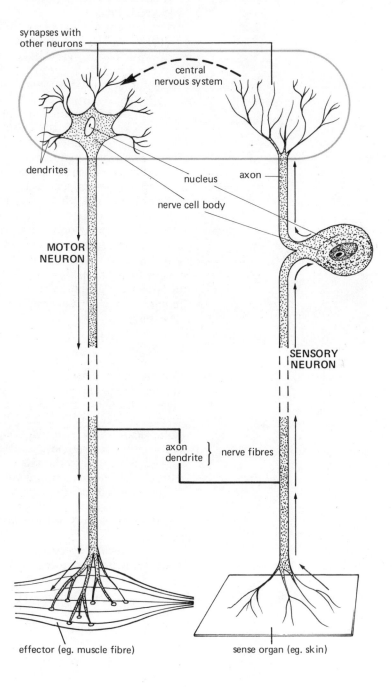

Figure 12.3 Sensory and motor neurons

Each neuron consists of three parts.
1. It has a **nerve cell-body** in which its nucleus is situated. This is either in the brain or spinal cord or in a **dorsal root ganglion,** a small swelling on a spinal nerve near its junction with the spinal cord.
2. It has one or more **dendrites,** which are fine fibres by which impulses enter the neuron.
3. It has a single **axon,** which is the fibre by which nerve impulses leave the neuron.

Nerves are made up of large numbers of **nerve fibres,** all running parallel to each other without branching or joining, rather like the many wires making up a large multi-core electric cable. Some of these fibres will be the dendrites of **sensory** neurons, running from a receptor to the CNS, while others will be the axons of **motor** neurons running from the CNS to an effector such as a muscle. There are no cell bodies along the length of the nerves, and these fibres can be up to a metre or more in length, stretching from the CNS to the extremities of our fingers or toes, and they are the longest cells in our bodies.

All spinal nerves are composed of both sensory and motor fibres. Some cranial nerves, such as the optic and auditory nerves, contain sensory fibres only, while those serving the eye muscles are exclusively motor. Remember that the rule for nerve impulse transmission is 'one-way traffic only'. Impulses in sensory fibres pass only inwards, from receptor to CNS, while motor fibres conduct exclusively outwards, from CNS to muscles or to other effectors. This is not due to any property of the fibres themselves, but to the fact that the **synapses,** or links between neurons, are so arranged that impulses can enter a neuron only by a dendrite and leave only by the axon.

12.4 Reflex action

You may now have some idea of how the nervous system works. A stimulus from the environment is detected by a receptor which triggers off a nerve impulse. This travels up the dendrite of a sensory neuron. Somewhere in the CNS this impulse is passed across to motor neurons and sent out along their axons to activate a muscle and so produce a response to the original stimulus.

There is one link in this chain of events to which we have not yet referred. In the brain and spinal cord there is a third type of neuron, the **intermediate** neuron; for the most part these are contained within the brain and spinal cord, having short dendrites and axons, and their function is to form the link between sensory and motor neurons.

The following experiment demonstrates these three types of neuron in action together.

Sit with your legs crossed so that the lowest part of the uppermost leg is hanging free, with the foot unsupported. Relax your muscles while someone gives you a sharp tap with the edge of the hand just below the kneecap. Note what happens. What change can you detect in the thigh of your uppermost leg if your hand is resting on it during the experiment?

The neurons and other structures involved in this action are shown diagrammatically in Figure 12.4. They, and the sequence of nerve impulses passing through them, constitute what is known as a **reflex arc.** The simple behaviour pattern resulting from the operation of a reflex arc is known as a **reflex action.** You can probably think of many other examples of reflex actions, such as blinking when some object approaches the eye, or the rapid withdrawal of your hand if a finger is burned or pricked. Reflex actions do not have to be learned and are not forgotten. They occur in the same fashion every time, they involve only part of the body, and they are very difficult to suppress. You may have tried to refrain from blinking while someone waves a hand in front of your eye, and discovered how very difficult it is.

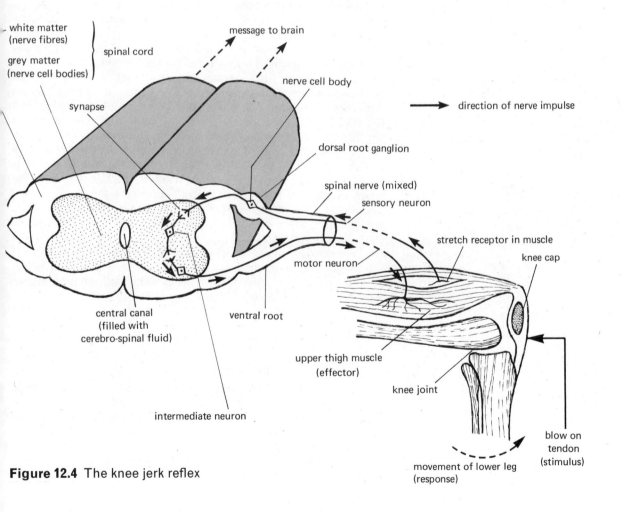

Figure 12.4 The knee jerk reflex

The arrangement of neurons involved is never as simple as in Figure 12.4, as there will be always more than one of each kind of neuron taking part. Most stimuli we receive will trigger off impulses in many sensory neurons. The CNS contains an enormous number of much branched intermediate neurons. These form a complex network through which impulses can pass out along a number of motor neurons, to produce a response which may involve the contraction of several muscles.

Furthermore, when a reflex arc operates, impulses are always sent along the spinal cord into parts of the brain. It is the spinal cord which controls the initial response, but it is through the brain that we are aware of what has occurred. If you burn your finger, the withdrawal of your hand begins a fraction of a second before you feel the pain. This is an example of the spinal cord in control, but if you cry out and rub the injured spot, it is the brain which is directing your actions.

12.5 Transmission of nerve impulses

It should be clear from what we have learned that selection must occur whenever a nerve impulse passes through the nervous system. Each neuron is potentially linked to every other, but when some activity such as a reflex arc occurs in the nervous system, only certain neurons are activated and the response is limited to the appropriate effectors. This is rather like the working of a telephone system. When you lift the receiver, you are not instantly in touch with all the other subscribers on the system. By dialling the appropriate digits, your call is made to take a particular route through the central exchange, equivalent to the CNS, and you are put in touch with the person of your choice.

In the nervous system, the nerve impulse has the form of a wave of electrical disturbance which passes through the neuron at speeds between 1 and 100 m per second. When it reaches the tip of the axon, as you may have noticed from Figure 12.4, there is not direct contact with the dendrites of the next neuron or neurons, but they are separated from one another by a very small gap, the synapse. Particular impulses may or may not cross particular synapses, and can be routed in almost limitless ways through the vast complex of intermediate neurons making up the CNS. It is this tremendous variety of response in the nervous system which allows the complex behaviour characteristic of man.

12.6 The brain

The brain is the most highly organised part of the nervous system. Like the spinal cord, it is hollow, and the central cavity is filled with **cerebro-spinal fluid.** The brain is composed of both **grey** and **white matter,** which are nerve cell-bodies and nerve fibres respectively. The arrangement in the brain is such that the grey matter is on the outside and the white matter inside: in the spinal cord, the arrangement is the reverse.

The brain is an enormous network of intermediate neurons, and the methods of impulse transmission and synapse action within it are the same as in any other part of the nervous system. Nevertheless, much more research has to be done before we are able to understand the precise details of what goes on inside the brain and to relate this to details of our behaviour, such as why we do one thing rather than another in a particular situation, and how memories are 'stored'.

We have a general idea of the functions of the different regions of the brain. This knowledge comes largely from experimental work on animals, and from observations on people who have suffered damage or injury to different parts of their brains.

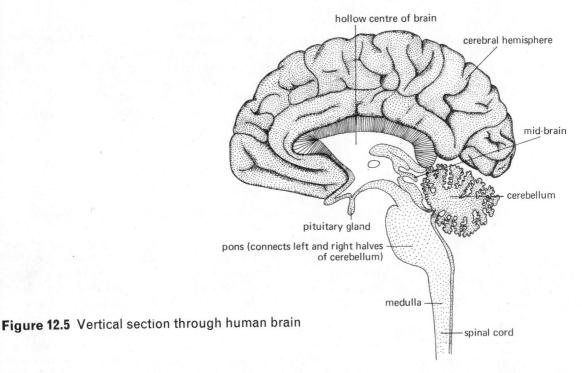

Figure 12.5 Vertical section through human brain

Figure 12.5 shows the various regions of the human brain. The largest and most conspicuous parts are the **cerebral hemispheres** constituting the **cerebrum.** In vertebrates such as fish, these are quite small outgrowths at the very front of the brain, but in mammals, especially man, they have become enormously developed, extending back over most of the remainder of the brain. The cerebrum is deeply grooved, and folded, which greatly increases the surface area and hence the number of nerve cell-bodies it contains. What effect do you think this will have on its function?

All parts of our body are connected, either directly or indirectly, with the cerebrum. Information from our eyes, ears and all other sense organs is fed into it, and conscious control of our muscular activities is located here. Thus, the cerebrum is the largest and most important of the **association centres** of the brain, where various types of sensory information are considered together and, with stored memories, determine the pattern of motor impulses which will be sent out to control any action which is to be taken.

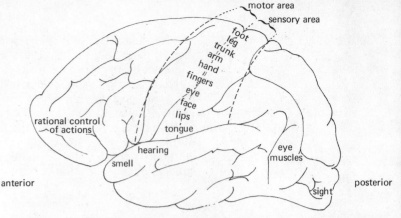

Figure 12.6 Functional areas of cerebrum.

Function in the cerebral hemispheres is to a considerable extent localised. Experiments have shown that the region responsible for conscious control of our muscles is located in a broad band of tissue running from the mid-dorsal regions of the brain over the top and side of each cerebral hemisphere, as shown in Figure 12.6.

It has also been possible to show, as indicated on the diagram, that particular parts of the **motor areas,** as they are called, are linked to, and hence control, the movements of various regions of the body.

The **sensory areas** are located just behind the motor areas and are divided into regions where skin sensations in different parts of the body are recorded.

The cerebrum is also involved in learning and in the storing of memories.

The **cerebellum** is a five-lobed outgrowth near the back of the brain (Figure 12.5). This region is concerned with balance and the co-ordination of muscular movement. The intricate patterns of muscular movement involved in such actions as riding a bicycle or catching a ball, come under the more or less automatic control of the cerebellum.

The third main region of the brain is the **medulla.** This leads back to the spinal cord and contains centres for the automatic control of a number of bodily activities such as the rate of heartbeat, respiration, and the distribution of the blood through the various parts of the circulatory system.

Looking Back at Chapter 12

1. Stimuli perceived by receptors may lead to responses carried out by effectors.
2. The nervous system provides the link between receptors and effectors.
3. The functional unit of the nervous system is the nerve cell, or neuron: millions of neurons are arranged to form brain, spinal cord and nerves.
4. Simple, involuntary reflex actions are operated through the spinal cord. Apart from these special cases, nerves and spinal cord are concerned with impulse transmission, the control and co-ordination of which are carried out in the brain.
5. The brain is divided into distinct structural and functional regions, such as the sensory and motor areas of the cerebral hemispheres.

13 GROWING AND MOVING

13.1 Response of plant roots

We have already mentioned that the behaviour of an organism is the sum total of its responses to the stimuli from its environment. In animals, the most obvious of these responses are those involving movement. Most plants remain fixed in one spot and have no obvious complex sense organs, and so we do not normally think of them as behaving in the same way as animals. But a plant, being a living organism, is subject to many stimuli from its environment; if it fails to make appropriate responses it will not be able to survive.

What sort of stimuli do you think would be important in the life of a plant?

The experiment in Figure 13.1 shows how to investigate the response of a growing root to an environmental stimulus.

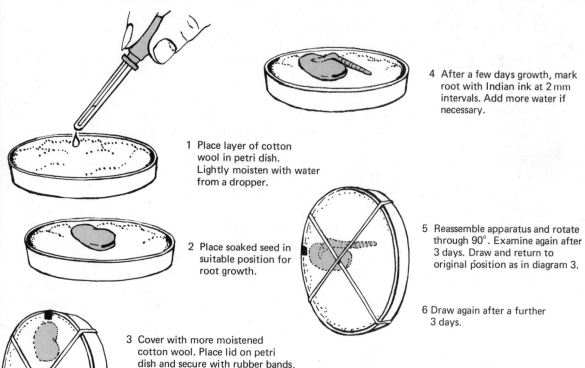

1 Place layer of cotton wool in petri dish. Lightly moisten with water from a dropper.

2 Place soaked seed in suitable position for root growth.

3 Cover with more moistened cotton wool. Place lid on petri dish and secure with rubber bands, Mark position of seed and stand dish upright with seed at top.

4 After a few days growth, mark root with Indian ink at 2 mm intervals. Add more water if necessary.

5 Reassemble apparatus and rotate through 90°. Examine again after 3 days. Draw and return to original position as in diagram 3.

6 Draw again after a further 3 days.

Figure 13.1 Investigating response in growing roots

To what stimulus do you suppose the root has been responding? In what region of the root did the visible response occur? What is the importance in the life of the plant of the stimulus and response which the experiment has demonstrated?

This experiment shows that plants, while not showing locomotion in the same way as animals, do make movements by changing the direction of their growth in response to stimuli from the environment. These growth movements are known as **tropisms.** In tropisms, the direction of the growth movements shows a relationship to the direction of the stimulus; that is to say, the plant organ involved turns either towards or away from the stimulus.

In the experiment, the bean root was responding to the stimulus of gravity by growing in a downward direction. This we call positive **geotropism.** When seeds fall to the ground, or if you are sowing seeds in the garden, the position in which they fall does not matter. The positive geotropism shown by the young root will ensure that it grows downwards into the soil. What factors other than gravity might affect the direction of growth of the root once it had become established in the soil?

13.2 Perception and response in shoots

What is negative geotropism? In what circumstances might some part of a plant show negative geotropism? If you can recall having seen garden plants beaten down flat by the wind or rain, you may get some help in answering this question.

Although shoots often show a negative response to gravity, light is a more important environmental factor controlling the direction of their growth. Why do you think this is so? You may have noticed what happens to the shoots of a geranium or of hyacinths kept on a table near a window. What should you do to prevent uneven growth of the shoots in this situation?

The following experiment will tell us something about the response of growing shoots to light, which is known as **phototropism.**

1. Fill four 6 cm diameter pots with moist sand or sawdust or vermiculite, and sow a dozen barley or oat grains in each, placing the grains 0·5 cm below the surface.
2. Place the pots in darkness in an incubator at 25°C. After four days they should have produced shoots about 1 cm long.
3. Arrange the pots as shown in Figure 13.2, so that the seedlings are illuminated in various ways, and leave them for a few days.
4. Now examine the pots of seedlings and note the direction of growth of the shoots.

What evidence is there to suggest that light affects the growth of the shoots? What evidence is there that the effect is directional?

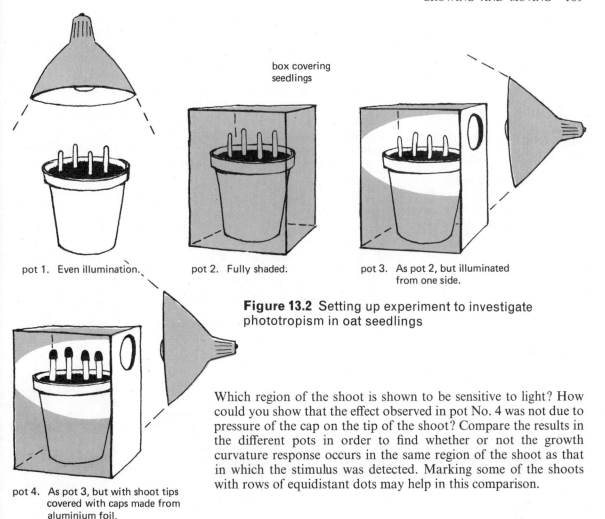

pot 1. Even illumination.

box covering
seedlings

pot 2. Fully shaded.

pot 3. As pot 2, but illuminated
from one side.

Figure 13.2 Setting up experiment to investigate
phototropism in oat seedlings

pot 4. As pot 3, but with shoot tips
covered with caps made from
aluminium foil.

Which region of the shoot is shown to be sensitive to light? How could you show that the effect observed in pot No. 4 was not due to pressure of the cap on the tip of the shoot? Compare the results in the different pots in order to find whether or not the growth curvature response occurs in the same region of the shoot as that in which the stimulus was detected. Marking some of the shoots with rows of equidistant dots may help in this comparison.

If light and gravitational stimuli are detected by the tips of growing roots and shoots, but the growth curvature responses occur in the elongating region, how do you suppose the elongating cells behave to produce the curvatures you have seen?

13.3 The mechanism of response in plants

As in animals, the receptor and effector regions of the plant in these examples are some distance apart. There must therefore be a linking system connecting the two. Which of the two types of linking systems discussed in the previous chapters do you suppose operates in plants? You have already learned that there are various types of cells which form the tissues of the roots and shoots of flowering plants. Do any of these resemble the neurons, specialised for nerve impulse conduction, which you learned about in Chapter 12? If not, one might expect that in plants the link between receptor and effector is more likely to be by means of diffusing chemicals. Why does the time lag between stimulus and response also support this hypothesis?

In 1910, a Danish botanist, Boysen-Jensen, carried out experiments on young oat seedlings. He found that the diffusion of a chemical provided the link between the receptor region in the shoot tip and the effector region in the zone of elongation. See Figure 13.3.

In the first experiment, what effect would the incision have on diffusion of any chemical from the shoot tip to the elongating region? In the second experiment, how might the watery contents of the cut cells cancel out the effect of the incision? In the third experiment, there was no continuous connection existing between receptor

Figure 13.3 Boysen-Jensen's experiments

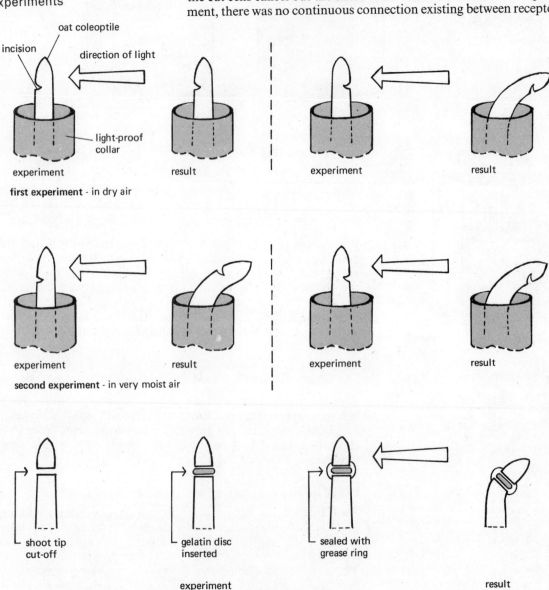

oat coleoptile
incision
direction of light
light-proof collar
experiment   result   experiment   result
first experiment - in dry air

experiment   result   experiment   result
second experiment - in very moist air

shoot tip cut-off   gelatin disc inserted   sealed with grease ring
experiment   result
third experiment - with several shoot tips stuck on with gelatin

and effector regions. Will this have any effect on substances travelling by diffusion down the shoot? What do these experiments indicate is the mechanism controlling the response of oat seedlings which are exposed to light from one side?

The chemical which controls these growth movements has since been isolated and analysed, and is now known to be indolyl acetic acid, IAA. Other substances having similar effects are also known. They are referred to as **auxins,** or plant hormones, and are responsible for governing the growth and development of plants and the responses they make to stimuli from their environment.

The following experiment investigates the effect of IAA in bringing about curvature in a growing shoot.

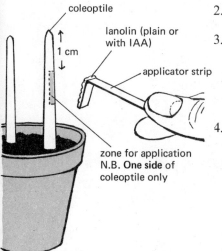

coleoptile

1 cm

lanolin (plain or with IAA)

applicator strip

zone for application
N.B. **One side** of coleoptile only

method of applying lanolin

Figure 13.4 Application of lanolin and IAA to oat coleoptiles

1. Prepare three 6 cm diameter pots of oat seedlings, following the procedure outlined in the phototropism experiment (Section 13.2).
2. During the experiment, avoid unilateral illumination of the seedlings. Why is this important?
3. The IAA used in the experiment is dissolved in a greasy substance known as lanolin. The solution is very dilute, equivalent to 1 g of IAA in 30 000 g of lanolin. You are also provided with lanolin which contains no IAA. Keep the samples of lanolin in separate test tubes in a beaker of water at 40°–50°C. This temperature will keep them soft enough for smearing.
4. Use the seedlings when they are 4 days old. Apply the lanolin + IAA carefully to one side only of each seedling in pot A; see Figure 13.4. Smear a small quantity on to a 0·5 cm length of the coleoptile, the young shoot, beginning 1·0 cm back from the tip. A narrow strip of thin plastic or photograph negative with an 0·5 cm length bent at right angles at one end makes a suitable applicator.

   Now, using lanolin without IAA, treat all the seedlings in pot B in the same way. Leave the seedlings in pot C untreated. Both pot B and pot C act as controls in this experiment. Explain why.
5. Return the pots to the incubator and examine again after 24 hours. Record any changes which have occurred in the seedlings.

   In which seedlings has curvature occurred? What factor has brought about the curvature? What is the direction of the curvature relative to the factor causing it?

Figure 13.5 shows other experiments on growth and growth curvature in oat seedlings and the results which have been obtained. How would you interpret these results in the light of what you have learned?

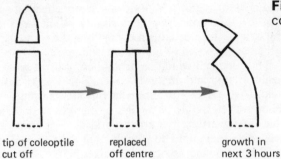

Figure 13.5 Further experiments on control of growth in oat seedlings

tip of coleoptile cut off → replaced off centre → growth in next 3 hours

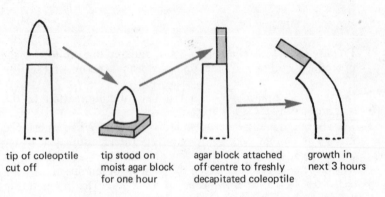

tip of coleoptile cut off → tip stood on moist agar block for one hour → agar block attached off centre to freshly decapitated coleoptile → growth in next 3 hours

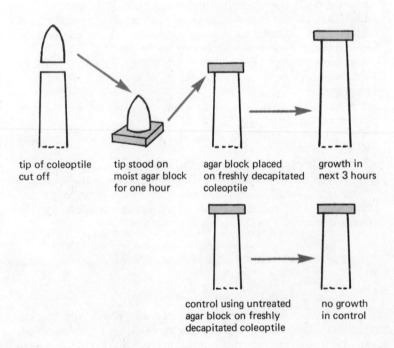

tip of coleoptile cut off → tip stood on moist agar block for one hour → agar block placed on freshly decapitated coleoptile → growth in next 3 hours

control using untreated agar block on freshly decapitated coleoptile → no growth in control

13.4 Locomotion as a response to stimuli

Locomotion, that is, the movement of the whole organism from place to place, is not common in plants, though it does occur in some unicellular forms which live in water and lash the long whip-like processes, or flagella, found at one end of their cells. What examples of such plants have you already found earlier in the course?

1. Place a drop of a culture of *Euglena* on a microscope slide, add a cover slip and examine under the low power of the microscope. Where are the organisms distributed?
2. Prepare a piece of thin cardboard, the same size as the microscope slide, with a narrow slit $0.1 \text{ cm} \times 1.0 \text{ cm}$ cut from its centre.
3. Slide this card under the microscope slide so that the slit is approximately under the centre of the cover slip. Leave the illumination of the microscope unchanged.
4. After 5 minutes examine the culture in the region of the slit with the low power of the microscope. Carefully remove the cardboard mask, and continue observing under low power.

What changes did you notice in the distribution of *Euglena* before and after using the mask? What environmental factor was responsible for these changes? What is the significance of such a behaviour pattern to these organisms?

Why do you think that this form of behaviour, involving locomotion, is less common in plants, whereas locomotion is common in the behaviour of most animals? The meaning of the terms autotrophic and heterotrophic may help you to answer this question.

In experiments involving locomotion in woodlice, you may have discovered that these animals come to rest in damp, dark situations. In the following experiment, you can make a more precise investigation of the factors controlling the distribution of these organisms, and the nature of the responses they make to them.

1. The first experiment investigates the response of woodlice to different degrees of humidity. Half fill one of the lower dishes of the apparatus shown in Figure 13.6 with distilled water, and in the other lower dish place some calcium chloride or silica gel, substances which will absorb moisture.
2. Place the perforated zinc platform in position and cover it with muslin. Then place a small piece of cobalt thiocyanate paper or cobalt chloride paper in both halves of the apparatus.
3. Place the tops of the dishes in position, and secure each side of the apparatus with an elastic band. The perforated zinc should project only a little way beyond the edges of the dishes. Take

great care to keep the apparatus horizontal to prevent spilling the liquid.

4. Observe the cobalt thiocyanate or cobalt chloride paper. Both of these are pink in moist air, but become lilac or blue when the humidity falls to a low level. Leave the apparatus until a distinct difference in humidity has been established between the two compartments, as indicated by the paper.

5. Now, work as quickly as possible without disturbing the liquid in the apparatus. Remove the top pair of dishes, place six woodlice of the same size and species in each dish and reassemble the apparatus.

6. Observe the apparatus over a period of time.

    (a) Record the number of woodlice in both sides of the apparatus at intervals of one minute.

    (b) Record the activity of the woodlice in both halves of the apparatus as shown by the speed of movement and frequency of turning. This may be recorded by drawing the path taken by one animal from each half of the apparatus over a period of a minute.

What responses do woodlice seem to make to different levels of humidity in their environment? How could you relate your results to the situations in which you normally find woodlice in their natural surroundings?

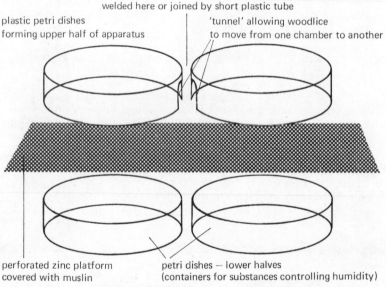

welded here or joined by short plastic tube

plastic petri dishes
forming upper half of apparatus

'tunnel' allowing woodlice
to move from one chamber to another

perforated zinc platform
covered with muslin

petri dishes — lower halves
(containers for substances controlling humidity)

components of choice chamber in their relative positions

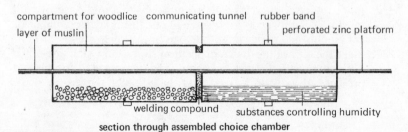

compartment for woodlice   communicating tunnel   rubber band

layer of muslin

perforated zinc platform

welding compound   substances controlling humidity

section through assembled choice chamber

Figure 13.6 Choice chamber for use in experiments on woodlice

How could this apparatus be modified to compare the responses of woodlice in light and in dark situations? Remember that other factors such as humidity should be constant throughout the experiment.

When you have suitably modified the apparatus, introduce six woodlice into each half, and as before, record the numbers in each half at intervals of 1 minute. How do light and darkness affect the behaviour of the woodlice in the apparatus? How is this related to their behaviour in the wild?

Repeat the experiment with ground beetles. Do they respond in the same way?

We can now offer an explanation for some aspects of the behaviour of woodlice along rather simpler lines than you might previously have supposed. There is no need, for example, to imagine that the woodlice actively 'seek' or 'select' moist dark places in the sense in which we normally understand these terms. The experiments show that woodlice tend to be more active in dry or light situations, and less active in moist or dark situations. This simple relationship between environmental factors and level of activity will usually bring woodlice in a natural habitat to rest in the places where we normally find them.

The behaviour of many small invertebrate animals can be very largely explained in terms of simple responses of this kind. For example, earwigs, woodlice and many other small animals tend to come to rest in cracks or crevices, where as much of their bodies as possible is in contact with a firm surface. How does this response play a part in keeping such animals in situations where they are likely to survive?

13.5 Animal locomotion

As animals need organic food, locomotion is vital for most of them, and many aspects of their shape and structure are determined by their need to move about from place to place in order to get food. This involves not only the organs of locomotion, but also a highly developed, fast-acting nervous system with sense organs. Such a nervous system, which is lacking in plants, is related to an animal's need to respond quickly to the changing stimuli which it encounters while moving.

Some unicellular animals move in much the same way as *Euglena*. Larger animals usually have complex and often quite large parts of their body set aside for movement.

Figure 13.7 shows a variety of animals from different habitats. Draw up a table showing the sort of movements they make and the organs which they use for locomotion, as shown in the first example.

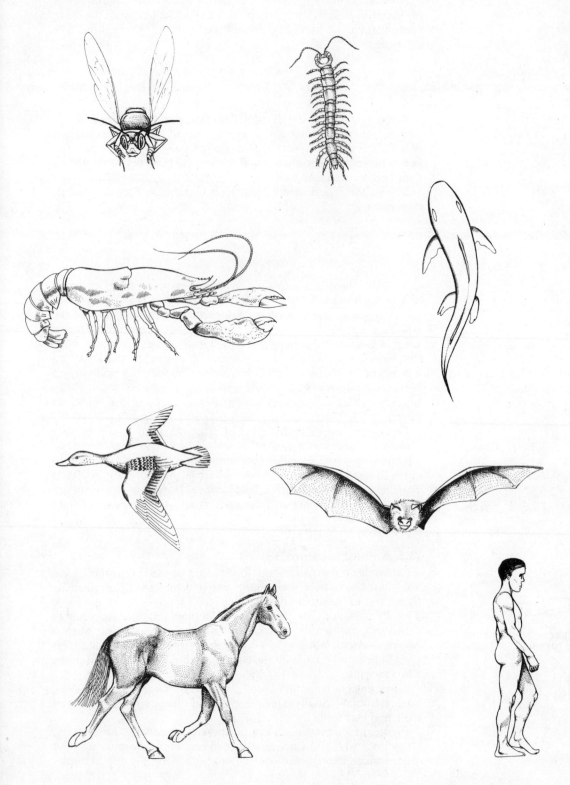

Figure 13.7 Animals showing various forms of locomotion

Include in your table any animals which you may have in the laboratory and which are not shown in Figure 13.7.

Table 13.1

Animal	Method of locomotion	Organs of locomotion
centipede	*walking*	*many pairs of jointed legs*

13.6 Bones for support and movement

Land vertebrates usually move by pushing with their legs against the ground. For this, legs must be made rigid by bone, as described in Chapter 1, but bones have no power of movement in themselves. What structures in your body cause your bones to move? You have already carried out an experiment to show muscles converting chemical to mechanical energy. Muscular contractions pull against the bones of the skeleton and produce movement.

In a sense, the needs for support and for movement make conflicting demands on the skeleton. For support, it must of course be rigid, but if your skeleton was merely a completely rigid scaffolding supporting the soft tissues of the body, there could be no possibility of movement. How is this difficulty overcome?

Examine Figure 13.8, or a model of a skeleton if one is available. Where does movement occur? The human skeleton consists of over two hundred separate bones. Some, such as those of the skull, are fused together. Others are **articulated** with one another; that is to say, where they come together, movement is possible. These regions are the movable **joints,** and by means of these the skeleton acts as a rigid yet movable framework, to which the muscles are attached. Contraction of the muscles produces movement of the bones at the joints.

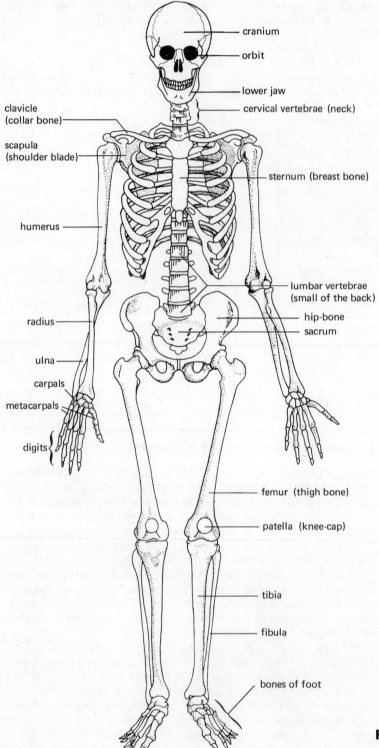

- cranium
- orbit
- lower jaw
- cervical vertebrae (neck)
- clavicle (collar bone)
- scapula (shoulder blade)
- sternum (breast bone)
- humerus
- lumbar vertebrae (small of the back)
- hip-bone
- radius
- sacrum
- ulna
- carpals
- metacarpals
- digits
- femur (thigh bone)
- patella (knee-cap)
- tibia
- fibula
- bones of foot

Figure 13.8 The human skeleton

13.7 Joints

Extend your right arm fully with the hand in the 'palm up' position. Grasp the upper part firmly with your left hand and bend your right arm slowly at the elbow. What change takes place in your upper arm? From this and from Figure 13.9, suggest what structure bends the arm at the elbow? The muscle which you feel bulging is called the **biceps** muscle.

Remember that a muscle can do work only by pulling, as it contracts. No muscle can push by elongation. How then can you extend your forearm after flexing it by the biceps muscle? Figure 13.9 shows that the **triceps** muscle is suitably arranged for this, and you may be able to feel it in action as you extend your forearm. These two muscles are said to be **antagonistic** to one another, and most joints in our body are operated by antagonistic pairs or sets of muscles. The muscle of an antagonistic pair which bends the limb is called the **flexor,** while the one which straightens it is the **extensor.** Which muscle operating the bending of the arm is the extensor, and which is the flexor? When one muscle of an antagonistic pair contracts, what happens to the other?

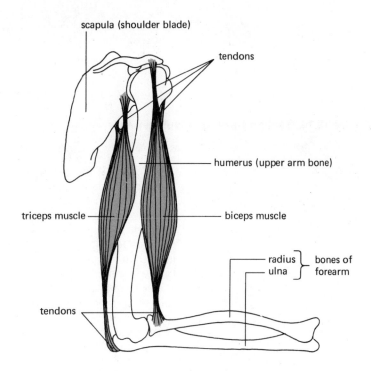

Figure 13.9 Human elbow joint

Figure 13.9 shows that muscles are attached to bones by **tendons.** Each is continuous with the tough sheet of tissue surrounding the muscle, and its other end grows right into the tissues of the bone. Feel the tendon of your biceps muscle just above the inside of your elbow joint as you bend your arm to and fro. A tendon must be flexible and very tough. What other property must it have to do its job effectively and transmit the pull of the contracting muscle to the bone? You may find the answer to this question by considering whether you would rather attach a piece of rope or a piece of elastic to a heavy weight to help lift it up.

Although both ends of a muscle are attached by tendons to bones, a contracting muscle produces movement at one of its ends only. The fixed end of a muscle is its **origin,** while the other end where movement occurs is its **insertion.** Where are the origins and insertions of the biceps and triceps muscles?

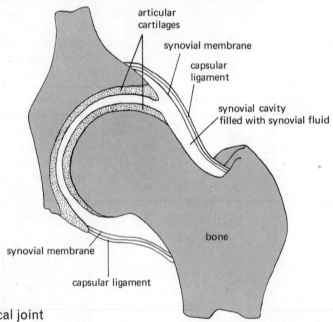

Figure 13.10 Section through a typical joint

We have seen that movements occur at joints. In a piece of moving machinery such as a motor car engine, what must you do to ensure that smooth movement occurs at the joints?

Figure 13.10 shows the structures responsible for various aspects of 'joint action'. The ends of bones at joints are covered with a thin, smooth layer of **cartilage** or gristle. Cartilage is slightly less hard than bone but rather more resilient or 'springy'. How will this help when the body receives jolts and bumps?

The joint is enclosed in a membrane which is fixed firmly around each bone just beyond the region of the joint, and it secretes a special fluid into the joint capsule. How does this help the action of the joint?

Look at Figure 13.10. What structures link two bones at a joint?

They may be strands of tissue running from one bone to the other, as in the drawing, or they may be in the form of a sleeve or cylinder enclosing the joint. They are tough and flexible, and they prevent dislocation if a strain is put on the joint. In what important property must **ligaments** differ from tendons?

13.8 The skeleton as a system of levers

The joints in our body operate as a system of levers. What acts as
(*a*) the fulcrum or pivot, where turning occurs?
(*b*) the effort by which movement is brought about?
(*c*) the load which is to be moved?
Simple models will help us to study these aspects of the skeleton's function.

In Figure 13.11 the pivoted end of the ruler represents the elbow joint; the weight on its end represents a weight held in the hand, and any upward force you exert on the ruler is equivalent to the biceps muscle supporting or lifting the weight. By exerting this upward force through a spring balance, you can measure the force which the biceps muscle exerts to support the weight in the hand.

Begin the experiment with the distance 'a' one tenth of the distance 'b' as shown in the diagram. Record the reading of the spring balance and the weight on the end of the ruler. Repeat the experiment with the balance attached at different points along the length of the ruler and with a series of different weights. Make a table of your results. What do the data indicate about the forces exerted by the muscles compared to the loads which they have to move?

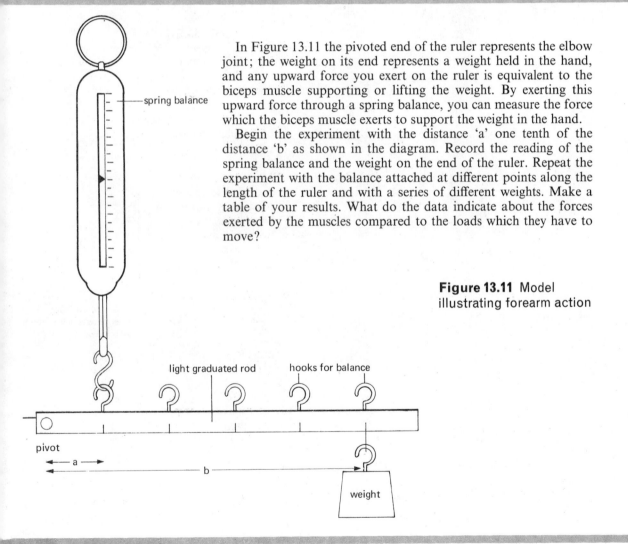

Figure 13.11 Model illustrating forearm action

Your results might suggest that most muscles have to exert forces many times greater than the loads they have to move. The experiment also indicates that these forces might be lessened by attaching the muscles at a greater distance from the joints. What two reasons can you give why this arrangement would be unsatisfactory and does not occur?

13.9 Types of joint

At some joints, the bones are firmly fused or joined together and no movement occurs. The sutures between the bones of the skull are an example of a rigid joint. Examine a skeleton, and try to find other examples.

Movable joints are described according to the type of movement they allow. Complete Table 13.2 by finding examples of the different types of movable joint in the skeleton. See Figure 13.12 for examples.

hip-joint

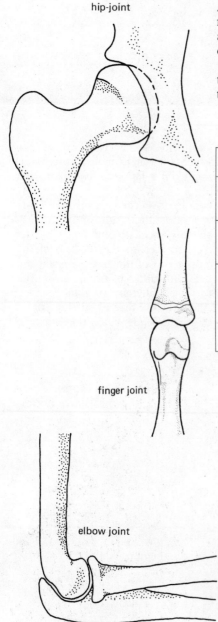

Table 13.2

Type of joint	Movement	Examples
1. Ball and socket joint	Movement in many planes	
2. Hinge joints	Movement in one plane only	
3. Gliding joints	More or less flat articular surfaces. Movement limited by arrangement of ligaments and muscles	

finger joint

elbow joint

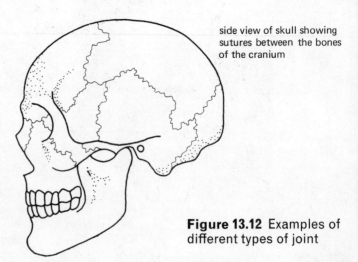

side view of skull showing sutures between the bones of the cranium

Figure 13.12 Examples of different types of joint

We sometimes speak of people as being 'double-jointed'. This does not of course mean that such people have two joints where most of us have one, but simply that they have supple ligaments which result in very flexible joints.

13.10 Animals on the move

Place a frog on the floor of the laboratory and make a quick, accurate drawing of it on a sketch pad. Follow your frog as it moves around the laboratory, and make as many outline sketches of it as you can over a period of 15–20 minutes. Replace the frog in its vivarium. From your observations and sketches, write an account of the way in which a frog moves.

What happens to the hind feet of a rabbit or hare as it bounds along?

Figure 13.13 shows the skeleton of a rabbit at rest. Examine a mounted skeleton of a rabbit. What features of the bones of the hind limb are related to the rabbit's method of locomotion? What is the advantage to the rabbit of its unusually long heel bone? The experiment in Section 13.8 may help you to answer this question. Make a drawing of the rabbit's hind limb as you think it would be at the moment the animal takes off from the ground.

If a rabbit is moving fast, we might well say that it is going 'flat out'. This is a very appropriate term, for as well as straightening its legs in movement, the rabbit's backbone, which is arched when at rest to give extra support to the body, is rapidly flicked out straight by the powerful muscles attached to its vertebrae. The

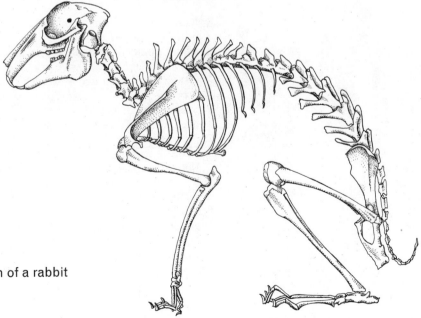

Figure 13.13 The skeleton of a rabbit

vertebrae, with the muscles and ligaments attached to them, act like a powerful spring, curving to help absorb the shock when the rabbit lands, and shooting out to help build up thrust as it leaves the ground. If you have ever eaten rabbit pie or rabbit stew, you will have seen the large powerful muscles of the hind limbs, and of the back, which are used for these movements.

The rabbit's fore limbs play no active part in jumping, but support its weight when it lands. Examine the shoulder region of the rabbit's skeleton. What features are associated with this part of its movement? How do the skeletons of a rabbit and a human differ in the shoulder region? Why should this be so? Do the frog and the rabbit move in the same way? What features of the frog's hind limbs make them less suitable for land locomotion than those of the rabbit?

What part does the rabbit's locomotion play in its way of life? What other features of the rabbit are important in ensuring its safety and survival?

13.11 Standing still

Muscles are not only for movement, but are equally important in maintaining posture; that is, holding the body still and steady in any required position. While you are awake, messages pass to the brain regarding the action of gravity on your body. What organ is important in the perception of gravity effects? As a result, your muscles are kept under an appropriate degree of tension, or **muscle tone,** so that the joints of your limbs and back are adjusted to keep your balance. In this way you can remain standing up or sitting down or in whatever position you choose. Any slight movements are automatically sensed and corrected, and so posture is maintained. This system fails to operate when you are unconscious.

Looking Back at Chapter 13

1. Responses to environmental stimuli often involve movement in both plants and animals.
2. Many plant movements are examples of tropisms, plant organs growing towards or away from a stimulus.
3. Gravity and light are examples of environmental factors which produce directional growth responses in roots and shoots.
4. Stimuli are detected at root and shoot tips, but the response occurs by **differential growth** of cells in the region of elongation.
5. Auxins, plant hormones, which diffuse from the receptor to the effector regions, control growth curvatures in roots and shoots.
6. Behaviour patterns in some plants and animals are often governed by simple relationships between locomotion and environmental factors.
7. Vertebrate skeletons form a jointed framework. Muscles are attached to this, and pull against it by contraction in order to produce movement at the joints or to maintain posture.
8. The proportions and arrangement of the bones in an animal are closely related to its method of locomotion.

14 MORE ABOUT MICRO-ORGANISMS

14.1 The history of bacteriology

You have already studied some aspects of bacteria. What is the order of size of a bacterium? Where in the human body would you expect to find bacteria? We shall consider how these organisms affect man and his environment.

Nowadays we assume that bacteria are present almost everywhere, but prior to the nineteenth century their existence was unknown, although the effects of bacteria have been known to man from his earliest days. We presume that prehistoric man suffered from some bacterial diseases, and that his food went rotten just as our food sometimes does today.

The existence of bacteria and the fact that they, and not the air, were responsible for food going rotten were shown in 1861 by Louis Pasteur.

Pasteur, a French scientist, proved that, when broth was boiled and kept in a special flask, it would remain fresh even when in contact with the air. Pasteur was sure that most bacteria dropped on to material from above, and he suspected that they were usually attached to dust particles. He designed a flask, Figure 14.1, which would prevent contamination from above but would still allow air to enter.

We cannot repeat Pasteur's experiment exactly, but we can carry out a similar investigation using simpler apparatus.

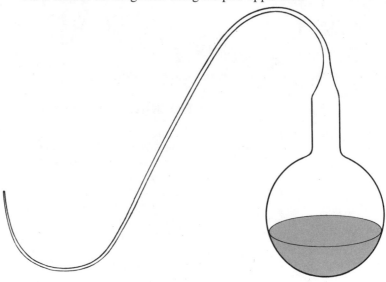

Figure 14.1 Pasteur's flask

1. Prepare four boiling tubes with nutrient broth, as shown in Figure 14.2.
2. Kill all the bacteria present in the broth by placing the tubes in a pressure cooker and boiling at a pressure of one atmosphere for 20 minutes.

   When Pasteur did his experiment, he boiled the broth vigorously for several minutes to kill the bacteria.
3. Leave the tubes aside, and observe any changes which take place in the broth over the next six weeks.

Explain the difference in the broths in the different tubes. Which tube corresponds to Pasteur's flask? Why have we used three additional tubes?

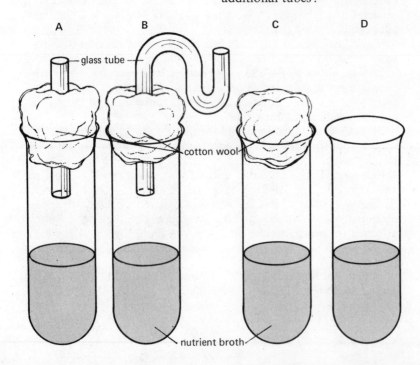

Figure 14.2 A version of Pasteur's experiment

14.2 Where are bacteria found?

The information about bacteria and rotting, which you have checked in this experiment, is used every day in the food industry. A very large sum of money is spent each year investigating aspects of bacterial action on food.

You have evidence from your previous work in Biology that bacteria exist in a number of places, including soil and milk. How widespread are bacteria? How many are there on the surfaces which we touch every day? To check the number of bacteria on a surface we must grow them on an agar plate, such as you prepared in the work of Chapter 2. In this way, one bacterium which we are unable to see will divide and multiply to form a colony which is visible.

1. Unroll a strip of adhesive tape 2 cm wide, and fold and cut as shown in Figure 14.3.

   Avoid contact with the sticky surface of the tape to ensure that it will remain sterile until it touches the surface to be investigated.

2. Handle the tape by holding the folded ends.

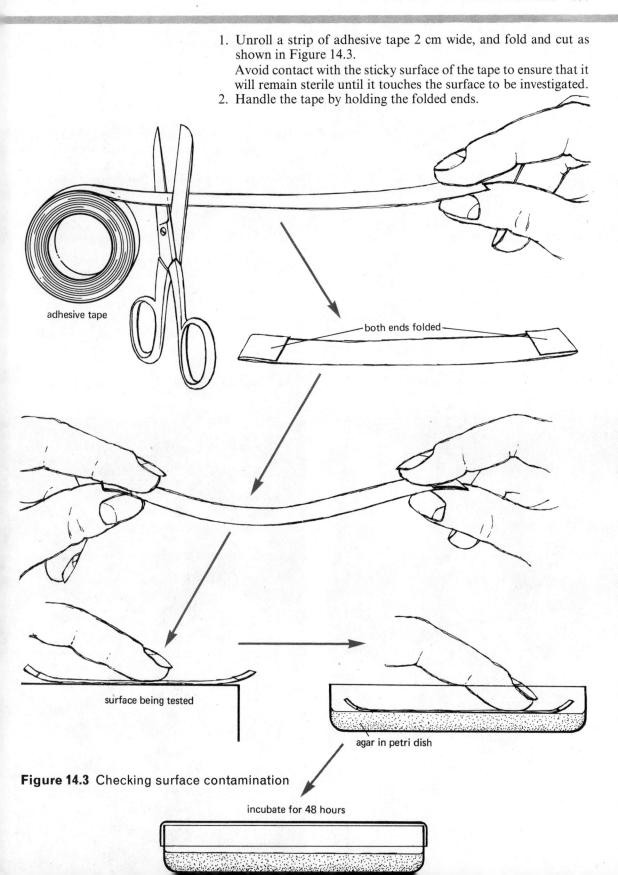

adhesive tape

both ends folded

surface being tested

agar in petri dish

Figure 14.3 Checking surface contamination

incubate for 48 hours

3. Press the sticky surface of the tape on to the surface to be investigated. Test any surface on which you think there will be bacteria. Likely places are your hands, desks, door handles and food containers.
4. Lift the tape from the surface and press it gently on to the surface of a sterile agar plate. Remove the tape from the agar.
5. Replace the lid of the petri dish and incubate for at least 48 hours at 35°C.
6. Bacteria from the tested surface will be transferred by the tape on to the plate, and each bacterium will form a visible colony after incubation.
7. Record the number of bacteria which you found in different places and consider the significance of the presence of these organisms in our everyday life.

Checks of this type are made every day in all large food factories. Large shops are also inspected from time to time. Instead of using adhesive tape, the Hygiene Officer uses a sterile, sausage-shaped block of agar, as in Figure 14.4(a). The end is cut from the sausage and the newly exposed agar is pressed on to the surface which is to be checked; in this case it is a bacon-slicing machine. Any bacteria on the machine stick to the agar as they did to your adhesive tape.

Figure 14.4(a) Checking a bacon slicer for bacteria

Figure 14.4(b) Bacterial colonies on the agar slices

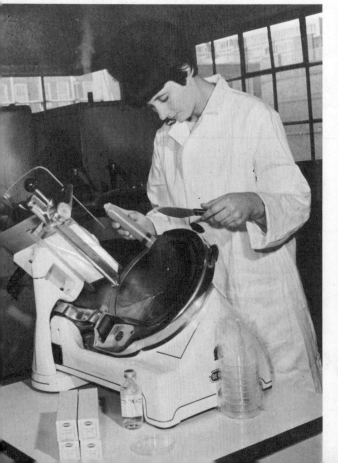

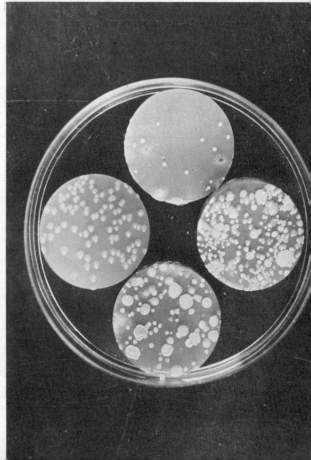

A slice from the end of the sausage is then cut off and placed in a petri dish. After incubation at 35°C for one or two days, colonies of bacteria in the agar indicate how many bacteria were present on the surface which was tested. Figure 14.4(b) shows incubated agar with bacterial colonies.

The widespread occurrence of bacteria means that special precautions must be taken to ensure that our food is not contaminated before it is eaten. Milk is heated to 73°C for 15 seconds to kill most of the bacteria present. This process is called **pasteurisation,** and is used for other materials, as you can see in Figure 14.8. Other ways in which bacteria are killed or prevented from spoiling our food are by boiling, by adding salt or sugar, by drying or by deep freezing. Good standards of personal hygiene are also important to make certain that pathogenic bacteria are not present on our hands or on food containers when we eat.

From your investigations, you will realise that all our surroundings are contaminated with bacteria. Luckily for us, most of these bacteria are harmless. If we take them into our bodies with our food they usually do us no harm, even if they survive the strongly acid conditions of the stomach.

14.3 Bacteria and disease

You found out earlier in the course that many bacteria are responsible for causing diseases in animals and plants. Bacteria obtain their food by digesting the organic material in which they live. If this material is the tissue of a larger organism, then the cells are damaged and the organism shows the symptom of the disease. As well as this direct effect on the cells, poisons produced by the bacteria spread round the body, affecting the general health of the host. What is the general name given to organisms that cause disease?

White blood corpuscles produce antibodies which react with the poisons or toxins produced by bacteria which have entered the body. Other organisms react in a similar way to the presence of bacteria, and produce antibodies which kill the bacteria and counteract toxic substances.

14.4 Antibiotics

Certain moulds can produce substances which kill or inhibit the growth of bacteria, and this is used in the commercial production of antibiotics. These substances are produced by the moulds, extracted, and then used to kill harmful bacteria inside our bodies. Study the account of the experiment described below, and answer the questions based on it to extend your knowledge and understanding of the interaction of fungi and bacteria.

Two agar plates were streaked with 6 types of bacteria, A, B, C, D, E and F. A mould was inoculated at the point X, on one of these plates, as shown in Figure 14.5. The mould alone was added to a third agar plate.

These plates were incubated at 35°C for 48 hours, and the Figure 14.5(b) shows the pattern of growth that developed.

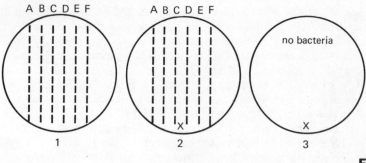

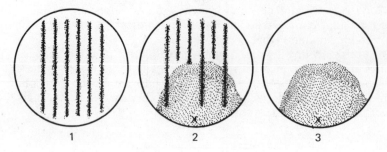

Figure 14.5*(a)* Inoculated plates

Figure 14.5*(b)* Plates after 48 hours

What evidence is there from this experiment for each of the following statements?
1. Moulds prevent the growth of bacteria.
2. The mould destroyed some of the bacteria.
3. Contact with the mould prevented the growth of bacteria.
4. The mould secreted something into the agar which prevented the growth of certain bacteria.
5. Moulds kill bacteria.

You have probably been able to answer each of these points, but no doubt you would prefer more evidence before you would agree with such sweeping statements about the effects of fungi on bacteria. You should try to investigate these relationships further, and to read about the development of this important branch of Biology.

14.5 Penicillin discovered

For centuries, moulds have been thought to have healing properties, and in ancient times, pads of moulds were often wrapped round wounds to aid healing. Most of these treatments made the wounds worse than if they had been left untreated. Why do you think this was so? Occasionally, however, the presence of the mould in the dressing did seem to heal the wound, although the reason for this was not understood.

The first scientific study of the effects of moulds on bacteria was carried out in 1928 by Alexander Fleming. He was investigating a bacterium called *Staphylococcus aureus* when he noticed the same sort of effect as shown in Figure 14.5. He decided that if the mould, in this case called *Penicillium notatum,* could affect some of the bacteria without apparently touching them, the mould probably secreted something into the agar. By careful and painstaking research, Fleming and his colleagues were able to produce an extract from the mould, and this had a marked effect on the growth of certain bacteria.

14.6 Penicillin in action

Although Fleming suggested that his extracts might have uses in the treatment of bacterial disease, the research was not continued until ten years later. In 1938, H. W. Florey and E. B. Chain working at Oxford began to investigate the use of antibacterial substances produced by living organisms, including the substance produced by *Penicillium*, and now given the name **penicillin.** At about the same time, the Second World War started, and this meant that, if a new drug with tremendous healing powers could be developed quickly, the country to possess it would be able to treat its wounded more effectively. An immense amount of money was expended on the research and development of antibiotics. In the United States of America, where most of the work then took place, the development of penicillin was considered the most important war project after that involving the production of the atom bomb. As a result of this research programme, penicillin was produced in large quantities in Britain and America and used extensively during the war, saving many lives and making almost harmless some diseases which had previously put servicemen out of action for a long time. Research has been continued since that time, and many different antibiotics are now in use, as you can see from Figure 14.6. Not all antibiotics are produced by moulds. Other soil micro-organisms sometimes produce useful antibacterial compounds.

Figure 14.6 Some of the antibiotics in a chemist's shop

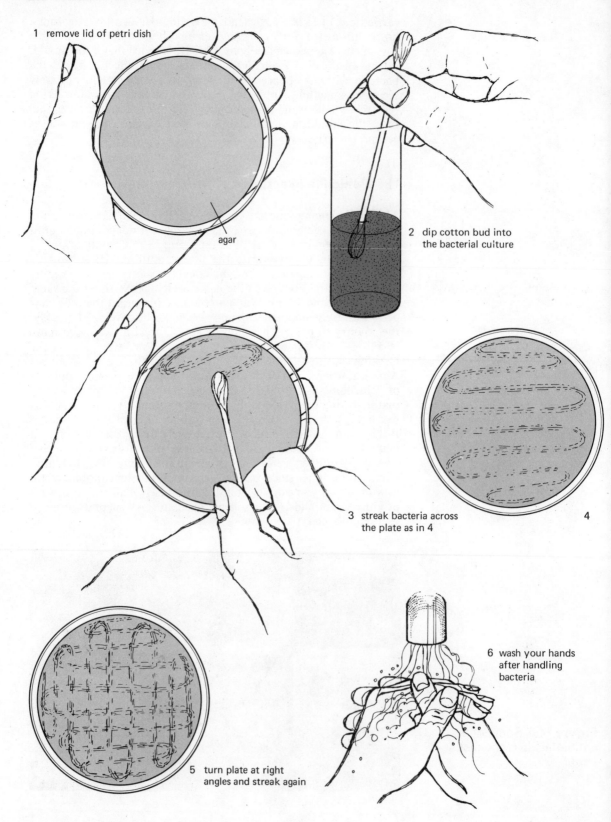

1 remove lid of petri dish

agar

2 dip cotton bud into
   the bacterial culture

3 streak bacteria across
   the plate as in 4

4

5 turn plate at right
   angles and streak again

6 wash your hands
   after handling
   bacteria

14.7 Bacteria versus antibiotics

Fleming investigated the effect of penicillin by using extracts which he had made himself from his moulds, but to carry out investigations we can now use discs of filter paper impregnated with penicillin and other antibiotics, at different strengths. Note that the concentration of antibiotic on the discs is given in terms of International Units (iu), or μg.

The agar plates for growing the bacteria have been prepared by adding a nutrient to agar and then allowing the medium to set in the petri dishes. Streak the agar as shown in Figure 14.7, to prepare 6 plates as follows:

(*a*) two plates with *Bacillus subtilis,* labelled A1 and A2,
(*b*) two plates with *Staphylococcus albus,* labelled B1 and B2,
(*c*) two plates with *Escherichia coli,* labelled C1 and C2.

To one of each pair, A1, B1 and C1, add a multodisc. Multodiscs have several different antibiotics impregnated in them. To each of the others, A2, B2 and C2, add the following four discs:

(i) penicillin 5 units, (ii) penicillin 10 units
(iii) streptomycin 10 μg, (iv) streptomycin 25 μg

Incubate the plates at 35°C for two days, and then record in a table, such as Table 14.1, the growth of the bacteria adjacent to each disc.

Table 14.1

	B. subtilis	*Staph. albus*	*E. coli*
Multodisc added	A1	B1	C1
5 units penicillin added	A2	B2	C2
10 units penicillin added			
10 μg streptomycin added			
25 μg streptomycin added			

You now have evidence of your own to add to that given in Figures 14.5(*a*) and 14.5(*b*), and you can consider similar questions to those asked at the beginning of the inquiry.

What evidence is there from your results that:
(i) antibiotics prevent the growth of bacteria?
(ii) some antibiotics destroy, or at least inhibit, the growth of some bacteria?

Figure 14.7 Instructions for streaking plates

(iii) only direct contact with moulds prevents the growth of bacteria?

Here are other questions which we can ask. Which bacteria were unaffected by all the antibiotics? Which antibiotics had the least effect on the bacteria? How does the strength of an antibiotic affect its action on a bacterium?

From your results, suggest why a range of antibiotics, as shown in Figure 14.6, is necessary in the treatment of human diseases.

14.8 A problem

Use the knowledge you now have about antibiotics to solve this problem. You are given unlabelled cultures of *Escherichia coli*, *Bacillus subtilis*, and *Staphylococcus albus*. Find out which is which by using the multodiscs and the impregnated small discs. Before doing this experiment you should think carefully about the way in which you will arrange the treatments.

When you are writing up the results of this work, explain why you carried out each step of the procedure.

14.9 Another problem

You are given a tube marked X which is a mixture of the above three bacteria. How could you use your knowledge of antibiotic effects to produce a pure strain of each of them? As in the first problem, the most important part of the report is the reason why you carried out each step of the experiment. Your answer must therefore include your reasons for each step of the experiment.

The second problem is very similar to one tackled by Fleming using his *Penicillium* extracts. He discovered that a bacterium called *Bacillus influenza* was insensitive to his extracts. This bacterium, despite its name, does not cause influenza, but it infects the back of the throat.

B. influenza had previously been very difficult to study because it was a problem to isolate a pure culture from a sample of sputum from the throat. The normal way to study disease organisms is to remove them from their habitat (in this case, the throat) and grow them in a petri dish. Each organism has to be separated from the others and grown separately before a detailed study can be carried out. *B. influenza* was very difficult to isolate until Fleming used penicillin. Only the *B. influenza* was able to grow in a medium containing penicillin, and it was thus isolated.

If you did not manage to solve the second problem, you should find that this summary of Fleming's work will give you a clue how to start.

14.10 Bread and cheese and beer

As well as using antibiotics from moulds and other organisms, man has made use of the activity of micro-organisms in a number of ways. Yeast is a fungus which man has used for centuries to produce alcohol and to make bread. Figures 14.8 and 14.9 show in summary the use of yeast in brewing and in baking.

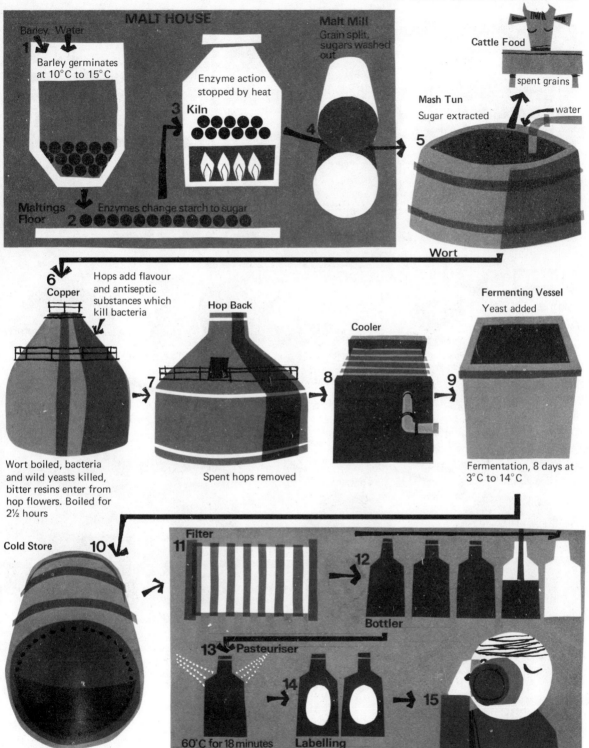

Figure 14.8 Brewing and bottling beer

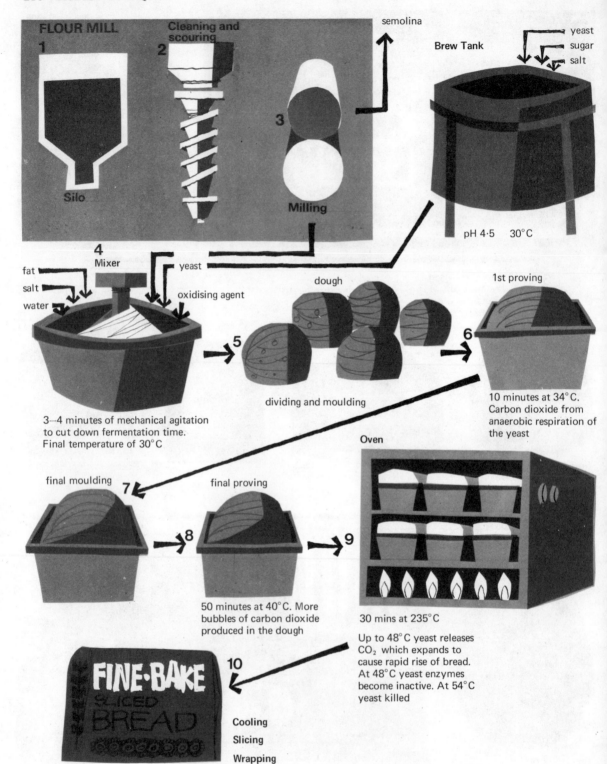

FLOUR MILL

1 Silo

2 Cleaning and scouring

3 Milling

semolina

Brew Tank

yeast
sugar
salt

pH 4·5   30°C

4 Mixer

fat
salt
water

yeast

oxidising agent

dough

5 dividing and moulding

6 1st proving

3—4 minutes of mechanical agitation to cut down fermentation time. Final temperature of 30°C

10 minutes at 34°C. Carbon dioxide from anaerobic respiration of the yeast

final moulding **7**

final proving

Oven

8

9

50 minutes at 40°C. More bubbles of carbon dioxide produced in the dough

30 mins at 235°C

Up to 48°C yeast releases CO_2 which expands to cause rapid rise of bread. At 48°C yeast enzymes become inactive. At 54°C yeast killed

FINE·BAKE SLICED BREAD

10

Cooling

Slicing

Wrapping

Figure 14.9 Baking bread

Cows

milk pasteurised
73°C for 15 sec

Yoghurt   Cheese

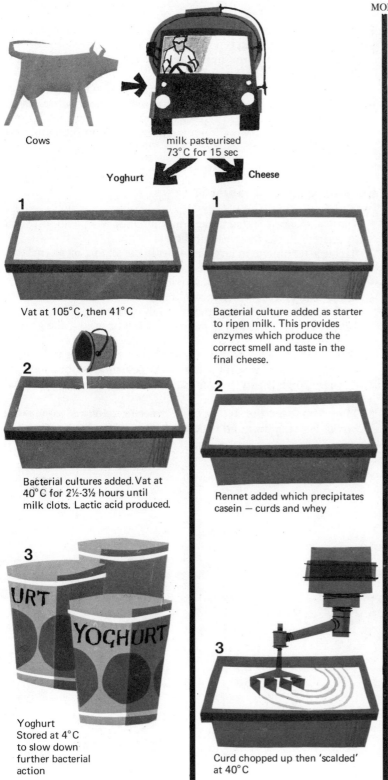

1

Vat at 105°C, then 41°C

2

Bacterial cultures added. Vat at
40°C for 2½-3½ hours until
milk clots. Lactic acid produced.

3

Yoghurt
Stored at 4°C
to slow down
further bacterial
action

1

Bacterial culture added as starter
to ripen milk. This provides
enzymes which produce the
correct smell and taste in the
final cheese.

2

Rennet added which precipitates
casein — curds and whey

3

Curd chopped up then 'scalded'
at 40°C

4

Whey run off, curds cut into blocks
and piled at one end of vat.

5

Blocks chopped up, salt added
to control bacterial growth

6

Salted curd, packed into
moulds and pressed

7

Ripening room at 10°C. Casein broken
down by bacterial action, and made
more digestible. Flavour develops.

Figure 14.10 Micro-organisms and milk

Find out more about baking and brewing. For example, are the same yeasts used in both types of process?

Figure 14.10 shows the importance of certain micro-organisms in the production of cheese and yoghurt.

In what ways are the biological principles which you have investigated earlier in the course involved in these processes of brewing, baking and cheese and yoghurt making? Consider enzyme action, bacterial contamination and anaerobic respiration amongst the topics involved.

Looking Back at Chapter 14

1. The significance of bacterial contamination was demonstrated by Pasteur in the nineteenth century.
2. Bacteria are present in large numbers in the air and on all surfaces that are not specially sterilised.
3. Precautions are taken to avoid bacterial contamination of food.
4. Many bacteria cause diseases, but many organisms produce antibodies in their tissues and thus kill bacteria.
5. Substances produced by some moulds kill or inhibit the growth of bacteria.
6. Fleming studied the antibacterial effect of extracts of the fungus *Penicillium*, from which the antibiotic penicillin is obtained.
7. A wide range of antibiotics is now used to combat bacterial diseases.
8. Man also uses the activities of micro-organisms in making bread, brewing beer and making cheese and yoghurt.

MORE ABOUT VARIATION

15.1 Variation

'They must be artificial; they are all the same size', said the young man in the restaurant. He was talking about the sea urchin 'shells' which were being used as lampshades, shown in Figure 15.1.

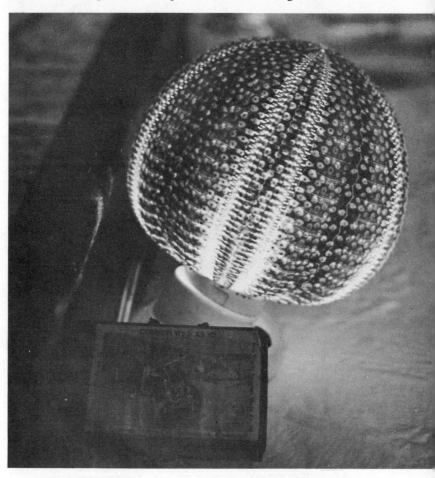

Figure 15.1 Sea urchin shell lampshade

Was he right? He was not, for they were real shells. Why did he think as he did? He realised that all living things, including sea urchins, vary from each other, and so someone must have taken a lot of trouble to find a number of shells which were all the same size.

This variation among organisms plays a very important part in

219

many human activities. How do the Olympic Games which were mentioned in Chapter 9 depend on human physical variation? How do flower, or agricultural shows, and horse racing depend on variation? The answer is, of course, that these and many other activities would not be possible if the individuals in the population of a species did not vary from each other. In earlier work you found that some of these variations were clear cut, and others showed a gradual change from one extreme of the feature to the other. Tongue rolling in humans is an example of a clear cut variation. You can either roll your tongue, or you cannot: on the other hand, the heights of a group of people show a wide variation from those who are very short to those who are very tall. Some groundsel plants have flower-heads with ray florets while others have not, and in this a clear cut difference is again noted. Are these differences **inherited**? In this chapter we are going to find out more about the causes of variation and about **heritable characteristics.**

15.2 Variation in fruit flies

We shall start by looking at variation in a fruit fly (*Drosophila*), an animal which has been used a great deal in investigating inheritance. What we shall do is to breed together flies which show certain characteristics and find if their offspring also have these characteristics. To give the results a more general significance, this should be done with several varieties of *Drosophila*.

Use a hand lens to examine the culture tubes of *Drosophila*, and look for differences between the flies in each tube. How do the flies differ from each other? Are the differences clear cut or graded? Take some flies from each tube and sort out males from females. Figure 15.2 shows the differences between the sexes. Put four

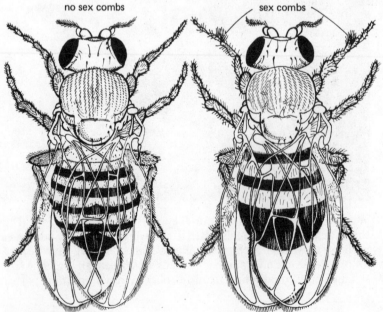

no sex combs

sex combs

Figure 15.2 Male and female *Drosophila*

abdomen pointed
dark bands separate along
entire abdomen
female

abdomen blunt
dark bands are merged together
at end of abdomen
male

females and two males of the same variety into each of several new culture tubes. The females will lay eggs which hatch into maggots, the larvae, in a few days and these larvae then change into pupae from which emerge the next generation of flies. Do these flies show the same variations as their parents?

To handle the flies it is necessary to anaesthetise them. Ether is used for this, and the technique is shown in Figure 15.3.

Figure 15.3 Anaesthetising flies

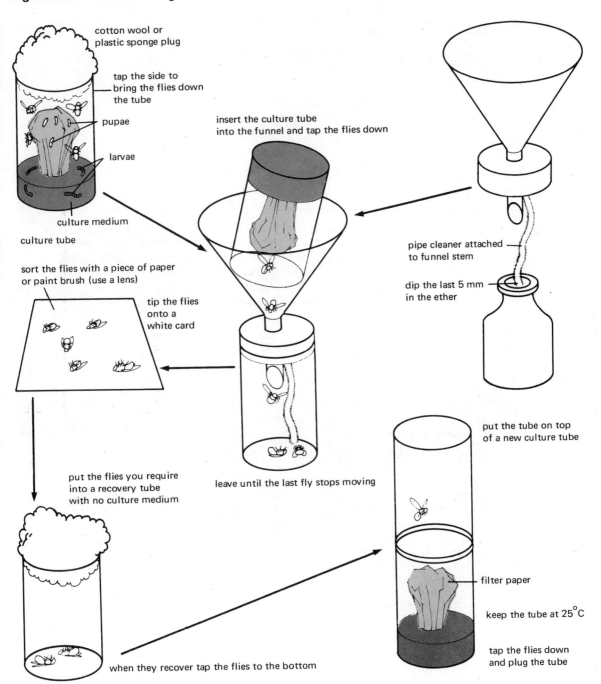

If flies start to revive while you are sorting them, use an emergency etheriser as in Figure 15.4. This is a glass petri dish lid with cotton

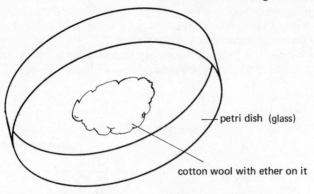

petri dish (glass)

cotton wool with ether on it

Figure 15.4 An emergency etheriser

wool glued to it. Ether is added to the cotton wool before use, and the lid can be put over the flies to anaesthetise them again.

Sometimes the culture medium becomes rather liquid and it may slip into the funnel. In this case, if there are not too many flies, a pooter can be used to catch them. See Figure 15.5.

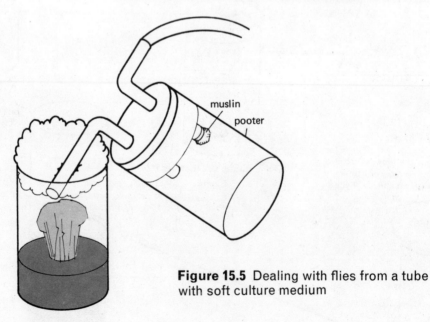

muslin

pooter

Figure 15.5 Dealing with flies from a tube with soft culture medium

You should carry out experiments, too, with plant material. What you are trying to find out is whether or not characteristics are passed from parent plants to their offspring. You can do this by collecting and growing seeds from plants which are of the same type, but which are different in some way. The plants which eventually grow must be examined to see if they have the same characteristics as the plants from which the seeds came. You may have tried this already with barley, earlier in the course. If you have found any groundsel plants with rayed florets you could use seed from them to find what sort of flowers develop on the plants which grow.

When you have done these experiments you should be able to decide whether the characteristics you have seen in the parent are also shown by the offspring of the organisms used. If they are, we can say that these characteristics are inherited.

15.3 Variation and the environment

Does anything else besides inheritance cause differences between individuals? If you compare the larvae of the fruit flies with the adults, there are clearly differences due to stage of development. (Someone who is two years older than you can probably run faster than you, and the effects of stage of development are again obvious. But perhaps another person could run faster than you because he or she had trained specially for the race, or perhaps had a better diet.) Someone who lives at 3 000 m all the time can play vigorous games at this height better than someone who normally lives at sea level, as you have found in the work of Chapter 9. It would seem that your surroundings and the conditions under which you live affect what you are like, and what you can do. Do your surroundings affect your behaviour? We can find out something about the way in which environment has an effect, by looking at specimens of *Drosophila* of a particular variety which have been cultured at different temperatures.

One variation in *Drosophila* is the characteristic 'bar-eye'. In flies with this characteristic only the 'eyes' in the middle of the compound eye are coloured; the rest are white, as shown in Figure 15.6.
This is a characteristic which is inherited. How could this be proved?
1. Look at the eyes of some anaesthetised bar-eyed flies which have been kept and reared at 25°C. Use the low power of the microscope with light reflected from the animal; shine the lamp on to the top of the slide rather than reflecting it upwards through the slide by the mirror. See Figure 15.7.
2. Count the number of 'eyes' which are coloured.
3. Record as many results as you can, and find the average number for the class.

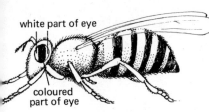

white part of eye

coloured part of eye

Figure 15.6 Bar-eyed *Drosophila*

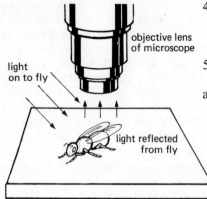

light
on to fly

objective lens
of microscope

light reflected
from fly

4. Now look at and count the number of coloured eyes in the compound eyes of flies which have been kept and reared at other temperatures (20°C and 30°C). Do the count again for as many flies as possible, and find average figures for each temperature.
5. Make tables and draw graphs of your results.

What effect does temperature have on the number of eyes that are coloured?

Figure 15.7 Using reflected light

In this experiment we have found that a feature of the environment in which the flies live, the temperature, has an effect on an inherited characteristic. This principle is also true of human beings. Several of you, because of your inherited characteristics, might be able to become first-class footballers or musicians. You will not, however, do this unless you learn and practise the game, or your musical instrument, a great deal. In other words, the characteristic does not develop in the same way if there are differences in the surroundings and in the way in which you use the characteristics.

You are more able than the fruit fly to control these surroundings. The difference in surroundings might be simply that you did not eat the right food. The surroundings of an individual organism have a great effect on the characteristics which it possesses. Does this happen also in plants? The following investigation will provide an answer to this question.

Grow in soil the two varieties of barley seed with which you are provided, watering as you are directed. Grow two lots of each variety of seed. One lot of each should be in darkness and one in the light.

Look at the plants when they have grown for 2 or 3 weeks and record the differences which you observe. Look for differences in height, colour, number and sizes of leaves. Record these in a table (Table 15.1). How can you explain the differences? Do both varieties respond to the different environments in the same way?

Table 15.1

Variety I		Variety II	
Light	Dark	Light	Dark

15.4 Breeding experiments

What will the offspring be like when two varieties of the same species of organism breed together? This question arises all the time, and we are beginning to see that although organisms can share characteristics, every individual is different from every other individual. For example, amongst six pupils with blue eyes, only three may be able to roll their tongues. Of these, only one may have a lobe on his ear, and so on. The shapes of noses are all different also. Hence we might ask the question, 'What types of noses will the children of a long-nosed father and a snub-nosed mother have?' This would take a long time to find out, from one generation to the next, so we shall use *Drosophila* again. You may also have some results of similar experiments which you have started some time ago, using mice.

Put four female *Drosophila* of one variety in a culture tube with four males of a second variety, or type. At the same time, set up another tube with four female flies of the second type with four males of the first type. Use the same methods for handling the flies as for the earlier *Drosophila* experiments. Once eggs have been laid and some larvae have hatched, remove the flies. This will be necessary after about four days. Then, after about twelve days, you will have a new generation of adults and you should obtain as many offspring as you can. Anaesthetise these flies and carefully count the number of each type which has emerged. Are there any intermediate types? Record your results in a table, similar to the one shown, Table 15.2.

Table 15.2

Parents	♀ Vestigial winged	♂ Normal winged	
F$_1$ Tubes	Normal	Vestigial	Intermediate
1.			
2.			
3.			
4.			
5.			
6.			
7.			
Class Total			

This generation of flies is called the **first filial generation,** and it is referred to as the **F$_1$ generation.**

The female flies we use in these experiments must be unmated, or virgin; this is because once a fly has mated, the sperms can be stored and can be used during the rest of its life, which is usually about six weeks. As we want the sperm to come from the males which are used in the experiment, you will be provided with virgin females which are collected from culture bottles within 8 hours of emerging. The flies will not have mated within this period.

You have now seen what happens in the F$_1$ generation, and so we shall breed the F$_1$ flies among themselves and find what happens in the **second filial generation** or **F$_2$.**

Collect four male F$_1$ flies and put them along with four F$_1$ female flies in a new culture tube, and await the emergence of the F$_2$ flies, removing the parents as before. Count the numbers of flies (F$_2$) of each type and make a table of results as before.

You can also try breeding experiments with plants. For example, grow dwarf and tall varieties of peas and breed them together. Figure 15.8 shows two pure breeding lines of pea plants. To cross-breed these varieties, pollen from one must be introduced on to the

Figure 15.8 Pea varieties

stigmas of the other, which is not allowed to produce pollen. To do this, these anthers must be cut out, and this must be done before the flower opens. By examining the anthers of different pea flower buds you can find the right stage which will be when the bud is at its largest, but before the anthers are burst open. Figure 15.9 shows the technique for crossing pea plants.

Collect together as many data as you can from the breeding experiments. This will mean collecting the results of the entire class. You may also have been breeding mice and so have results from these experiments too. Look at these results carefully. Is there anything similar about them? Try to explain what you have found out.

A class result of crosses between ebony-bodied and grey-bodied *Drosophila* gave an F_1, all of which had grey bodies; these, when bred together, gave a total of 1 280 grey-bodied flies and 422 ebony-bodied flies.

The first interesting thing is that none of the F_1 are intermediate in colour and that they are all grey-bodied. Secondly, these F_1 grey-bodied flies collectively are different from their parents in that when bred together they give some grey-bodied and some ebony-bodied flies. The total number of F_2 flies is 1 280 + 422 = 1 702 flies.

$$\frac{422}{1\,702} \text{ of them are ebony-bodied}$$

i.e. $\frac{1}{4{\cdot}04}$ of them are ebony-bodied

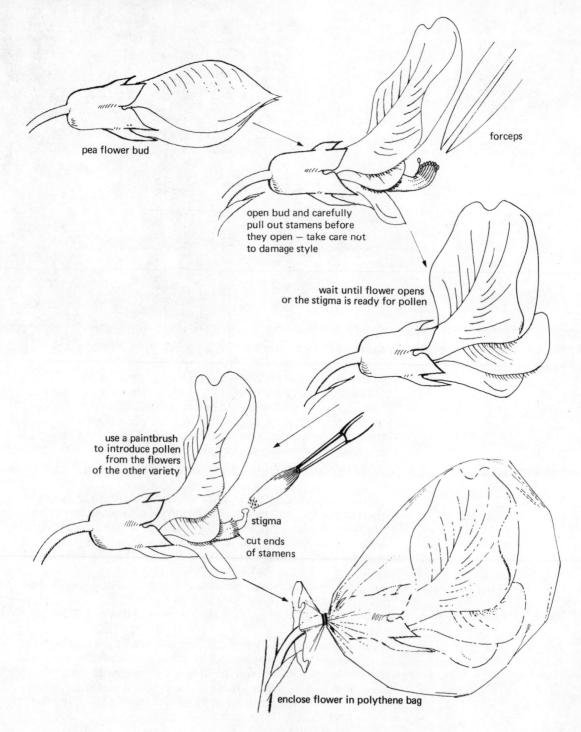

pea flower bud

forceps

open bud and carefully
pull out stamens before
they open — take care not
to damage style

wait until flower opens
or the stigma is ready for pollen

use a paintbrush
to introduce pollen
from the flowers
of the other variety

stigma

cut ends
of stamens

enclose flower in polythene bag

Figure 15.9 Crossing pea plants

It appears that about one-quarter of them are ebony-bodied. This is a ratio of three grey-bodied flies to one ebony-bodied fly in the F_2 generation. Are any of your results similar to these? If you have results of plant or mouse breeding experiments that are also giving a three to one ratio in the F_2 generation, this suggests that this ratio may be significant, since it has occurred for more than one type of organism.

We have to explain the following observations.

(a) All the F_1 generation have the characteristics of one type of parent.

(b) Flies with the characteristics of the other type of parent appear again in the F_2 generation.

(c) In the F_2 generation one-quarter of the individuals are of the type that did not appear in the F_1 generation.

We might first ask if the grey F_1 flies are exactly the same as the grey parents. They have the same appearance. The appearance of an individual characteristic is called its **phenotype**; for example, the ebony-bodied flies have an ebony-bodied phenotype. The F_1 generation flies and their grey parents have the same phenotype, but are they the same? The F_1 generation flies have one grey parent and one ebony parent. The grey parent flies had parents which were both grey: they were from a pure breeding line.

Suppose that the pure-breeding grey flies produced eggs or sperms which we call B, and that the ebony flies produce eggs or sperms which we call b. Then the F_1 generation flies could be called Bb, as they are formed by the fertilisation of B eggs by b sperm. A pure breeding grey fly would be BB and a pure breeding ebony fly bb.

When pure breeding flies are crossed amongst themselves the schemes would be as follows.

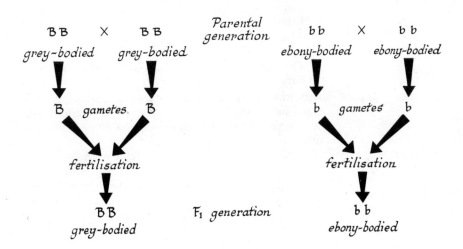

However, when different types are crossed, we would have a scheme like that shown on the next page:

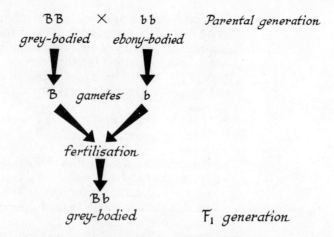

The F$_1$ generation would be called Bb.
Now what happens when the F$_1$ organisms produce gametes?
Perhaps they can produce both types of gametes. A model will help you to understand this idea better.

1. Make up pairs of poppet beads in which one of each pair is one colour and the other a different colour. One colour of bead represents the factor 'B' and the other, the factor 'b'. The pairs are Bb, and represent the F$_1$ generation of flies.
2. Put not less than 40 pairs into each of two containers. These pairs of beads represent males in one container and females in the other.
3. Separate the members of each pair from each other. You have now formed 'eggs' in one container and 'sperms' in the other.
4. Take 'sperms' from one container and join them to 'eggs' from the other. You must select the beads at random without looking at the colours.
5. The pairs you have now obtained represent the F$_2$ generation. How many different types do you have?

Record your results and the results of other groups in the class. Combine all the results. What numbers of different types of fly do you have? Remember that one colour of bead was 'B' and the other 'b'.

In this experiment we have made the following four assumptions.
(a) Only one of the factors of a pair is present in a gamete. Pairs of contrasted factors like this are called **allelomorphs.**
(b) These allelomorphs retain their identity and do not blend with each other.
(c) A fly carrying both of these allelomorphs produces two types of sperms or eggs in equal quantities.
(d) Sperm of either type have an equal chance of meeting eggs of either type.

Now you must consider if these assumptions were justified. To help us to decide, we can sum up our ideas in a scheme, and we shall introduce the units within the gametes which are responsible for producing characteristics in the organism. They are called **genes**.

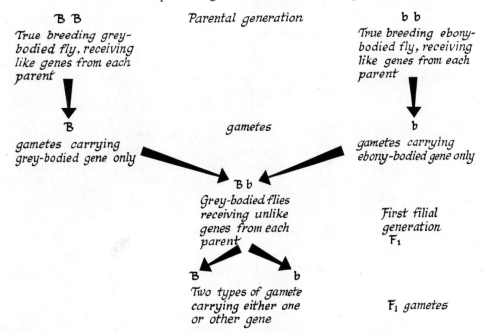

B B

True breeding grey-bodied fly, receiving like genes from each parent

Parental generation

b b

True breeding ebony-bodied fly, receiving like genes from each parent

B

gametes carrying grey-bodied gene only

gametes

b

gametes carrying ebony-bodied gene only

B b
Grey-bodied flies receiving unlike genes from each parent

First filial generation
F_1

B   b
Two types of gamete carrying either one or other gene

F_1 *gametes*

The mating of the two types of sperms and eggs can be shown on a chequer board, where sperms of both types have an equal

SPERMS

		B	b
E G G S	B	BB grey-bodied	Bb grey-bodied
	b	Bb grey-bodied	bb ebony-bodied

chance of meeting either type of egg. The phenotypes of the F_2 generation are written into this chequer board.

This scheme results in three grey-bodied flies for every one ebony-bodied fly in the F_2 generation. It thus explains the facts we set out to investigate.

Before accepting this explanation there are two things you should consider.
1. Why it was that your results did not give exactly the ratio $3:1$ in the F_2 generation.
2. Consider experiments to test the ideas put forward here. For example, what would happen if you crossed the F_1 grey-bodied flies with ebony-bodied flies? You can predict from the theory what results you would expect, and then try the cross.

The **BB** and **Bb** flies have the same phenotype, but different **genotypes** or genetical constitutions. With genotype Bb, the phenotype is grey-bodied and the grey-body gene is said to be the **dominant** allelomorph of the pair.

Sometimes neither of the allelomorphs is dominant; for example, when a red Shorthorn bull was crossed with a white Shorthorn cow, all the calves were roan coloured. A roan bull crossed with a roan cow gave ten calves over ten years, six were roan, three were red and one was white. Analyse and explain these figures, using the theory we have developed.

In the arguments in this section, our schemes have involved the production of various types of gamete. Gametes are formed as the result of cell division. What happens to the chromosomes at the cell divisions which give rise to gametes? What parallels are there between the process of meiosis, in which chromosome number in the cells is halved, and in the distribution of genes between parent and gametes?

15.5 Cross fertilisation

The only contribution from a male animal to the new organism is a sperm. You may remember that many sperm consist almost entirely of a nucleus with a small amount of surrounding cytoplasm in the tail. The characteristics which are contributed by the male must be carried by the sperm, and in the same way the egg carries the characteristics of the female. In the majority of animals the sexes are separate, and the offspring show some of the characteristics of the mother and some of the father.

Some animals, such as the earthworm, have both testes and ovaries in the same individual. In these cases, the animals still mate with others, and sperm from one individual fertilises the eggs of another. What is the significance of this cross-fertilisation? Find out other examples of animals which have both sexes in the same individual. How is cross-fertilisation achieved in these organisms?

In flowering plants it is quite normal to have both sexes on the same individual. Most flowers have anthers, which produce pollen grains containing the male nucleus, and they also have ovules, which contain the egg cell. Does pollen fertilise the ovule of the same flower? If so, this is called self-fertilisation. Does cross-fertilisation take place?

Enclose flower buds of different plants separately in small plastic bags so that pollen cannot reach these flowers from outside. Peas, beans and antirrhinums would all be suitable for this investigation. Observe these flowers as they grow older, and, as seeds and fruits develop, make a table to record how many of the flowers produce seeds. If they produce seeds, fertilisation must have taken place, using the pollen grains of the same flower.

Do all the flowers of one species give the same results? Do different types of flowers give different results?

You will have obtained a variety of results from this experiment. How do you think the pollen is transported when cross-fertilisation occurs? Earlier in the course, wind and insects were suggested as agents of pollen transfer. If you look carefully at conspicuous flowers like foxgloves, buttercups or antirrhinums, you will often find insects in or on them.

Watch insects visiting flowers of various kinds, and make notes of what you observe. A list of the sort of questions you should try to answer is given below.

1. What kind of insects visit particular flowers? While keys will help you to identify the insects, the important thing is to be able to recognise the type of insects involved rather than to name each kind.
2. Do the insects visit only one type of flower?
3. Do they visit more than one flower of the same type? If so, do they visit flowers on different plants?
4. Is there any connection between the colour of the flowers and the insects which visit them?
5. Do the insects collect pollen? Do they collect anything else from the flowers? A hand lens will help you to see pollen on insects, but you will have to anaesthetise the insects to make these observations.
6. Do the insects have any special structures for collecting the pollen?
7. Is the shape of the flower related to the type of insect which visits it?
8. What happens when an insect visits a flower such as that of broom?

Try to design a table in which all the information gathered by the whole class can be recorded.

What general conclusions can you draw?

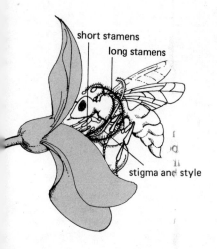

Figure 15.10 Broom flower being visited by a bee

short stamens
long stamens
stigma and style

It seems clear that insects do carry pollen from flower to flower and that the structure of the flowers is often related to the structure of the insects; for example, the broom flower shown in Figure 15.10 is especially suited for the visits of bees. Perhaps the most astonishing example of a pollination method is what happens in the plant, *Yucca*. The moth which pollinates this flower visits a number of flowers and collects a ball of pollen. It then lays its own eggs in the ovary of the flower and puts the pollen on the stigma. The ovules are fertilised and then the larvae feed on the developing seeds. However, some seeds do survive. The interesting thing is that neither the plant nor the insect could continue to exist without the other. What kind of symbiotic association is this?

In your investigation you have probably come across less conspicuous flowers. These are not visited often by insects, and their pollen does not stick to those that do alight on them. Could it be that these flowers have their pollen transported by the wind?

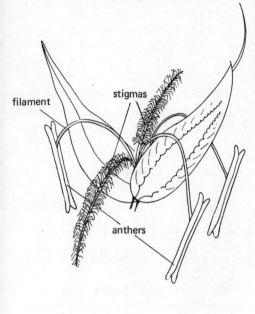

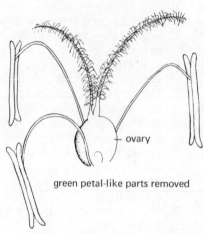

Figure 15.11 A grass flower

Make a full investigation of the structure of a flower of a grass or of a plantain. Look at the petals, anthers, pollen grains and stigmas and describe them. What features suggest that pollen is carried from flower to flower by the wind?

Either as a class or individually, look at more than one type of flower, and try to tabulate your results. Figure 15.11 shows an example of a flower of this sort.

15.6 Reproduction of a fungus

The mechanisms involved in reproduction in grass and broom plants are seen to be complicated. What happens when simple plants such as fungi reproduce? Let us grow some and see. We shall culture a fungus in patches which grow towards each other, and observe what happens when they meet.

You are provided with two strains of the fungus *Mucor*. This fungus will grow on potato dextrose agar medium. Using a sterilised wire loop, inoculate some of one strain of the fungus on one side of a petri dish containing the agar and then place some of the other strain on the opposite side of the dish. On another dish, use the same technique to put some of the same strain on both sides of the dish. On a third dish repeat this with the second strain. Figure 15.12 illustrates the technique.

Incubate the dishes at 25°C. Some of the material which has grown together can be transferred to a microscope slide and mounted in water. With a microscope, examine what happens at the point where the fungal colonies meet.

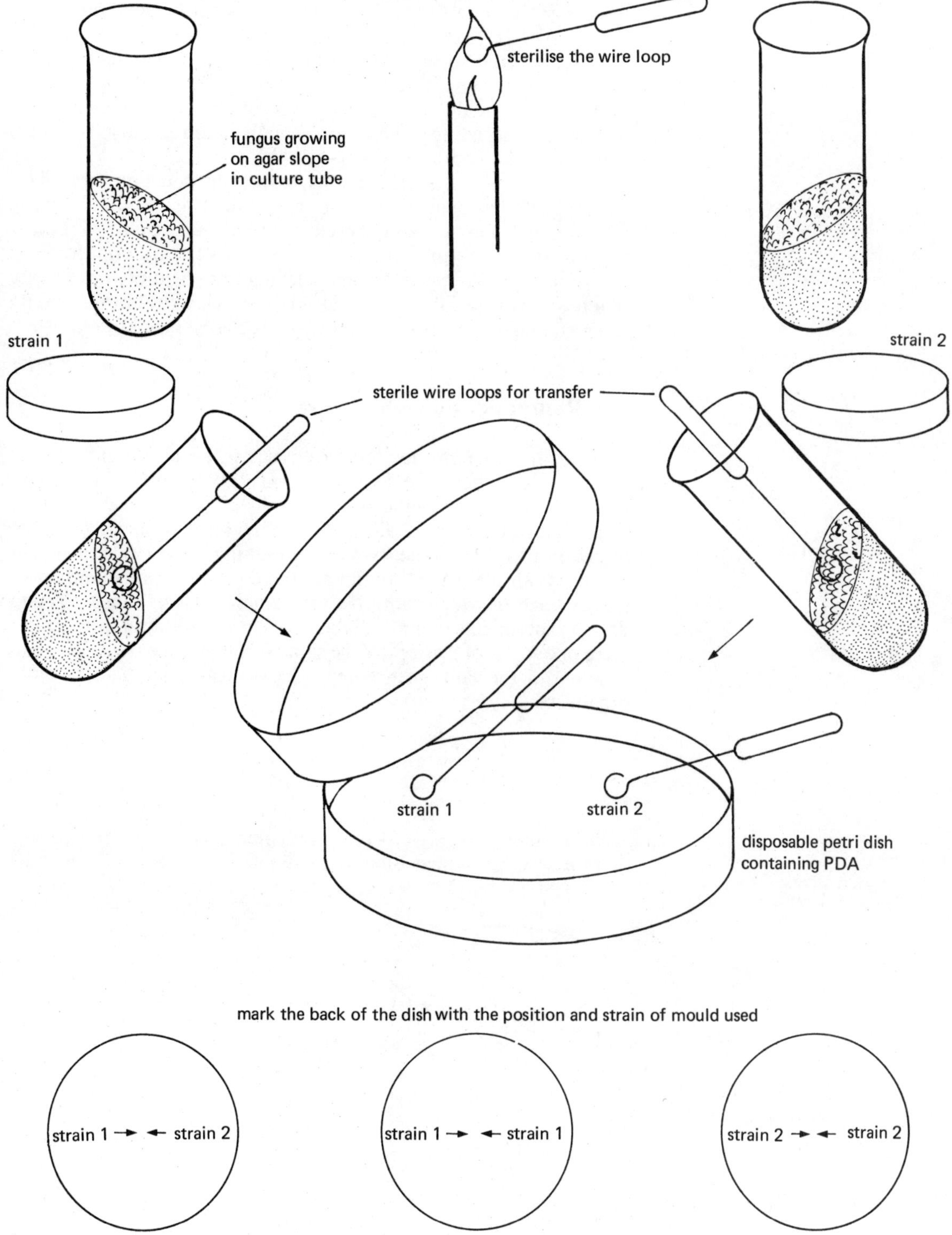

Figure 15.12 Crossing
Mucor strains

What evidence is there that reproduction has taken place between the two strains? Does reproduction take place between colonies of the same strain?

sterilise the wire loop

fungus growing
on agar slope
in culture tube

strain 1

strain 2

sterile wire loops for transfer

strain 1   strain 2

disposable petri dish
containing PDA

mark the back of the dish with the position and strain of mould used

strain 1 → ← strain 2   strain 1 → ← strain 1   strain 2 → ← strain 2

Have you any evidence of the nuclei of two cells fusing together? Have you seen any nuclei in the fungus? Certainly you will not have seen any sperms or eggs, but material from two individuals has fused together and this will be followed by the production of new individuals. It seems reasonable to call this fusion of material fertilisation, and to say that sexual reproduction has taken place. The two strains could be called male and female, but they do not show any visible differences from each other even when examined under the microscope. They are usually referred to as + (plus) and − (minus) strains of *Mucor*.

In *Mucor* and in flowering plants, sexual reproduction takes place between different individuals. The structure of the flowers ensuring that this will happen and the existence of two strains of *Mucor* suggest that it is important for this cross-fertilisation between individuals to take place. From breeding investigations we can see that the more often cross-fertilisation takes place, the more variation there will tend to be between individuals of one type of organism.

15.7 Reproduction without sex

Does a form of reproduction take place in which the individuals produced are the same as the parents? We have already seen evidence of this in simple organisms like *Pleurococcus*, bacteria, and yeast. In these cases, all the new individuals are exactly like the original individual. When you were looking at *Mucor* you would see spore capsules called sporangia; these produce large numbers of spores, each of which can grow into a new mass of *Mucor*. Try to design experiments to find whether the *Mucor* produced from spores from one strain of *Mucor* are the same strain as the parent. We shall now find if the same sort of reproduction can take place in other organisms.

Place a single duckweed plant on some pond water in a beaker or in a large specimen tube as in Figure 15.13. Keep it near the

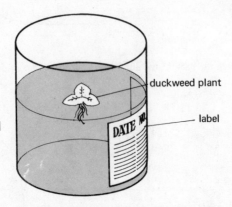

Figure 15.13 Growing duckweed

window or in the greenhouse so that it is well illuminated. Why should you do this? Keep records of the growth of the duckweed and of the numbers of duckweed plants. You can keep the daily records on a label on the side of the container and transfer them to a book later. Are any new plants formed? Are they like the original plant?

Figure 15.14 A *Bryophyllum* plant. Insert shows details of a plantlet

Look at a *Bryophyllum* plant, like the one shown in Figure 15.14. What signs of reproduction does it show? Take off some of the plantlets and grow them in separate pots of soil. How have they been produced? Are they the same as the parent plant?

A number of plants are able to produce new ones in this 'one parent only' way. There is no joining of cells such as we have seen occur in sexual reproduction. In this **asexual** reproduction some part of an organism grows to form a new individual. The new organism is exactly like the parent, for it has been formed from the cells of one parent only. Make a list of examples of plants which reproduce vegetatively.

We can now ask the question, does asexual reproduction also occur in animals?

Set up a small aquarium. A beaker with pond water and a piece of water weed is quite satisfactory. Put one *Hydra* in your aquarium, and watch it carefully over a period of about three weeks. Add water fleas to provide food for the animal from time to time. Record your observations, and observations on the main culture of *Hydra* that may be kept in your school. You have probably watched *Hydra* previously, when looking at a pond or at an aquarium tank. Is there any evidence of asexual reproduction? What other examples of asexual reproduction in animals can you think of?

Many organisms can reproduce asexually, and in this type of reproduction the offspring are the same as the parent organism. This fact can be very useful to us if we want to maintain a particularly useful variety of flowering plant, or strain of yeast. For example, if by careful breeding a special type of chrysanthemum has been produced, cuttings can be taken from it and planted in soil. These cuttings are exactly the same as the parent plant, and they will produce flowers of the same colour and characteristics. Why might the seeds of this plant not produce flowers of the same colour? In this case we have propagated the plant by artificial cultivation. In maintaining a potato variety we can simply grow new plants from the potato tubers produced by the plants of the variety we want. Why would growing seeds from the flowers of these plants not be satisfactory?

Another way of using asexual reproduction to maintain the variety must be adopted in cases in which cuttings do not grow well and in which there is no natural method of multiplying in this way. This can often be done by grafting twigs from the plant which you

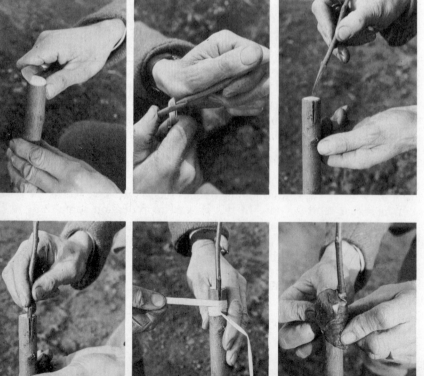

Figure 15.15 A grafting technique

Figure 15.16 Nettles

want to increase in numbers, on to the already well-established stems of other plants which are of the same type but which are of different varieties. If the graft is successful, the twig grows on the existing tree, but this new part of the plant keeps its own characteristics. This grafting technique is used a great deal in the wine industry in maintaining special varieties of grapes. Apple, cherry, and pear and rose varieties are maintained and propagated in the same way. Figure 15.15 shows a method of grafting.

What, if any, are the advantages in reproducing asexually? Usually this form of reproduction is rapid, and it forms a method of fast colonisation of a suitable environment. An example of this is shown in Figure 15.16. How do you think such a clump of nettles has been produced? Did a lot of seeds grow, or has asexual reproduction taken place? Dig up some nettle plants and find the answer.

Many plants occur in clumps like this which have been produced by rapid asexual reproduction. Do you think they have an advantage over plants without this ability? What are the possible disadvantages of this form of reproduction?

Looking Back at Chapter 15

1. Organisms of the same species vary: some variations are clear cut while others are not.
2. Varieties of organisms often breed true. Hereditary characteristics are transmitted from generation to generation.
3. Variation among organisms may be influenced by environmental factors.
4. Breeding experiments between different varieties reveal a regular pattern of inheritance which can be explained by a theory of 'factors'. These factors do not blend, but separate during the production of gametes and then come together at fertilisation.
5. Organisms reproduce sexually, usually by a mechanism involving cross-fertilisation. The occurrence of variation is enhanced as a result of sexual reproduction.
6. Asexual reproduction also takes place in some organisms. In such cases, the offspring are exactly the same as the parent.

16 MAKING USE OF VARIATION

16.1 Classifying living things

When we use reference books and keys to identify organisms, we find that the differences between organisms are used to sort them out and to classify them. To find out more about how classification is done, we shall look at some of the animals found in soil and litter.

Collect as many animals as you can from the following habitats.
(*a*) under stones
(*b*) amongst litter, leaves, twigs, on the surface of the soil
(*c*) the soil itself

You will need a pooter to collect some of the animals, but for others in the soil you will need special methods. You may have ideas of your own which you can try, but some suggestions are given here.

1. A jam jar or bottle buried in the soil, as in Figure 16.1, will catch animals which move about amongst the litter and on the surface of the soil. A cover of some sort, supported on sticks or pebbles, prevents rain entering the jar. If a lot of water does get into the jar, the animals can easily be filtered off.

Figure 16.1 A jam jar trap

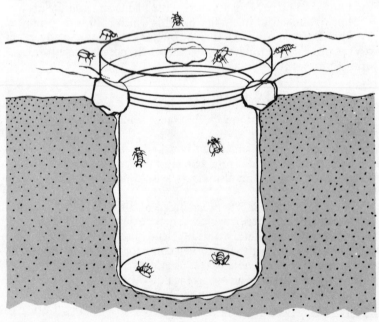

2. One method of extracting animals from soil depends on the fact that many soil animals move away from light, and from dry places, and are sensitive to temperature changes. A Tullgren funnel is designed so that soil or leaf litter gradually dries out, and is warmer on one side than the other. The animals move away from the hotter part, which is also the driest, and eventually out of the soil into a collecting device. Two designs are shown here in Figures 16.2 and 16.3, one made out of a roll of stiff paper and the other from a one-gallon can. In both cases a lamp provides the source of heat. Leave the apparatus set up for several hours and then sort out the animals you have collected.

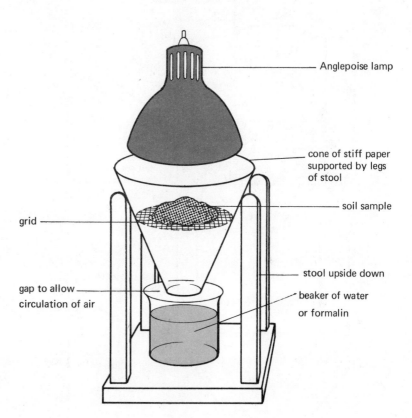

Figure 16.2 A Tullgren funnel

Anglepoise lamp

cone of stiff paper supported by legs of stool

soil sample

grid

stool upside down

gap to allow circulation of air

beaker of water or formalin

3. Some of the animals may not be able to move in dried-out soil, as they may be living in the soil water and be semi-aquatic organisms. To extract these, a Baermann funnel can be used. In its simplest form, a sample of soil, or litter, is hung in water in a large funnel warmed by an electric lamp. See Figure 16.4. There will again be a temperature gradient in the funnel, and the animals move out of the bag of soil and into the stem of the funnel. The clip can be opened periodically and some of the water containing the animals run into a beaker.

Sort out the animals you have collected into groups, or sets, which are similar. All the members of a set should have at least one characteristic in common. Within each set you will have smaller sub-sets and your smallest sub-sets will consist of animals which are all of the same type.

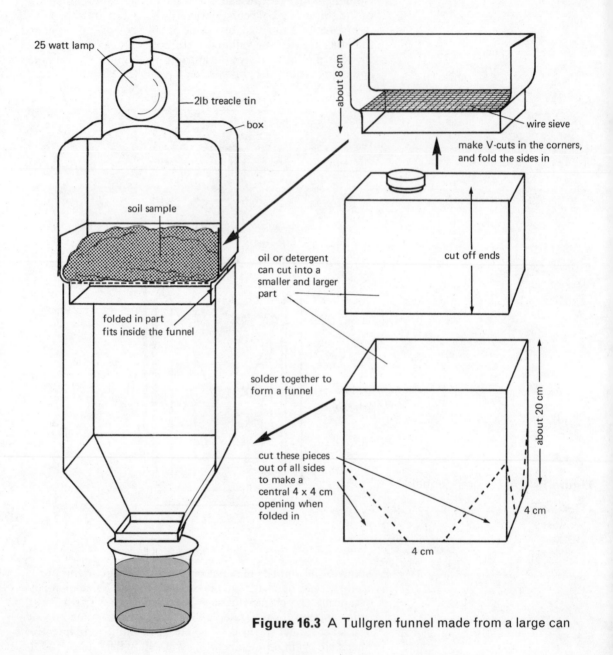

25 watt lamp

2lb treacle tin

box

soil sample

folded in part fits inside the funnel

about 8 cm

wire sieve

make V-cuts in the corners, and fold the sides in

cut off ends

oil or detergent can cut into a smaller and larger part

solder together to form a funnel

about 20 cm

cut these pieces out of all sides to make a central 4 x 4 cm opening when folded in

4 cm

4 cm

Figure 16.3 A Tullgren funnel made from a large can

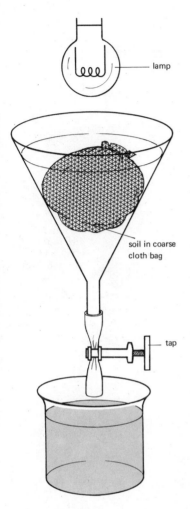

Figure 16.4 A Baermann funnel

Sorting out of pupils has already been done in your school. You are a member of a group of people in your class and all are probably about the same age. There may be four or five other classes in your year group, and there are other classes in other year groups. Thus, the whole school is divided into groups which can be divided into smaller groups. You are using 'pigeon-holed' classifications like this all the time. For example, when you watch traffic, you automatically classify it into buses, lorries and cars, and the cars into different makes. Amongst the makes of car there are different models and amongst the models, different kinds which have slightly different bodies or engines. It is convenient to have names for them all. Below is a classification of Ford Cortina cars made in 1968. Think how complicated it becomes when we add to this scheme cars of different models from this and other years, and how impossible it would be for buyers, salesmen and manufacturers if they were not classified.

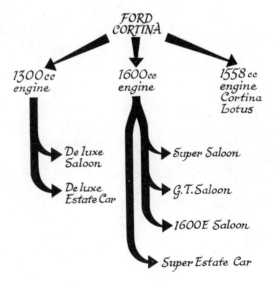

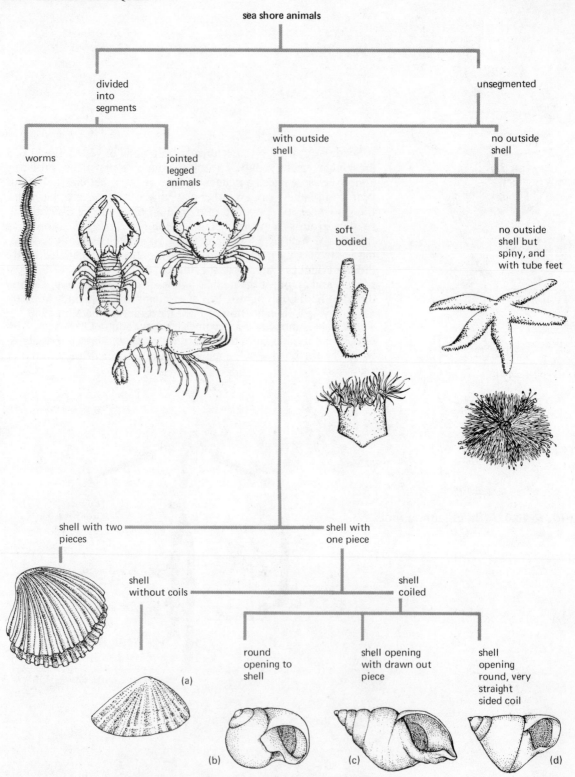

sea shore animals

divided into segments

unsegmented

worms

jointed legged animals

with outside shell

no outside shell

soft bodied

no outside shell but spiny, and with tube feet

shell with two pieces

shell with one piece

shell without coils

shell coiled

round opening to shell

shell opening with drawn out piece

shell opening round, very straight sided coil

(a)

(b)

(c)

(d)

Figure 16.5 A classification of some animals from the sea shore

The scheme in Figure 16.5 shows the possible classification of a collection of animals from the sea shore.

Imagine the unsorted collection of animals. Some of them have hard outer coverings, and it would be possible to divide the animals into hard and soft sets. This would put the crabs with the whelks and the anemones with the worms. It is still possible to separate these groups in the next part of the sorting out.

Instead, they have been sorted out firstly on the basis of whether their bodies are divided into segments or not. This has put the worms with the prawns and the lobsters. All the groups could be subdivided further, but in this scheme only the group with the outside shells and no segments has been divided further. Consider how you would have grouped these organisms and decide how you would further divide the groups.

The car classification we have used is a **natural classification.** The different models are related to each other in that they come from the same factory or production line, or one type may have been developed from another. In a natural classification, the members in each group are related to each other. Do you think any of the groups into which you have placed your organisms are natural groups? Amongst the sea shore groups there are several natural groups; for example, all the **Echinoderms** are animals which have numerous tube feet, which are small projections that can be extended and moved about, and which usually have suckers on them. It seems likely that all these animals have come from a common ancestor, and that the group is a natural one. However, in classifying living things and in drawing up keys, we place organisms into convenient groups such as has been done, for example, in the endpapers of this book. It is important to realise that this may result in an **artificial classification,** in which the members of each group are not related to each other.

We shall look at this problem in more detail in two or three very similar types of organisms.

Look carefully at the plants or animals which you have been given. Record in a table any differences and similarities they might have. You will find it easier if you look at the features in a definite order; for example, for the plants, examine the roots, then stems, leaves, flower arrangement and numbers, the structure of an individual flower, fruits and any other special features.

Would you classify these plants in one group? How would you distinguish between the different types? What difficulties have you come across in doing this work?

We can see some of the difficulties in classification by looking at three types of periwinkles. On the sea shore several types occur, three of which are shown in Figure 16.6. Look at Table 16.1 which shows the differences, including the distribution, of these animals on the shore.

Littorina littoralis

Figure 16.6 Three species of periwinkles

Littorina littorea   Littorina saxatilis

Table 16.1

	Shell size	Shell shape	Nature of shell	Colour	Dis-tribution
Common periwinkle	1–3 cm	pointed high spire	sculptured heavy shell	grey-black	middle and lower shore
Flat periwinkle	less than 1·5 cm	flat-topped no pointed spire	surface smooth with fine sculp-turing	very variable, red, black, yellow, brown	middle and top of lower shore
Rough periwinkle	0·5–1·5 cm	curve of shell aper-ture meets spire at right angles	surface rough some-times ribbed	very variable, red to black	upper and top of middle shore

Observations on the periwinkles show differences in their behaviour, the sort of eggs which they lay, and the type of micro-habitat in which they are found.

It becomes clear that these three types of periwinkles, though similar in general structure, and though the individuals of each type differ from each other, do form distinct populations on the shore. A 'type' of organism like this which forms a distinct population, the members of which interbreed freely, is what we call a **species** of organism. A species is given two names, the first of which refers to a group of similar species and the second only to the particular species. These are always Latin names. Why is it a good idea to use Latin names?

The three periwinkle species are given the following names.

Littorina littorea—the common periwinkle

Littorina littoralis—the flat periwinkle

Littorina saxatilis—the rough periwinkle

This way of naming things was established by a Swedish biologist called Carl Linnaeus in a book called *Systema Naturae* in 1758. He classified a large number of organisms, and his scheme is still the basis of modern classification.

The group of similar species is called a **genus,** and the name of the genus is always given a capital letter. The second, or specific, name is given a small letter. Sometimes populations are found which are only slightly different: for example, the Shetland wren is called *Troglodytes troglodytes zetlandicus* and the mainland wren is called *Troglodytes troglodytes troglodytes*. The sub-species is referred to by the third name. A sub-species is a population of organisms within a species which is not thought to be sufficiently different to be called a separate species. If you discovered a new species or a sub-species, it might be named after you.

Genera (plural of genus) are gathered into families, and the families into orders; orders into classes, and classes into large groups called Phyla (singular, Phylum).

You belong to the species *Homo sapiens*. Table 16.2 shows how man fits into the classification scheme.

Table 16.2

Grouping	Latin Name	Other Members of the Group
Species	sapiens	Modern Man
Genus	Homo	Other types of man
Family	Hominidae	Man-like apes
Order	Primates	Apes, monkeys, lemurs, man
Class	Mammalia	All hairy animals, warm-blooded, and suckling their young
Phylum	Chordata	All animals which have back-bones (and a few without)

In making classifications it is important to remember that the divisions into sets such as orders and classes are artificial and convenient. We are making use of the variation between species to be able to distinguish between them and to classify them. The main difficulty in doing this is that the individuals of a species vary from each other, as well as from the individuals of other species. If we think of a species as a population of organisms that interbreeds freely to produce fertile offspring, then classification at this level becomes easier.

16.2 Plant and animal breeding

One of the striking features of many domestic animals and plant species is the great variation within them. Cows, sheep, cats and dogs show this very well amongst animal species, and practically every cultivated plant also shows it. How do you think the great variety of roses has come about?

In earlier work you grew a crop of barley, and you should have selected the seeds from the different types of plant and grown plants from them. By selecting seed from the plants with certain special features, and by growing them and selecting seeds from the next generation of plants, it is sometimes possible to produce plants with the particular characteristics which are the ones you want. For instance, if we continually select seed from the plants with the shortest stems, we might eventually produce seed which gives only short-stemmed plants. Why could this idea be incorrect? Man started selecting seed in this way, and thus changed the characteristics of his crop plants from the time he started growing them.

Another possibility is to deliberately cross varieties of plants to form hybrids which combine the characteristics of both varieties.

Most species of plants have both sexes in each flower. This was not realised until the eighteenth century, following the work of Linnaeus. Once this was discovered, the way was open to the artificial crossing of plants, although as early as about 700 BC the Assyrians and Babylonians crossed date palms in which the flowers have only anthers on male trees and ovaries containing ovules on female trees.

The laws of inheritance were not appreciated before 1900, but since then plant and animal improvement has gone ahead rapidly. One feature of the story of the breeding of plants in particular has been the collection of plants from all over the world. Our gardens and fields have many of these plants and varieties produced from them.

Plants of different species can sometimes be crossed successfully. It has been found that hybrids between varieties of one species, or between species, are often more vigorous than the original parent plants. This is an unexpected result not fully understood.

When we talk of improving plants we mean producing varieties which yield a larger crop or which are more resistant to disease. Plant breeding was mentioned in Chapter 6 as one of the important ways in which food production has been and still is being increased. This may mean breeding in order to obtain plants which produce a higher yield, or it may mean breeding varieties which are resistant to fungus or virus disease, or which are not attacked by insect pests. Sometimes plants are bred which can grow in areas formerly thought to be unsuitable for the particular crop.

The seed used to grow a crop may be obtained by the plant breeder in quite a complicated way. Maize seed is an example, as is shown in Figure 16.7. Maize plants have male flowers, at the top of the plant, which produce pollen, and female flowers producing seeds farther down the stem, and so this makes artificial pollination easy.

In animals, it takes longer to obtain genetic information, and breeding programmes depend more on chance. In spite of this,

The 4 inbred lines, S,T,Y and Z have
been produced by selection

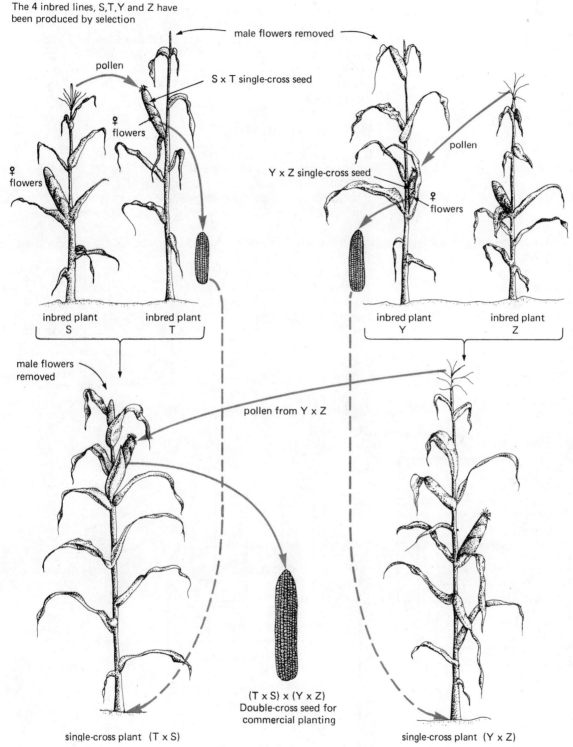

Figure 16.7 Producing maize seed

knowledge of the principles of inheritance helps in designing the programmes, and can save time in selecting a particular individual for breeding stock. The family tree of breeding stock of cattle, pigs, and other farm animals is usually well known, and has a good deal to do with the value of these animals and their offspring for producing particular types of animals with good food-yielding characteristics.

16.3 Selection in nature

It seems likely that, within an ecosystem in which competition goes on between members of a population, the varieties most suited for particular conditions will be selected naturally. We can do a simple experiment on this setting up populations of two types of *Drosophila*, and watch changes in the composition of the populations.

Set up populations of fruit flies in containers like the ones shown in Figure 16.8, which are small plastic sandwich boxes. The lids of the containers have holes in them for three 14 mm × 75 mm tubes containing food. There is a small hole in the middle plugged with cotton wool. The chambers are set up with populations of flies as follows.

1. 20 pairs of wild type
2. 20 pairs of vestigial winged
3. 10 pairs of vestigial winged, 10 pairs of wild type

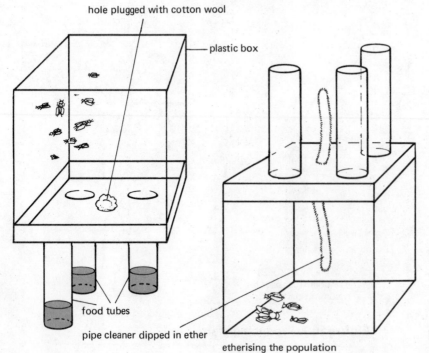

Figure 16.8 *Drosophila*

You will have to etherise the flies from stock bottles first, and then sort out the males and females before making up the population. The flies can be put in the container and the apparatus kept on its side until the flies revive from the anaesthetic.

Every week, for as many weeks as possible, etherise the flies by taking out the cotton wool plug and putting in a pipe cleaner which has been dipped in ether. Then count the numbers of different types present. Each week replace one of the food tubes. The one you take off must be kept with a cotton wool plug in it, as flies will hatch out in it and must be returned to the population at the next count. Be very careful to label all the tubes.

Set out your results in a table to show the changes in populations in all three containers, and draw graphs of these results showing the population changes against time. What explanation can you give for the changes? Is there any evidence for one variety being favoured, that is, being selected, compared with the other?

In a wild population, the situation will be more complex, as there will be more varieties and there will not be such large proportions of each one. From your experiments, how do you think that changes take place in the proportions of varieties in a natural population?

Looking Back at Chapter 16

1. It is convenient to classify and name different kinds of organism. The classification we devise may or may not show the natural relationship between the organisms.
2. A species is an interbreeding population of similar organisms.
3. Variation between individuals in a population has allowed man to select and to breed a wide variety of domestic animals and cultivated plants.

17 MAN IN HIS ECOSYSTEM

17.1 Man's demands on the environment

The population of animals which has most effect on the environment is the species we call man. In Chapter 6 we thought about the human population of the world, which was 3 300 million in 1965 and which could be 7 000 million by AD 2000, at the present rate of increase. What did you estimate the total population might be by AD 2050? Part of this increase is inevitable. How could part of the increase be controlled? Man needs food, water, shelter, sources of energy, and the means of disposing of waste materials. Figure 17.1 gives some idea of the amount of land used in construction of motorways. Leisure activities also make demands on our national resources. As the population increases in size, the demands will become greater. All these needs of man affect the ecosystems of which he is a part.

Figure 17.1 Land use for mobility

17.2 Whales and man

We shall consider one resource which man has used. Whales have been hunted in various ways and used as a source of food, fuel, and other useful materials, for a very long time. What has been the effect of this hunting on the whales? In considering this, we must first realise that there is a large number of different species of whale, as shown in Figure 17.2, and in studying their populations and man's effect on them, their classification and the differences between them are very important.

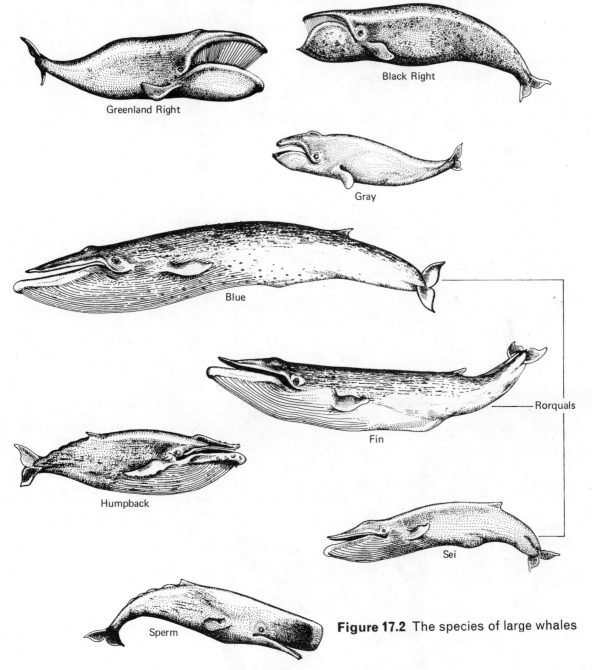

Greenland Right

Black Right

Gray

Blue

Rorquals

Fin

Humpback

Sei

Sperm

Figure 17.2 The species of large whales

One important difference is that sperm and right whales float when they are killed but fin and blue whales do not. This meant that until the method of using compressed air to blow up whales to make them float was used in the late nineteenth century, fin and blue whales were not caught in large numbers.

Numbers are given below in Table 17.1 of Greenland right whales caught by ships from the port of Dundee. Data are also given in Table 17.2 for catches from other ports in the four years up to 1817.

Table 17.1
Catches of whales by
Dundee-based ships

Year	No. of whales	No. of ships
1874	190	11
1884	79	16
1885	17	27
1893	29	5
1911	7	8
1912	0	1

Table 17.2
Catches of Greenland right whales
(1814–1817)

Port	No. of whales
English Ports	3 348
Aberdeen	427
Leith	278
Peterhead	402
Dundee	248
Montrose	127
Others	200
Total	5 030

Figure 17.3 A blue whale

Table 17.3
Total whale catches in the Antarctic

Year	Blue whales	Fin whales
1930	20 150	17 518
1932	29 263	16 171
1935	17 214	14 003
1939	12 323	19 936
1941	1 170	1 402
1944	1 201	1 311
1947	7 534	22 310
1950	5 231	19 503
1955	2 298	29 013
1960	1 740	27 374
1961	1 118	26 438
1962	947	18 668
1963	112	13 870
1964	20	7 308
1965	1	2 318
1966	4	2 893
1967	0	2 155

Figures are given in Table 17.3 for catches of blue and fin whales in the Antarctic during recent years.

What conclusions can you draw from these figures? Drawing graphs may help you to understand them better. What information would help you in analysing these data?

It is obvious from the figures that man has had a great effect on the whale populations. To a large extent, the history of whaling shows hunting of the animals until they were nearly extinct, followed by a change of either hunting area or of the species hunted. You may ask what has been done to conserve whale populations? Before the Second World War there was a certain amount of international

Figure 17.4 A factory ship

Figure 17.5 A whale is caught

regulation of whaling, but the most important measure, an overall limit to the Antarctic catch, was agreed upon in 1945. Nowadays, the International Whaling Commission sets a limit on the catch in 'Blue Whale Units' for each whaling season. (1 Blue Whale Unit = 1 blue whale, or 2 fin whales, or $2\frac{1}{2}$ humpback whales, or 6 sei whales, or 5 sperm whales.)

Each factory ship radios weekly details of its catch to the Bureau of International Whaling Statistics in Norway, which estimates from the increasing total the date on which the limit will be reached. The Bureau then sends out a signal one week in advance of the day when whaling should cease. The ships then return to port, possibly catching a few sperm whales on the way back. There are great problems in enforcing regulations which depend on a great deal of co-operation between people of different nations.

Do you think the measures have been effective? The figure for the limit to each year's catch is arrived at by calculation. Supposing a population of adult whales, that is whales capable of breeding, is 100 000 and that 10 000 new adult whales are added to this population each year, then, if 9 500 are caught, there is a surplus of new whales and the population will increase, but if 10 100 are caught the population will decrease. The catch must be below the figure for the new number of adult whales produced, in addition to those required to make up for normal losses. It follows that a great deal of knowledge of the breeding rates and seasons, total numbers, and general biology of whales is required in order to discover this figure. Information is collected by factory ships.

$$\text{Fishing mortality} + \text{Death by other causes} = \text{Total mortality}$$

Total mortality must be less than the number of new adults, if the population is to remain the same size or is to increase.

We are dealing in this example with an animal whose population has been reduced below the level which the environment could support if the whales were not hunted.

The principles which govern the size of the populations of whales apply to other organisms such as elephants, lions, red deer, crested tits and to the many other animals and plants which are near extinction in the world.

17.3 Man and the soil

For a population of 3 300 million humans, a good deal of food is required. It has been estimated that, to provide enough animals to keep one man alive by hunting, one square mile of land is required. There are 56 million square miles of land surface, and so hunting is clearly not the way by which we can support our population. Disregarding the sea as a source of food, it means that man must turn to plants and domesticated animals as sources of food. Certain plants like wheat, potatoes, rice, maize and many others produce a great deal of food per unit area. Man has cleared away natural plant ecosystems and grown these plants by themselves in large areas. See Figure 17.6. What effect does this **monoculture** of plants have on our surroundings? This is a very broad and complicated question, some aspects of which we can investigate. We shall start by looking at an area where cultivation is not going on.

Figure 17.6 Monoculture. The aeroplane is spraying insecticide

Examine the surface and upper layers of soil in a piece of woodland or under a hedge. What is the material like in the various layers? Use an auger to collect samples of soil at different depths, and compare this soil with that from a cultivated field. The upper layers probably contain the recognisable remains of leaves. How deep in the soil can you find leaves? What do you think happens to them?

The soil consists of a mineral part which is formed by the weathering of rocks, as shown in Table 17.4. This mineral part is

Table 17.4

	Diameter of Particles (mm)	Chemical Composition
Sand	2–0·02	Silica
Silt	0·02–0·002	Silica
Clay	Less than 0·002	Alumino-Silicates

partly sand, which is silicon dioxide (silica), and smaller clay particles which are complicated salts called alumino-silicates. In addition to this, the soil contains the dead and decaying remains of plants; in a woodland this is largely made up of leaves. The leaves and other plant remains become a dark complex of partly broken down materials in the soil in which the structure of the plants is no longer visible. This material is called **soil organic material,** or sometimes humus. You will remember from earlier work that the micro-organisms in soil, such as bacteria and fungi, cause the decay of the remains of plants and animals in order to obtain energy for their own life processes. In an experiment which you carried out, various organic materials added to the soil decayed away. We suggested that chemicals which could be used by plants were released into the soil as a result of the process of decay.

The first stage in decay is the production of soil organic material. Perhaps in cultivated soil fewer plant remains are available for decay. If this is so, then cultivated soil should contain less organic material than a woodland soil. Let us investigate this.

1. Put some soil in a drying oven at 90°C for two days. Use two types of soil, some uncultivated soil, preferably from a woodland area, and some cultivated soil.
2. Put some of each sample in weighed crucibles and weigh again.
3. Heat each crucible very strongly for about three hours in order to burn away the organic material.
4. Cool the crucibles and weigh them again.

From these results calculate the percentage of soil organic material in the samples. What differences are there between the samples, and how can you explain them?

The problem now is to find what is produced by the decay of the soil organic material? We have already suggested that chemicals which plants can use are the products.

What are the chemicals that plants require from soil? If you found out about Van Helmont's experiment earlier in the course, you will remember he discovered that a willow branch, in growing from 2·5 kg to 80 kg, took 56 g of mineral material from soil over a period of 5 years. What minerals made up this 56 g?

Photosynthesis provides the plant with carbohydrates, but to make proteins, other elements in addition to carbon, hydrogen and oxygen are necessary. What are these elements, and from where does the plant get them? In an earlier experiment we used ammonium sulphate to make the grass of a turf grow better. Presumably the nitrogen and sulphur in ammonium sulphate can be taken up from the soil. Potassium nitrate added as fertiliser is another source of nitrogen.

Design experiments to find the effects of these and other substances on the growth of plants. You will need seeds of suitable crop plants, pots of soil, or plots of land with uniform soil, and, if possible, controlled growing conditions. Other elements like phosphorus, potassium, calcium and iron are all present in plants and are obtained from the soil. How could you demonstrate that plants needed molybdenum for growth? The photograph Figure 17.7 shows the amazing effect of adding only 84 g per hectare of sodium molybdate to a crop of rape.

The plants on the left had sodium molybdate added to the soil in which they were growing.

Does the photograph provide evidence that molybdenum is required for the growth of rape?

The source of these mineral compounds required by plants is the soil. Elements like potassium and magnesium can be found in the clay minerals from which they are gradually released. Nitrogen is not present in the clay minerals, though a little comes into the soil as nitric acid formed in the air during lightning flashes. Its source must be the plant remains from which mineral salts are released by bacterial and fungal action, in decomposition.

What is the characteristic smell of a manure heap or compost heap? Those of you who are good chemists will recognise it as the smell of ammonia. Can it be that this is produced from the decay of the proteins in the plant remains?

Figure 17.7 Molybdenum and plant growth

Set up two flasks with a little horse dung or mouse droppings and some straw in them. Sterilise one flask and its contents in an autoclave, or in a pressure cooker. What is the difference between the two flasks at this stage? (Figure 17.8.)

Leave the flasks aside, and after a few days remove the stoppers and smell the contents. What differences do you notice?

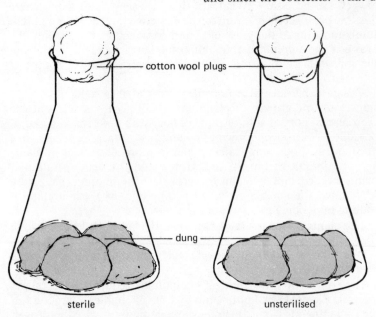

cotton wool plugs

dung

sterile   unsterilised

Figure 17.8 Decaying dung

In the eighteenth century, the French army needed saltpetre, which is potassium nitrate, to make gunpowder. They made it in heaps of decaying organic matter which were kept under cover and not allowed to cool down. After a time, the saltpetre was washed out with water and the solution was evaporated to crystallise out the saltpetre. The process was called **nitrification** because chemists found that the nitrate had been formed by the oxidation of ammonia which was produced in the heaps.

Schloesing and Muny, two chemists studying sewage in Paris, found out more about nitrification at the end of the nineteenth century. Consider these two pieces of evidence which they discovered.

(a) When sewage water, containing organic matter, trickled through a column of chalk, it was much the same for several days, but after that it contained more nitrate and less organic matter than it did before. Where did the nitrate come from? Why do you think there was a delay in its formation?

(b) Once the column was established and producing nitrate, they blew chloroform vapour through the chalk and started again to run sewage through the tube. (The chloroform killed anything living in the chalk.) There was no nitrate production for some time after this treatment. Does this confirm any of your ideas about (a)?

From the results of these and earlier experiments it has been found that nitrates are formed by bacteria from the nitrogenous materials in soil organic matter. You have already considered the re-cycling of minerals in earlier work in your course. The circulation of nitrogen is summed up in Figure 17.9.

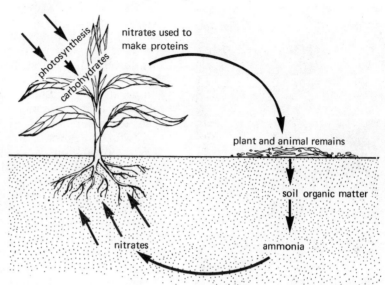

Figure 17.9
The circulation of nitrogen

At this stage it is worth while considering the nature of the soil habitat in which the bacteria live. It consists of about 50 per cent by volume of solid matter, the rest being filled by either water or air. The solid matter is made up of mineral and organic matter. The surface area of the solid matter varies from a relatively low figure to about 11 000 m^2 in 1 g of soil. The soil organic material provides the main food source for the ecosystem. Salts are released from the soil particles and also from the soil organic material and are taken up by plants. In this fascinating habitat, populations of bacteria, protozoa, insects, nematodes and other organisms form a delicately balanced ecosystem.

When a crop is grown in monoculture, a good deal of the plant is harvested and taken away, so that the natural circulation of nitrogen and other elements is disturbed. The following are ways in which this problem has been solved by man:

1. by growing plants for several years until the crops start to fail and then moving somewhere else. Why do you think the crops fail? There is very little possibility of supporting the world's population by this nomadic method of agriculture.

2. by the addition of organic material which has been formed in compost heaps or by the addition of organic matter of other types such as horse dung, dried blood, wool or fur. How does this method help to solve the problem? It cannot completely solve the world problem, as organic manure is available only in small quantities. Waste material from city populations can be rendered useful, and attempts are being made to process more of the sludge produced from sewage in order to make organic fertilisers.

3. by the addition of artificial fertilisers such as ammonium sulphate, potassium nitrate, phosphates and other salts in smaller amounts. Millions of tons of such fertilisers are used every year.

4. by the rotation of crops. Man found out a very long time ago that the continuous growing of one crop in the same soil led to a decrease in yield. In the eighteenth century it was discovered that if different crops were grown in successive years the yield was more satisfactory. For example, a farmer could grow wheat, then turnips, then barley, then clover and then wheat again and produce good yields. The actual rotations on a modern farm are complicated by consideration of the sort of crops which will make money, by differing soil conditions and by other problems, such as the amount of labour a particular crop requires for successful cultivation.

Why do rotations work and, particularly, why do they help to maintain soil conditions? Here are some ideas for investigations which you might try to carry out, using pots or plots of land.

(a) Different plants have different mineral requirements. One crop may use large quantities of one salt and small quantities of another. The next crop may have large demands on the second salt but only use small quantities of the first. What will happen to the soil concentrations of these salts while (i) the first crop, (ii) the second crop, is growing? If the crops are grown one after the other how does this help to maintain soil fertility?

(b) Roots of different crops reach different levels and thus take salts from different depths in the soil. You could investigate the root system of crops on a farm or in a garden, or grow plants under equivalent conditions in pots or plots and then map the root systems. The photograph, Figure 17.10 shows part of a root system.

A comparison of wheat, barley and a root crop will provide interesting differences in root systems.

(c) Clover and other plants belonging to the same family have small structures on the roots called **root nodules.** The following experiment with clover, or bean plants, will give more information about these nodules.

Figure 17.10 Part of the root system of a sugar beet plant

1. Sterilise some sand by heating it strongly.
2. Plant some French bean or clover seeds in pots or trays of this sterile sand.
3. Plant some more seeds of the same sort in sterile sand to which has been added some soil in the proportions of 1 part of soil to 20 of sterile sand, well mixed together.
4. When the plants have produced several sets of leaves, dig them up and examine the roots. If nodules are present try to measure the number there are relative to the size of the plant.
5. Try to explain any differences in numbers of nodules on the plant.

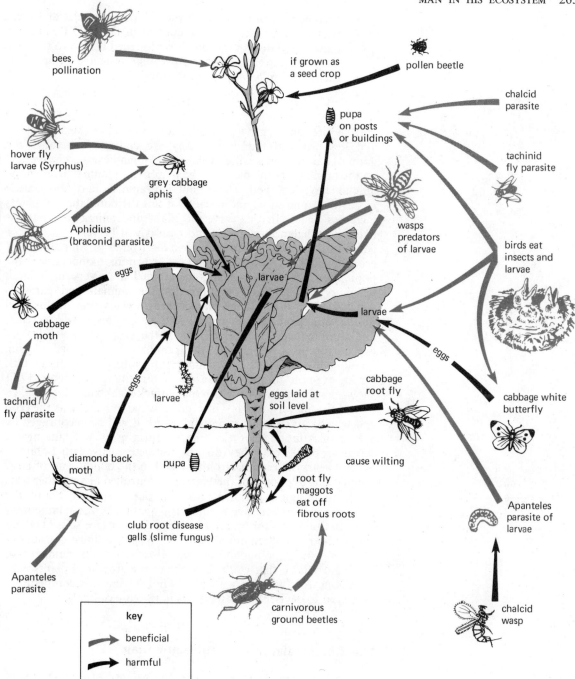

bees, pollination

pollen beetle

if grown as a seed crop

chalcid parasite

tachinid fly parasite

pupa on posts or buildings

hover fly larvae (Syrphus)

grey cabbage aphis

Aphidius (braconid parasite)

wasps predators of larvae

birds eat insects and larvae

eggs

larvae

larvae

cabbage moth

tachnid fly parasite

eggs

larvae

eggs

cabbage white butterfly

diamond back moth

pupa

cabbage root fly

eggs laid at soil level

cause wilting

Apanteles parasite of larvae

Apanteles parasite

club root disease galls (slime fungus)

root fly maggots eat off fibrous roots

carnivorous ground beetles

chalcid wasp

key

beneficial

harmful

Figure 17.11 Pests and diseases of cabbage plants

Experiments have shown that these nodules are growths on the roots produced by bacteria which entered the root. These bacteria have been shown to be able to make compounds using nitrogen from the air and materials in the plant which contain no nitrogen. Some of these nitrogen-containing compounds are used by the plant to make protein and they become part of the plant. How will these nodules and their bacteria affect the nitrogen content of the soil? Remember that a good deal of the clover is ploughed back into the soil. Why are clover and other crops, like peas and beans from the same family, important in rotations?

In nature, plants grow in populations which are usually smaller and less crowded than when they are cultivated, because the animals and parasites which feed on them may exert some control on the numbers of the plant. If the number of plants falls, then the animals have less food. The numbers of animals may fall because of death or migration, and because of this the population of plants increases again. In this way, the plant and animal populations maintain a balance, which in most cases will be very much more complex than this, as you may have discovered in your studies of ecosystems. Now, when a plant is grown in monoculture, the population of plants is being maintained at a very high level, which produces ideal conditions for the animals and parasites which feed on them. If the plant is grown every year at this level on the same land, the population of these organisms will increase, and thus reduce the productivity of the crop. How would you expect rotations to change the populations of pests? Again, investigation of a farm gives interesting information about this. As an example of the complexity of the situation, Figure 17.11 shows pests and diseases which may attack a cabbage plant.

In the same way, weeds which grow at the same time as the crop and which can compete successfully with it will be encouraged by a lack of rotation. For example, poppies grow well amongst a cereal crop, whereas they do not compete easily with potatoes. Several years of cereal crops may result in the building up of large populations of poppies if these are not controlled in any other way.

Try to design experiments to find out something about the competition between weeds and crop plants. Is the competition between the shoots for light, or between the roots for salts? Is there any method of finding out about this? What you must consider in designing your experiments are methods of preventing competition between roots so that you can compare the growth of plants with competing root systems with plants not having this competition. You need to devise similar methods in the case of light.

17.4 Chemicals, pests, eagles and man

In growing plants in monoculture, the balance of populations of living things is disturbed, and insects, fungi and weeds may increase in numbers alarmingly. These problems have led to the use of chemicals to control the populations of pests and weeds. Chemicals with names like DDT, BHC, Aldrin, Dieldrin, Paraquat, Simazin have been used. If you go to a gardening shop you will find there are all sorts of aerosol sprays, and other chemicals in powder or liquid form, which can be used to kill weeds, fungi, insects or slugs. These are used on a much larger scale in farming. We should ask at least three questions before using these chemicals.

1. How effective are these substances?
2. What other effects do these substances have?
3. What is done to control the use of the chemicals?

We will now discuss each of these questions in turn.

1. *How effective are these substances?*

Sheep suffer from a number of parasites, for example, ticks which carry diseases from animal to animal, mites which cause sheep scab, and blowflies which are responsible for the condition called 'strike' in which the sheep is parasitised by the larvae of the blowfly. In the 1930s it was not unusual for up to 40 per cent of a flock to be 'struck'.

Scottish flockmasters considered that blowfly strike was becoming an increasing problem as the years went by. In the 1940s DDT and BHC were used in dips. DDT killed the adult flies and the BHC killed the larvae and protected the flocks for six weeks. Dieldrin was used in the 1950s and its activity lasted twelve weeks, and so saved money on shepherding and inspection of flocks. The reduction of losses due to strike has been dramatic. Similarly, by careful use of proper dipping programmes, sheep scab has been eliminated from England, Scotland and Wales.

Figure 17.12 An eagle's eyrie

Table 17.5

Estimated effectiveness of organochlorine insecticides (O/C's) in the field

(All data given as equivalent acres per annum)

Crop	Pest	Maximum likely loss	Possible average loss	Possible average annual loss if O/C's continue to be used as at present	Possible average annual loss if O/C's are not used at all
Winter wheat	Wheat bulb fly	60 000	30 000	—	30 000
All cereals	Wireworm	400 000	56 400	—	32 400
Sugar beet	Wireworm	172 000	10,300	—	10 300
Sugar beet	Mangold fly	20 400	5 100	—	—
Potatoes	Wireworm	18 100	1 600	1 500	1 600
Potatoes	Aphids	25 800	3 700	—	—
Peas	Moth and weevil	20 500	4 200	2 100	4 200
Mustard	Beetles	8 000	3 300	—	2 000
Carrots and celery	Carrot fly	30 000	17 000	200	700
Culinary apples	Caterpillars	86 500	33 400	1 000	1 000
Totals		841 300	165 000	4 800	82 200

Look at Table 17.5, giving data for 1963. It shows the possible losses to crops with and without the use of a particular group of pesticides. What do you think is meant by one equivalent acre per annum? How do you think this information was obtained? Do you think that these chemicals are effective? What other comments can you make on these figures? What other information would you like to have to help your interpretation?

It is also worth commenting that modern pesticides have been very effective in controlling insects which carry disease-causing parasites. Control measures in Europe, using insecticides like DDT against lice, during and after the Second World War, were dramatically successful in controlling typhus fever. Equally effective has been the control of mosquitoes carrying malaria and other diseases in tropical countries.

2. *What other effects do these substances have?*

We shall approach this question by examining a particular problem, that of the breeding of golden eagles. Look at the figures in Tables 17.6 and 17.7. At first sight these data may seem to have

Table 17.6

Breeding success of golden eagles in West Scotland during 1937–1960 and 1961–1963

The percentage in the 'broken eggs' column excludes pairs robbed or not breeding, and the percentage in the last column excludes eyries with eggs where the outcome was unknown. The broken eggs are broken by the eagles and do not hatch.

Years	Total number of pairs studied	Number of pairs not breeding	Number of pairs robbed	Number of eyries with broken eggs	Number of eyries with eggs but outcome unknown	Number of eyries with young
1937–1960	40	1	4	5	4	26
1961–1963	39	16	1	8	4	10

Table 17.7

Proportion of eyries of golden eagle in West Scotland which had broken eggs during 1937–1963

Years	Number of eyries examined (excluding ones robbed or where birds not breeding)	Number of eyries with broken eggs	Percentage of eyries with broken eggs
1937–1950	9	1	11%
1951–1960	26	4	15%
1961	6	1	17%
1962	7	2	29%
1963	9	5	56%

little connection with the problem of pesticide effects.

What facts are shown by these tables? What comments can you make on the information in them? Suggest explanations for any differences in the figures.

What you must consider is the breeding success of the eagles during the periods 1937–1960 and 1961–1963. You should look at the differences between the figures for these two periods and consider the differences in

(a) the number of pairs breeding,

(b) the number of pairs robbed of their eggs,

(c) the number of eyries with broken eggs.

How do the eggs get broken? If the eagles break them, why do they do this?

Table 17.7 gives more detailed information about the change in proportion of nests with broken eggs. Make a graph of these results.

Table 17.8
Details of organochlorine pesticide residues found in eggs of golden eagles in 7 eyries in West Scotland, in 1963

Eyrie and location	Weight of egg contents (g)	Dieldrin (µg)	Total chlorinated hydrocarbon (µg)
(1) Argyll	131·3	903·00	1 347·2
(2) Argyll	112·6 103·9	167·00 177·00	330·6 346·5
(3) Sutherland	128·2	142·00	560·6
(4) Inverness-shire	63·0	85·80	103·8
(5) Wester Ross	147·4 140·7	54·60 24·00	140·6 70·6
(6) Inverness-shire	134·1 128·2	38·80 41·60	60·3 85·5
(7) Wester Ross	102·5	4·75	31.1

The breeding success of eagles in the Eastern Highlands has been greater than in the West. In these areas the eagles do not feed on dead sheep to any great extent. Look at Tables 17.8 and 17.9. What these figures suggest is that there may be a relationship between the pesticides and the breeding success of the eagles. How do you think the residues of the chemicals have got into the eggs?

From this example, and from others like it that you may have discussed, it is clear that, if used at all, chemicals of certain types must be used with great care.

Table 17.9

Dieldrin residues in eggs of golden eagle in West Scotland in 1963 in relation to recent history of breeding success at the eyries concerned

Although golden eagles pair for life, it is impossible to be certain that there had been no changes in these pairs through the death and subsequent replacement of individuals. Eyries 4 and 7 were counted as successful, in spite of the addled eggs, because a single eaglet was reared in each; the residue figure for the egg from eyrie 4 is an estimate.

Eyrie	Recent history of breeding success	Residues in 1963 (parts per million)
(1)	1962: eggs broken by eagle. 1963: one egg broken by eagle and one egg taken for analysis	6·90
(2)	1962: no young reared. 1963: one egg broken by eagle and the other two, which failed to hatch, taken for analysis	1·30 1·58
(3)	1962: bred successfully. 1963: one egg taken for analysis and the other failed to hatch	1·11
(4)	1962: unknown. 1963: one young reared and addled egg taken for analysis	0·68*
(5)	1961: bred successfully. 1962: eggs broken (possibly by Pine Marten). 1963: one egg taken for analysis; second egg later kicked out of nest and also taken	0·37 0·17
(6)	1961: eggs in eyrie at end of April. 1962: unknown. 1963: both eggs taken for analysis	0·32 0·29
(7)	1962: unknown. 1963: one young reared and addled egg taken for analysis	0·04

* Figure is suspect because egg was addled.

Consider the following problems.

(*a*) What insects and animals are killed by pesticides, apart from the pests? How will food chains be affected?

(*b*) What happens to the remains of the pesticides? This may be particularly important in the case of such substances as DDT and Dieldrin, which do not seem to be broken down within organisms or to decay in the soil.

(*c*) What is the effect of a herbicide which kills more than one type of plant in an ecosystem?

(*d*) What is the significance of the fact that residues of some of these chemicals are found in many animals, even in penguins in the Antarctic?

(*e*) What are the effects of chemicals on the very complex ecosystem in the soil?

(*f*) What are the effects of the residues in human food on health, both immediately and also over a long period?

(*g*) How can we obtain more information about the effects of chemical pesticides?

(*h*) What alternative methods are there for controlling pests?

3. *What is done to control the use of chemicals and to make sure that they are safe to use?*

There are three Government schemes dealing with pesticides, of which the Pesticides Safety Precautions Scheme is typical. It is a voluntary scheme, agreed between the associations representing pesticide manufacturers and the Government departments concerned, whereby manufacturers notify the Ministry of Agriculture, Fisheries and Food, before selling new chemicals. They supply extensive data on the chemistry of the products, their persistence, how they work, and details of experimental work on the effect of them on mammals, including man, and their effects on wild life of all kinds. The data are considered, and, if the information is satisfactory, the compound is approved for use. It is important to remember that this is a voluntary scheme, so that it is possible for compounds to be manufactured and used even though they have not been approved.

Recently the Government has restricted the use of Dieldrin and related compounds. There has also been an investigation by a Government Advisory Committee on Pesticides into the safety arrangements for the use of toxic chemicals. The main recommendation is the establishing of a full compulsory licensing scheme for pesticides.

Something then is being done, but you must ask yourself these questions.

(*a*) Is the action being taken really effective?

(*b*) Must chemicals of the sort named be used?

(*c*) Is it too late? Are there too many potentially harmful chemicals in organisms and in the soil and water already?

(*d*) Can experiments in laboratory and field provide information and help on both the short- and long-term effects of these substances?

Figure 17.13 Air pollution

17.5 Air pollution

Not only does man discharge industrial chemicals intentionally, he also releases waste materials into the air and water from other activities. It is estimated that $1\frac{1}{2}$ million tons of ash and grit, 2 million tons of smoke, and 5 million tons of sulphur gases are discharged into the atmosphere in Britain every year. An example of this discharge is shown in Figure 17.13.

These substances affect plants and animals, and we considered some of their effects on man in Chapter 9. In December 1952, smoke and fog in London produced a deadly 'smog' in which at least 4 000 people died of respiratory diseases.

We can attempt to measure the effect of pollution of the air on plants, as follows.

Collect twigs from privet, holly, laurel or rhododendron, and from conifers such as pine or yew. Try to collect leaves from plants which are in polluted areas and others from cleaner areas. Measure the sizes of the leaves and the amount of growth in each year of these twigs. What precautions must you take in order to get a true comparison? How are the plants affected by pollution?

As wiping polluted leaves with filter paper will give a dirty smear, you can now devise a method to compare the amount of pollution on leaves from different places. You can also use this method to compare the pollution on pine needles of various ages, since pine needles remain on the tree for several years.

A good deal is being done about air pollution. There is control of fuel use and the establishment of smokeless zones; factory and other tall chimneys are better designed; and studies of movement of air masses may also contribute to future planning. The pollutants produced by man's industries, essential though these industries are, may overshadow his future health and well-being.

17.6 Water pollution

Man discharges many waste materials into rivers or into the sea. Although most of this discharge is made deliberately, toxic materials are occasionally discharged by accident. Figure 17.14 shows dead fish being taken out of the River Rhine in June 1969. At that time millions of fish were killed because of the accidental discharge of a very powerful insecticide into the river.

The materials discharged into water are of different types. Sewage contains organic material, both in suspension and in solution. This material provides food for micro-organisms which thrive on it. Simple experiments on the effects of water pollution are easy to perform.

Figure 17.14
The effects of water pollution

Set up two aquarium tanks, using plastic tanks or basins. If possible, have water from the same pond in both, and also the same amount of weed of the same type in the tanks. To one of them add some sugar, which is an organic substance. This tank is now polluted with additional organic material. Does pollution affect the numbers of bacteria present? There is a special way of estimating numbers of bacteria in water samples.

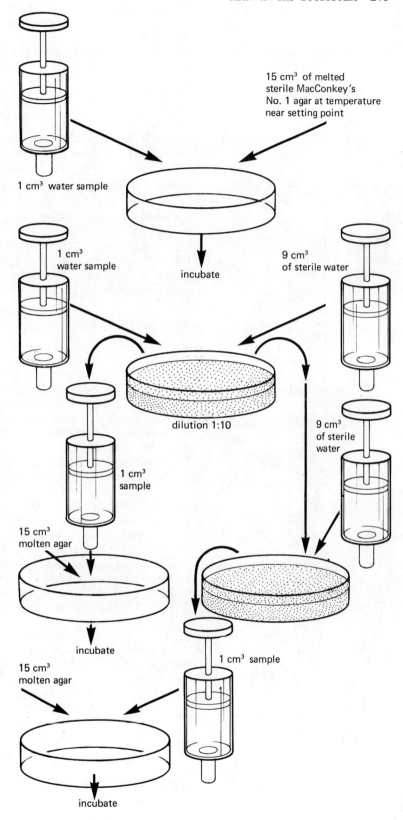

Figure 17.15 Counting bacteria in water samples

15 cm³ of melted sterile MacConkey's No. 1 agar at temperature near setting point

1 cm³ water sample

incubate

1 cm³ water sample

9 cm³ of sterile water

dilution 1:10

1 cm³ sample

9 cm³ of sterile water

15 cm³ molten agar

incubate

15 cm³ molten agar

1 cm³ sample

incubate

Using the technique shown in Figure 17.15 three dishes of agar are prepared by dilution, one of which has 1.0 cm^3 of water from the tank mixed with it, another has 0.1 cm^3 of the water mixed with it, and a third has 0.01 cm^3 of water mixed into it. (Further dilutions can also be tried.) If the plates are incubated and the colonies of bacteria which develop are counted, we have a measure of the number of bacteria there were in the original water. We are assuming that each colony has originated from a single bacterium or spore. Why was the first sample of water diluted? Is there any difference between the bacterial count of the water in the tanks (a) after 24 hours, (b) after one week, (c) after several weeks?

If there are large numbers of bacteria in the water, they will use up much of the oxygen, and this will reduce the amount available for animals living in the water. In fact, the oxygen content of the water is sometimes used as an indication of the amount of organic pollution it contains. The following is one method which can be used to estimate oxygen concentrations in water.

When ferrous sulphate solution is run into water, the oxygen dissolved in the water reacts with it and changes it. If we put in more ferrous sulphate when all the oxygen is used up, some of it will not be changed. If we also have phenosaffranin present, which is a coloured dye, as soon as there is some ferrous sulphate left over, it reacts with the dye and decolourises it. The following are the stages in the analysis.

1. Fill a burette with ferrous sulphate solution.
2. Use a pipette to take a 50 cm^3 sample of water from one of the tanks and run it into a small beaker or flask; keep the end of the pipette at the bottom of the vessel.
3. Add 3 drops of phenosaffranin to this sample.
4. Then add 10 cm^3 of Fehlings' solution B.
5. Arrange the end of the burette tube so that it is below the surface of the water in the beaker or flask, as in Figure 17.16.
6. Run in ferrous sulphate until the colour of the dye has gone, stirring with a glass rod while doing this.
7. Record how much ferrous sulphate was necessary to decolourise the dye.
8. Repeat this with water from the other tank.

What differences are there in the oxygen concentrations of the tanks as indicated by the volume of ferrous sulphate needed in each case?

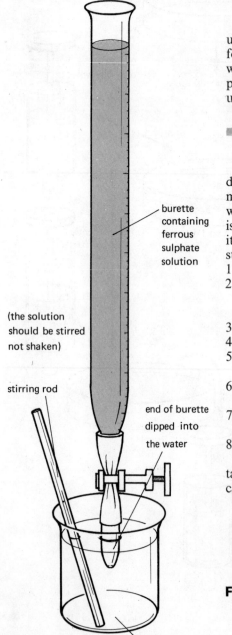

burette containing ferrous sulphate solution

(the solution should be stirred not shaken)

stirring rod

end of burette dipped into the water

50 cm^3 of water from the tank

Figure 17.16 Measuring the oxygen content of water

Is there any relationship between oxygen concentration, bacterial count and organic content of the water? How is this type of pollution going to affect animal and plant populations?

Chemicals discharged by works of various types will have various effects. Some will kill organisms, while others may react with other chemicals to produce dangerous substances. In Alsace it is estimated that 15 000 tons of potassium salts are discharged into the Rhine in one day. Downstream, the Ruhr mines discharge more, and by the time the water reaches Holland it is useless for human consumption, or for industrial purposes except for floating ships and barges.

Detergents are another type of substance which frequently pollutes rivers. Devise experiments to find out how detergents affect the growth of water weeds or the populations of different animals in the aquarium.

There has been considerable control over discharges into rivers since the beginning of this century, and particularly since 1951. Rivers which became excessively polluted in Victorian times have improved during this period. In Europe there is considerable international control of discharge into rivers. Why is this necessary?

The difficulties caused by sewage discharge into the sea have now become apparent. All waters can remove organic matter by means of micro-organisms in them if the conditions are suitable, but problems arise when the discharges become too great. Concern about pollution in Scottish estuaries and also along the south coast of England is growing, and the situation is being carefully watched.

A special marine problem is the discharge of oil, either deliberately or by accident. In March 1967 a large tanker, *The Torrey Canyon,* went on the rocks south of Land's End. About 60 000 tons of oil were released and spread on to beaches along the south coast of England and also on the French coast. Sea birds and other marine life were gravely affected: on some beaches nearly all the animals and many of the plants died. Such widespread effects may last for years.

In 1968 there were nine major oil-pollution incidents, one of which was a result of the release of a mere 87 tons of oil from a

Figure 17.17 Oiled eider duck

damaged tanker in the Tay Estuary. Figure 17.17 shows an eider duck which was caught by this oil. The Tay Estuary is very rich in bird-life, the winter population of eider ducks being the largest in Britain, perhaps as many as 20 000. At the time of the incident there were many other duck present with the eiders, such as mallard, wigeon, scaup, goldeneye, and merganser, as well as swans and geese. Oiling clogs a bird's feathers and permits water to get between them, destroying their heat insulating properties which depend on the air amongst the feathers. As a result the bird loses heat rapidly and the body mobilises all its reserves, burning them in a vain effort to keep the temperature from dropping. Eventually, even the muscle-tissues are used as fuel by the body: the bird becomes weak, cannot feed and dies of exposure, starvation, and shock. In the Tay incident, 1 368 birds were found oiled, of which 1 127 were eider ducks. Many of the affected birds were not, of course, found and it is likely that about 10 per cent of the British eider duck population perished in this one incident.

Oil itself has little effect on marine life other than on the birds, though it may taint the flesh of fish. However, the detergents which are often used to combat the oil are more deadly: some animals are killed by less than one part per million of detergent in sea-water. Fortunately it is rarely necessary to use detergents since methods of cleaning up the oil are known which are just as effective as detergents but less dangerous to wildlife. During the Tay incident, water-proofed limestone dust was used successfully to remove oil from rocky beaches. Even so, the best method of control is to prevent the release of oil in the first place.

17.7 Conservation

This chapter started with a statement of the increased demands man is making on his environment and on its resources. In the past, his demands have caused great changes. The men of the Stone Age, and later invaders like the Romans, Anglo-Saxons and Danes, cleared the forests to grow crops, using the wood for fuel and for building houses. The early iron industry depended on charcoal, and charcoal burners cleared a great deal of forest. In the fifteenth century, oak was in great demand for ship building due to expansion of trade. About that time some people began to realise what was happening, and sufficient replanting of oak took place to provide enough wood to build the ships that Lord Nelson used at Trafalgar 300 years later.

In the Scottish highlands, forest has been cleared extensively to provide grazing for animals. Originally, cattle were as numerous as sheep, but during the last two centuries there have been many more sheep. Sheep are more selective in their feeding. They prefer some grasses to others, and the result of this is that the grasses they do not prefer tend to win in competition with the more useful ones, and the quality of the grazing deteriorates.

The older heather and grass are often burned off in the hope that the plants will grow again in the same proportions as before grazing. However, some species of plants do not return, and burning may encourage erosion of the soil. Cattle are heavier than sheep, and they seem to destroy the underground stems of bracken; sheep do not destroy these stems, and bracken spreads rapidly on sheep-grazed land.

These examples are quoted to emphasise man's dilemma. He must use his resources and yet conserve them. Conservation of resources is necessary, not only to prevent the whole world becoming ugly and defaced, but also to ensure man's survival. Not the least of the difficulties is that man can never be absolutely certain of the consequences of his activities.

In all the examples we have studied, such as whaling and the use of pesticides and herbicides, the needs of man have been immediate, whereas the full consequences of his actions in exploiting a resource or in using the chemicals, only become apparent over a longer period. This is a fundamental aspect of the whole problem of conservation of resources.

When you look at an area of countryside, you should think not only of its beauty, but also of the extent to which it can be used without deterioration. Resources of the land and sea must be exploited for social and economic benefit, and yet be conserved. Within this general principle, there is room for the conservation of areas of special interest as nature or game reserves. In some cases it may be that this leads to the best use of land. In the savannahs of East Africa, large herds of cattle are raised, which eat only the grasses, and from their tracks erosion gullies develop. More meat could probably be producing by conserving the variety of wild animals which feed on the different trees and on the other plants, rather than solely on the grasses. The populations of different species can be 'cropped' in a controlled way in a game reserve, while conserving these areas is also the best way of looking after rare or nearly extinct species which may live in them.

Looking Back at Chapter 17

1. Man has an enormous and increasing effect on his surroundings, the devastation of whale populations being an example of this.
2. Land can be changed by man's monoculture of crop plants, and the natural recycling of minerals is interrupted by the harvesting of crops.
3. Certain chemicals can be used to control pests and weeds, so that more crops can be grown and animals can be protected against parasites. The use of these chemicals has long-term consequences, not all of which are understood.
4. Man releases waste substances into the air and he also pollutes water.
5. Conservation of natural resources is not only aesthetically desirable, but it is vital for man's continued existence.

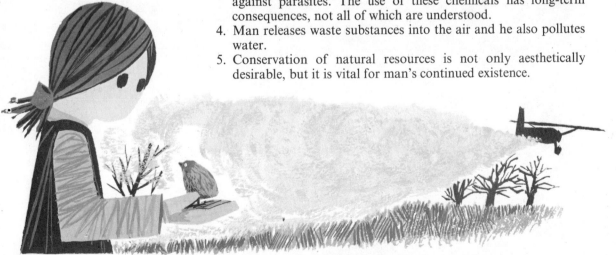

INDEX

The letter (F) after a page number indicates reference to a Figure

The Plant Kingdom

PLANT CLASSIFICATION IN SETS AND

Non-seed bearing plants

Division Algae

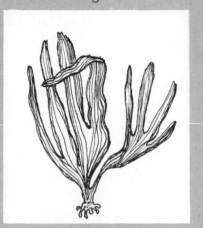

Division Fungi

Class Eumycetae

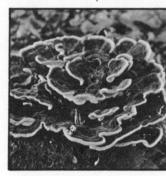

Class Lichenes

Division Bryophyta

Class Musci

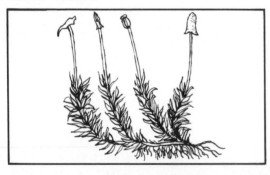

Class Hepaticae

Division Pteridophyta

Class Filicinae

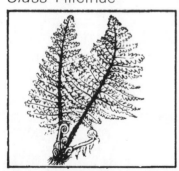

Class Equisetinae

Class Lycopodinae